Hamlet

Online resources to accompany this book are available at https://www.bloomsburyonlineresources.com/hamlet-the-state-of-play. Please type the URL into your web browser and follow the instructions to access the Companion Website. If you experience any problems, please contact Bloomsbury at: contact@bloomsbury.com.

ARDEN SHAKESPEARE STATE OF PLAY SERIES

General Editors: Lena Cowen Orlin and Ann Thompson

Elizabethan Narrative Poems: The State of Play, edited by Lynn Enterline

Macbeth: The State of Play, edited by Ann Thompson

Othello: The State of Play, edited by Lena Cowen Orlin

The Revenger's Tragedy: The State of Play, edited by Gretchen E. Minton

The Sonnets: The State of Play, edited by Hannah Crawforth, Elizabeth Scott-Baumann and Clare Whitehead

Titus Andronicus: The State of Play, edited by Farah Karim-Cooper

The Taming of the Shrew: The State of Play, edited by Heather C. Easterling and Jennifer Flaherty

The Changeling: The State of Play, edited by Gordon McMullan and Kelly Stage

The Merchant of Venice: The State of Play, edited by M. Lindsay Kaplan

Hamlet

The State of Play

Edited by Sonia Massai and Lucy Munro

THE ARDEN SHAKESPEARE
LONDON • NEW YORK • OXFORD • NEW DELHI • SYDNEY

THE ARDEN SHAKESPEARE
Bloomsbury Publishing Plc
50 Bedford Square, London, WC1B 3DP, UK
1385 Broadway, New York, NY 10018, USA
29 Earlsfort Terrace, Dublin 2, Ireland

BLOOMSBURY, THE ARDEN SHAKESPEARE and the Arden Shakespeare logo are trademarks of Bloomsbury Publishing Plc

First published in hardback in Great Britain 2021
This paperback edition 2023

A catalogue record for this book is available from the British Library.

Library of Congress Cataloging-in-Publication Data

Names: Massai, Sonia, editor. | Munro, Lucy, editor.
Title: Hamlet : the state of play / edited by Sonia Massai and Lucy Munro.
Description: London ; New York : The Arden Shakespeare, 2021. | Series: Arden Shakespeare state of play series | Includes bibliographical references and index.
Identifiers: LCCN 2020055169 (print) | LCCN 2020055170 (ebook) | ISBN 9781350117723 (hardback) | ISBN 9781350117730 (epub) | ISBN 9781350117747 (ebook)
Subjects: LCSH: Shakespeare, William, 1564-1616. Hamlet. | Hamlet (Legendary character)
Classification: LCC PR2807 .H2677 2021 (print) | LCC PR2807 (ebook) | DDC 822.3/3—dc23
LC record available at https://lccn.loc.gov/2020055169
LC ebook record available at https://lccn.loc.gov/2020055170

ISBN: HB: 978-1-3501-1772-3
PB: 978-1-3502-3274-7
ePDF: 978-1-3501-1774-7
eBook: 978-1-3501-1773-0

Series: Arden Shakespeare The State of Play

Typeset by RefineCatch Limited, Bungay, Suffolk
Printed and bound in Great Britain

To find out more about our authors and books visit www.bloomsbury.com and sign up for our newsletters.

CONTENTS

LIST OF ILLUSTRATIONS

Web Figures are available at https://www.bloomsburyonlineresources.com/hamlet-the-state-of-play.

LIST OF TABLES

Web Tables are available at https://www.bloomsburyonlineresources.com/hamlet-the-state-of-play.

Part 3 for the Norton Shakespeare (2015), all three texts of *Hamlet* (with Ann Thompson) for the Arden Shakespeare (2006, 2016) and *Thomas Middleton: Five Plays* (with Bryan Loughrey) for Penguin Classics (1988).

Ann Thompson is Emeritus Professor of English at King's College London. She is a General Editor of the Arden Shakespeare (third series) and has (with Neil Taylor) edited all three texts of *Hamlet* for Arden (2006). An updated edition of *Hamlet* appeared in 2016, along with a volume of essays on the play in Arden's 'Critical Reader' series. Other publications include an edition of *The Taming of the Shrew* for Cambridge (1984, updated 2003 and 2017), an edition of *Cymbeline* for the Norton Shakespeare (2016), *Shakespeare's Chaucer* (1978), *Shakespeare, Meaning and Metaphor* (with John O. Thompson, 1987), *Teaching Women: Feminism and English Studies* (edited with Helen Wilcox, 1989), *Women Reading Shakespeare, 1660–1900* (edited with Sasha Roberts, 1996), *In Arden: Editing Shakespeare* (with Gordon McMullan, 2003) and *Macbeth: The State of Play* (edited, 2014).

PREFACE

All quotations from *Hamlet* are from Ann Thompson and Neil Taylor (eds), *Hamlet*, Arden Third Series, rev. ed. (London: Bloomsbury, 2016) (referred to as 'vol. 1' when citing introduction and commentaries) and Ann Thompson and Neil Taylor (eds), *Hamlet: The Texts of 1603 and 1623* (London: Thomson Learning, 2006) (referred to as 'vol. 2'), unless otherwise specified. All quotations from other Shakespeare plays are from the editions in the Arden Third Series.

The editors are very grateful to the contributors to the 2017 Shakespeare Association of America seminar '*Hamlet:* Shifting Perspectives', to the series editors Lena Cowen Orlin and Ann Thompson, to Mark Dudgeon and Lara Bateman at Bloomsbury, to project manager Merv Honeywood and copy-editor Paul King, and to Emer McHugh for compiling the index.

SERIES PREFACE

The Arden Shakespeare
State of Play
Series editors: Lena Cowen Orlin and Ann Thompson

This series represents a collaboration between King's College London and Georgetown University. King's is the home of the London Shakespeare Centre and Georgetown is the home of the Shakespeare Association of America (SAA). Each volume in the series is an expedition to discover the 'state of play' with respect to specific works by Shakespeare. Our method is to convene a seminar at the annual convention of the SAA and see what it is that preoccupies scholars now. SAA seminars are enrolled through an open registration process that brings together academics from all stages of their careers. Participants prepare short papers that are circulated in advance and then discussed when the seminar convenes on conference weekend. From the papers submitted, the seminar leader selects a group for inclusion in a collection that aims to include fresh work by emerging voices and established scholars both. The general editors are grateful for the further collaboration of Bloomsbury Publishing, and especially our commissioning editors Margaret Bartley and Mark Dudgeon.

Introduction

Sonia Massai and Lucy Munro

一千个人眼中有一千个哈姆雷特

'There are a thousand Hamlets in a thousand people's eyes'

CHINESE SAYING[1]

Shakespeare's popularity as a global cultural icon is a unique phenomenon in terms of the amount of cultural capital he has accrued when compared to any other author, both classical and modern. *Hamlet* in turn has a special place among the other works in the Shakespearean canon. It is not only most readily associated with Shakespeare in our own time than any of his other works,[2] but it has also been intensely read and re-read, regularly revived on the English-speaking stage and increasingly translated and adapted to reach new audiences across different languages and art forms.

This collection captures a representative range of significant interventions in the critical debate that *Hamlet* has continued to generate as an exciting sub-field in its own right, within the wider context of Shakespeare Studies as a whole. Our introduction contextualizes these interventions by discussing first the features of the play that seem to have catalysed both popular and critical attention over time and then by placing special emphasis on recent critical developments which relate more directly to the essays included in this collection.

§

Suggestive evidence attests to the popularity of *Hamlet* in its own time as both a performance and reading text. Little more than a third of plays written for the commercial stage reached the press in Shakespeare's time, and only one playbook out of five was reprinted within nine years from the publication of its first edition. *Hamlet* was first published in quarto format in 1603 (henceforth Q1). The title page in Q1 mentions that the play had been performed 'in the Cittie of London: as also in the two Vniuersities of Cambridge and Oxford, and else-where'.[3] This unusual reference to Cambridge and Oxford, the most established seats of learning at the time, besides the Inns of Court in London, seems in keeping with a contemporary reference to *Hamlet* as being especially popular with 'the wiser sort'.[4] A second quarto edition followed in 1604–5 (henceforth Q2). Q2 boosts on its title page the fact that it is 'Newly imprinted and enlarged to almost as much againe as it was', that is, almost twice the length of Q1, and that it is set from a better manuscript ('according to the true and perfect Coppie').[5] The provenance of the printer's copy from which Q1 and Q2 were set and the relationship between these two versions of the play are complex questions, as two of the essays included in this collection eloquently demonstrate.[6] But the publication of Q1 and Q2 in quick succession one after the other, followed by the publication of another quarto edition in 1611 (Q3) and a further undated edition (Q4) now believed to have preceded the publication of the first collected edition of Shakespeare's works in 1623 (F1),[7] plus two further quartos in 1632 and 1637, unequivocally suggest a strong demand for *Hamlet* among its early readers.

Hamlet seems to have been just as popular with early modern theatre audiences. When it was entered in the Stationers' Register on 26 July 1602 it was referred to as '"*the Revenge of HAMLETT Prince [of] Denmarke" as yt was lately Acted by the Lord Chamberleyne his seruantes*'.[8] Q1, published after the accession of James I, updates this ascription by stating that the play has 'beene diuerse times acted by his Highnesse seruants in the Cittie of London', and its references to the performances in Oxford and Cambridge also suggest that it was a staple in the company's touring repertory. The performance record in the early seventeenth century is extremely patchy, but we nonetheless know that *Hamlet* was being considered for performance at court in 1619–20, and it was selected for performance there on 24 January 1637.

More than this, the company's own plays treat it as material for adaptation, appropriation and quotation. Only six years after *Hamlet* was first performed at the newly built Globe Theatre around 1600, the King's Men staged another play, Thomas Middleton's *The Revenger's Tragedy*, which was steeped in memorable stage images and turns of phrase drawn from *Hamlet*. Its most iconic of moments, Hamlet's address to Yorick's skull in Act 5, was already highly recognizable, as Kaara L. Peterson reminds us in her contribution to this volume,[9] and as suggested by the fact that Middleton decided to open his play with its main character, Vindice, addressing the skull of his fiancée, Gloriana:

> Thou sallow picture of my poisoned love,
> My study's ornament, thou shell of death,
> Once the bright face of my betrothéd lady,
> When life and beauty naturally filled out
> These ragged imperfections[.]
>
> (1.1.14–18)[10]

Vindice's lines echo with Hamlet's earlier address to Yorick: 'Alas, poor Yorick. I knew him, Horatio . . . Here hung those lips that I have kissed I know not how oft. Where be your gibes now[?]' (5.1.174, 178–9). Middleton deploys a series of strategic similarities and differences between the two speeches and characters. The pedigree of this stage image is unmistakable, and it would have been underlined in performance if – as is likely – Vindice and Hamlet were played on the Globe stage by the same actor, Richard Burbage.

There are stylistic differences between the two speeches. Vindice, for example, speaks his lines in verse, Hamlet in prose. Vindice does not quote Hamlet verbatim here, even though he evokes Hamlet's morbid obsession with the decomposition of the body after death. But other lines in Middleton's play replicate Shakespeare's language quite literally. When, for example, Vindice describes how he murdered the Duke earlier in the play – 'how quaintly he died – like a politician in hugger-mugger' (5.1.18–19) – he borrows the distinctive adverbial phrase 'in hugger-mugger' from Claudius's lines in *Hamlet*, where Claudius expresses his regret at not having taken better care of Polonius's funeral: 'we have done but greenly / In hugger-mugger to inter him' (4.5.83–4). Similarly, when Vindice upbraids his mother Gratiana for her moral looseness, the latter begs her son to 'Take this infectious spot out of my soul' (4.4.52), echoing Gertrude's lines from the closet scene, when Hamlet gets her to admit that she feels ashamed:

> Thou turn'st my very eyes into my soul
> And there I see such black and grieved spots
> As will leave there their tinct.
>
> (3.4.87–9)

The influence of *Hamlet* on *The Revenger's Tragedy*, ranging from the use of recognizable stage images to local verbal echoes, is pervasive. We can therefore safely assume that Middleton borrowed from Shakespeare so often because he knew that his audience would identify and enjoy each parallel and allusion in his play.

Shakespeare was not singularly responsible for *Hamlet*'s popularity on the early modern stage and among its early readers. *Hamlet* was in fact a late example of plays modelled on Senecan tragedy, and it exploited the popularity of this form. The Latin playwright Lucius Annaeus Seneca had become vastly popular on the English stage after ten of his tragedies were translated and published in the first collected edition of his works in English in 1581. These translations sparked the demand for tragedies about murder, madness and revenge. These tragedies generally opened with the vengeful ghost of the victim of a terrible crime who returns to haunt the living and to demand retribution and ended with a play-within-the-play or a highly ritualized event, such as a trial by combat, a banquet or a masque, which gives the revenger the opportunity to surprise and kill his enemies. The sheer magnitude of the violence unleashed by the revenger, far from redressing the original crime, magnifies it, thus producing an effect of breathtaking escalation; hence the moral ambiguity of the character of revenger. Hamlet's dismissive comment about sending Guildenstern and Rosencrantz to their death, 'They are not near my conscience' (5.2.57), marks a distinctive departure from Hamlet's preoccupation with his conscience earlier in the play. This line also signals the fast-approaching, tragic ending early modern audiences would have expected as the conventional resolution of a revenge tragedy. As Vindice puts it in *The Revenger's Tragedy*, ''[t]is time to die when we are ourselves our foes' (5.3.109). Or, in other words, it is time for the play to end when it becomes clear that the revenger is unable to remedy or rectify the original crime by rising morally and unequivocally above it.

By the late 1580s, Seneca had become the most popular model for English playwrights who were writing tragedies for the early modern stage. As early as 1589, Thomas Nashe complained about those writers who read 'English *Seneca* . . . by candlelight' and then, by imitation, wrote 'whole *Hamlets*', filling them with 'handfulls of tragical speaches'.[11] Similarly, in 1596 Thomas Lodge declared that the ghost in an earlier Elizabethan play about the Danish Prince Hamlet, whose story had been first recorded by Saxo Grammaticus in his chronicle,

Gesta Danorum, and which is generally known as the *Ur-Hamlet*, cried '*Hamlet, reuenge*' like 'an oisterwife'.[12]

Shakespeare himself had already written a popular revenge tragedy about ten years earlier, called *Titus Andronicus*, which was printed in multiple editions before it was included in F1 in 1623. However, while *Titus Andronicus* went on to be regarded as increasingly grotesque and distasteful when the English commercial stage was revived after the Interregnum in 1660, *Hamlet* grew in reputation and popularity. Like other Shakespearean plays revived on the Restoration stage, *Hamlet* was adapted to suit a very different stage: on returning from France, where drama had a distinctive neo-classical quality to it, the English court brought back with it a different set of expectations as to what constituted dramatic decorum. As a result, pre-Restoration drama was routinely adapted, when revived to entertain post-Restoration audiences. However, when *Hamlet* was reprinted for Restoration readers in 1676, the Shakespearean text was reproduced in its entirety in this edition, and not in the redacted version that, as the title page informs its readers, was being staged at the Duke of York's Theatre at the Haymarket.[13] An address to the reader on the next page goes on to explain that

> *This Play being too long to be conveniently Acted, such places as might be least prejudicial to the Plot or Sense, are left out upon the Stage: but that we may no way wrong the incomparable Author, are here inserted according to the Original Copy with this Mark* "
>
> (sig. A2r)

Shakespeare had by now become 'the incomparable Author'. Even so, some of his other plays were being performed and reprinted in heavily altered versions – most notoriously Nahum Tate's version of *King Lear* with a happy ending. *Hamlet*, on the other hand, was singled out in this edition as being worthy of its readers' attention in its original Shakespearean incarnation. *Hamlet*, in other words, had already started to acquire the canonical aura of a modern classic.

Starting from the Restoration period, the character of Hamlet became the most popular star vehicle for male actors who wanted to make a name for themselves on the English-speaking stage. Thomas Betterton, the leading actor on the Restoration stage, played Hamlet for nearly fifty years, from the time when he was put in charge of the Duke's Company as a young man in the early 1660s until he was well into his seventies. The London periodical, *The Tatler*, noted the 'force of action in perfection' in his performance but nonetheless teased him about the way in which he 'acted youth' as an old man.[14] However, Betterton was only the first in a long line of actors who also went on to play this role throughout their acting career, including David Garrick in the eighteenth century and Edmund Kean and John Philip Kemble in the nineteenth century. Edwin Booth similarly played Hamlet for nearly forty years in the United States in the second half of the nineteenth century, while Henry Irving made the role his own at the Lyceum Theatre over a period of thirty years, from the early 1870s to the early 1900s.

John Gielgud's Hamlet is also worth mentioning because it represented an important connecting link between a late Victorian elegant and high-sounding acting style associated with *Hamlet* and Shakespearean tragedy more generally and a movement towards a more natural approach to delivery and towards psychological realism. Gielgud, who played Hamlet in the 1930s, then played Claudius next to Richard Burton's electrifying Hamlet in 1964. The striking difference in the delivery styles used by Gielgud and Burton inspired The Wooster Group, a New York-based experimental company, to perform *Hamlet* against a recording of the Gielgud-Burton production projected on a giant screen at the back of the stage. The layered acoustic dimensions of this production offered a unique point of access into a century-long theatrical tradition centred on *Hamlet*.

Also central to the reception of *Hamlet* on the twentieth-century, English-speaking stage was Laurence Olivier's interpretation of Hamlet's tragedy as stemming from his repressed Oedipal desire for his mother, which was in turn taken to fuel his jealousy and hatred for Claudius, whom he unconsciously wishes to replace on the throne of Denmark and in his mother's bed. This peculiarly Freudian interpretation lost its appeal when Freudian psychoanalysis started to be critiqued and replaced by other critical and theatrical approaches in the late twentieth century. But Olivier's Hamlet remains an important milestone. Olivier went on to direct *Hamlet* as the inaugural production of the newly founded National Theatre, when its first season opened at the Old Vic in 1963. This production was echoed when the National Theatre moved to the South Bank in 1976 and artistic director Peter Hall directed *Hamlet* as one of his first productions there. And Olivier's Hamlet continues to have a palpable, material presence at the National Theatre: a statue of Olivier, holding up his sword like a cross and swearing to revenge his father's death, was erected on the South Bank, just outside the National Theatre, to commemorate the centenary of his birth in 2007.

Olivier's statue is a perfect example of how influential but also how problematic *Hamlet*'s legacy has become. We must pause and reflect on the choice not only of playwright and play, but also of actor and the iconic moment the actor is remembered by, to celebrate the National Theatre as the prime site of a British acting tradition that reaches back to Shakespeare. It is unsettling to think that this tradition is celebrated by remembering the moment when Hamlet vows to revenge the death of his father. Revenge poses an important moral dilemma and was already perceived in the early modern period as challenging both a legal and a Christian need to refrain from retaliating in order to allow a higher authority, a court of justice or God, to redress a crime. Francis Bacon, politician, essayist and philosopher, memorably wrote in his essay 'Of Revenge' that '*Revenge* is a kinde of Wilde Iustice; which the more Mans Nature runs to, the more ought Law to weed it out'.[15] Hamlet's misogyny, encapsulated in his infamous line 'Frailty, thy name is Woman' (1.2.146), the way in which he rejects Ophelia in the 'nunnery scene', as much as his arraignment of Gertrude in the 'closet scene', have also come to be regarded as deeply troubling.

Writers, directors, critics and scholars have unsurprisingly felt the need to address these and other disturbing aspects of *Hamlet*'s legacy in their work. Various counter-traditions exist in the performance and adaptation of the play. For example, there is a tradition that stretches back as far as the eighteenth century in which women have played Hamlet. As Tony Howard has reminded us, the first Hamlet to appear on screen in 1900 was played by Sarah Bernhardt; it is highly likely that the first Hamlet on radio was Eve Donne, who played the role in 1923.[16] Female Hamlets have appeared across global theatre and film cultures, including Fatma Girik in the Turkish film *Intikam Melegi* (*Angel of Vengeance*), also known as *Kadin Hamlet* (*Lady Hamlet*) in 1976, Angela Winkler in the Berlin Schaubühne's *Hamlet* (2000), and, more recently, Maxine Peake at the Royal Exchange in Manchester in 2014, Ruth Negga at the Gate Theatre, Dublin, and Michelle Terry at Shakespeare's Globe, both in 2018. Hamlet has also been more open than many of Shakespeare's leading roles to actors of colour, notable performances including not only Girik and Negga's but also those of Samuel Morgan Smith – who in the 1860s appears to have become the first black actor to play the role, which he performed in white face – Adrian Lester at the Bouffes du Nord in Paris (2000; and 2000–1 on tour in London and New York) and Paapa Essiedu for the Royal Shakespeare Company (2016).[17]

Creative responses have often focused on giving the female characters a stronger voice and more explicit motivations. T. S. Eliot refers to *Hamlet* as a failed work of art because of the ambiguity of Gertrude's character, which he described as 'negative' and 'insignificant'.[18] His reading, while problematic, does highlight an important fact about Gertrude, namely that she speaks only 4 per cent of the lines in the play and that, when she speaks, she speaks to others and never directly to the audience. Her lines amount to only twice as many as the lines spoken by the Ghost, who speaks 2 per cent of all lines in the play. Also, while Gertrude speaks about the same number of lines as Ophelia, Gertrude features in ten scenes, Ophelia in five, so even Ophelia speaks twice as often as Gertrude when their characters are on stage. It is therefore true that we get to find out very little about her and her motives in the play.[19] But her ambiguity has inspired modern writers to re-imagine her character in ways that challenge older, pejorative ways of reading her, which Eliot's famous essay about *Hamlet* had reinforced. In John Updike's novel, *Gertrude and Claudius* (2000), Gertrude is, for example, the passive victim of an arranged marriage to Old Hamlet, who is a rather stereotypical, brutal Viking warlord. She awakens to desire and sensuality only when she gives in to her attraction for Claudius. Similarly, Margaret Atwood turns Gertrude into one of her notoriously radical murderesses: in her short story, 'Gertrude Talks Back', Gertrude memorably informs Hamlet that 'It wasn't Claudius, darling, it was me'.[20]

§

Critical responses to *Hamlet* have also presented a rich variety of approaches, addressing both its complex textual transmission and the problems that it poses in interpretation. It is also one of the few Shakespeare plays to regularly receive book-length studies and dedicated special issues; it is, furthermore, the only individual play to have a journal dedicated to it, *Hamlet Studies*, which was founded by its editor, R. W. Desai, in 1979. As David Bevington notes, 'the history of *Hamlet* can be seen paradigmatically as a history of cultural change'.[21] Scholars have used *Hamlet* to intervene in many of the most prominent areas of early modern studies, engaging in depth with the theatrical, textual and intellectual contexts of the play and its afterlife. Yet this is a history with its own preoccupations and lacunae, as a brief survey of book-length studies of the play published in the last twenty years reveals.

Analyses of the texts of *Hamlet* by Paul Menzer, Terri Bouros and Zachary Lesser have probed the relationships between the various early versions of the play that have come down to us.[22] In particular – as we set out in a little more detail below – such studies have offered alternative histories of Q1, its theatrical and textual background, and its own history since it was rediscovered in 1823. Connections between text and performance are approached from another angle in *Shakespeare's Hamlet in an Era of Textual Exhaustion* (2018), edited by Sonya Freeman Loftis, Allison Kellar and Lisa Ulevich, which shows how audiences in the early twenty-first century make use of *Hamlet* in ways that challenge and play with textual authority.[23] In doing so, the volume also points to the prominence of *Hamlet* in studies of Shakespeare across media, and in various educational and institutional settings. *Hamlet* features here in various shapes and guises – for instance, in the Japanese responses to Q1 on page and stage surveyed by Yi-Hsin Hsu, or in Christopher Wheeldon's *Misericordes/Elisinore*, examined by Elizabeth Klett – and in the school and prison settings analysed by Sheila T. Cavanagh, Deneen Senasi and Erin M. Presley.

When the Arden Third Series edition of *Hamlet*, edited by Ann Thompson and Neil Taylor, was published in 2006, its cover provoked some critical commentary because it featured not Hamlet but Ophelia. 'Maybe it was to be expected that the jacket of the first major edition of Hamlet to be prepared, at least in part, by a woman would carry an image not of the play's hero, but of mad Ophelia', grumbled Stanley Wells in the opening sentence of his review in *The Observer*.[24] The women of Hamlet have long been central to feminist scholarship on Shakespeare, but recent criticism has paid special attention to Ophelia, taking up the challenge posed by earlier scholars such as Elaine Showalter, Carol Thomas Neely and Carol Chillington Rutter.[25] Ophelia features prominently in essays by Chloe Owen and Victoria Farmer in *Shakespeare's Hamlet in an Era of Textual Exhaustion*, and receives a book-length account of her own in Kaara L. Peterson and Deanne Williams's collection

The Afterlife of Ophelia (2012). Ranging beyond stage and screen, the book includes studies of Ophelia in social media by Sujata Iyengar and Christy Desmet, in the scholarly theatre review by Jeremy Lopez, and in painting and photography by Delphine Gervais de Lafond and Remedios Perni. As the editors note, 'there is no story of Ophelia that is not properly the history of her representation, reflecting each era or culture's characteristic notions of women's roles, madness, and essentialized notions of femininity'.[26] Within our collection, Kathryn M. Moncrief readdresses such issues.

Other recent book-length studies of adaptations of *Hamlet* have offered reappraisals of canonical figures, such as Patrick J. Cook's 2011 study of the *Hamlet* films of Olivier, Franco Zeffirelli, Kenneth Branagh and Michael Almereyda, or ranged more widely outside the Anglophone tradition, such as Mark Thornton Burnett's *'Hamlet' and World Cinema* (2019) and Howard's *Women as Hamlet* (2007).[27] They have also explored the uses that visual artists have made of *Hamlet* – for instance, in Alan R. Young's 2002 study of the place of the play in eighteenth-century art.[28]

Hamlet scholarship has a long tradition of philosophical engagement, continued in recent years in *Shakespeare's Hamlet: Philosophical Perspectives* (2018), which opens with editor Tzachi Zamir's provocative question, 'Is Hamlet a genuine philosopher or a pseudophilosopher?'[29] Scholars have also asked 'Does Hamlet have a self?', a question that has also been linked with the idea that *Hamlet* is a text that somehow prefigures or embodies modernity. Alexander Welsh's *Hamlet in his Modern Guises*, a study of responses to the play in the work of Goethe, Scott, Dickens, Melville and Joyce, published in 2001, opens by claiming that 'Hamlet became a modern hero . . . as soon as Shakespeare put his hands on him four hundred years ago'.[30] Stephen Greenblatt's *Hamlet in Purgatory*, published in the same year, in contrast focuses on *Hamlet* in its own cultural moment, one at which English culture was struggling to get to grips with the pressures that the Reformation and its aftermath had put on the ways in which the dead were managed and mourned.[31] Yet this intensely historicist project is also one that positions *Hamlet* as uncannily ever-present – 'into what cultural artery', Greenblatt asks, 'did [Shakespeare] plunge his needle in order to release the startling rush of vital energy?' (xiii). John Lee's *Shakespeare's Hamlet and the Controversies of Self* (2000) wonders whether 'Prince Hamlet has a self-constituting sense of self', and in probing the question of subjectivity in *Hamlet* he enters into a squabble between medievalists and early modernists that had been bubbling during the 1990s.[32]

Contrasting views are offered by Linda Charnes and Margreta de Grazia in two books published in the middle of the decade. In *Hamlet's Heirs: Shakespeare and the Politics of a New Millennium* (2006), Charnes suggests that '[t]he problem is not that Hamlet is a "modern" character ahead of his time, a prematurely Cartesian figure . . . but that Hamlet is always already postmodern, or rather *amodern* – since . . . one cannot "post" something that has not yet happened'.[33] In contrast, de Grazia declares in the opening pages of *'Hamlet' Without Hamlet* (2007) '[t]he Hamlet this book would do without is the modern Hamlet, the one distinguished by an inner being so transcendent that it barely comes into contact with the play from which it emerges'.[34] As this statement suggests, it is often unclear whether the focus of scholarly interest is *Hamlet* the play or Hamlet the character, the latter being more open to critical refashioning if he can be detached from the ghosts, violence and awkward gender relations of the play in which he appears. Yet, as Rhodri Lewis writes in his 2017 *Hamlet and the Vision of Darkness,* a study that returns explicitly to these questions, 'something about the way in which Hamlet speaks and acts . . . is surely meant to be unusual and arresting'.[35]

Lewis argues that this 'something' in Hamlet can best be understood when it is read against what he terms 'the textual contours of the psychological, rhetorical, and moral-political theorizing that lay at the heart of sixteenth-century humanism'.[36] As such, his approach is part of a particular mode in current historicist scholarship, which presents both the intellectual and affective contours of early modern political and textual culture. It is perhaps appropriate that scholarship on *Hamlet* – a play centring on a man who both feels and thinks excessively – should pursue this project. A complementary approach to the question of political culture in *Hamlet* appears in András Kiséry's *Hamlet's Moment: Drama and Political Knowledge in Early Modern England*, published a year before Lewis's book in 2016.[37] Where Lewis situates *Hamlet* within a network of mainly non-dramatic humanist texts, Kiséry studies its connections with other plays of the commercial stage. Juxtaposing *Hamlet* with the political theatre of Jonson and Chapman, he examines 'the connections between political knowledge and dramatic form' and 'how the plays engaged with (and also contributed to) the professionalization, popular dissemination, and aestheticization of politics' (2). Kiséry thus returns formal questions to the heart of *Hamlet* criticism.

Viewed as a group, these book-length studies of *Hamlet* suggest some of the strengths of recent scholarship on the play: rigorous attention to questions surrounding textual variation and book history; in-depth work with histories of performance and adaptation, from 1600 to the present day; and major interventions in questions around character, history, politics and religion within early modern studies. There are, however, some lacunae in these works that also point to broader questions that have so far been neglected in *Hamlet* criticism. It is perhaps unsurprising that *Hamlet* scholarship has drawn heavily on Western intellectual frameworks established in the twentieth century, from psychanalysis to postmodernism, given that the play has acted as an inspiration for many of these frameworks.[38] Among the most famous examples, *Hamlet* features repeatedly in Sigmund Freud's writing on mourning and desire, and it facilitates the postmodern aesthetics of Tom Stoppard's 1966 play *Rosencrantz and Guildenstern are Dead*. Ayanna Thompson refers in her account of the film *Suture* – which uses *Hamlet* as a reference point rather than *Othello* despite its overt presentation of racial difference through its casting strategies – to its favouring of 'cultural models that do not account for cultural or racial differences: Descartes, *Hamlet*, Freud, Lacan'.[39]

Perhaps as a result, some modes of thinking that challenge the centrality of traditional Western thought – such as critical race studies, ecocriticism, queer theory and disability studies – have had a harder time with *Hamlet*. Nearly twenty years ago, Peter Erickson asked 'Can we talk about race in *Hamlet*?' – a question that David Sterling Brown addresses in our collection – while Goran Stanivukovic writes that '*Hamlet* does not come to mind immediately as a queer text'.[40] Yet recent essays have offered ways of thinking with and about *Hamlet* that do not elide cultural, racial or bodily difference. Urvashi Chakravarty and Emily C. Bartels both present approaches to *Hamlet* that consider connections between race, gender and sexuality in early modern contexts.[41] A recent essay by Jami Rogers picks up the topic of black actors' performances as Hamlet, previously examined at length in Errol Hill's 1986 book *Shakespeare in Sable: A History of Black Shakespearean Actors*.[42] Another perspective is offered by *Hamlet* adaptation and reception studies. For example, in recent years, Vishal Bhardwaj's *Haider* has yielded a particularly rich set of critical responses to questions of place, politics and nation, from scholars such as Pompa Banerjee, Abhishek Sarkar, Amrita Sen, Jyotsna G. Singh and Sandra Young.[43]

Adaptations similarly offer a way into thinking in detail about non-normative sexualities in *Hamlet*. Bettina Bildhauer, for instance, examines 'queer medieval time' in the 1920 silent film *Hamlet: The Drama of Vengeance*, directed by Svend Gade and Heinz Schall and featuring Asta Nielsen as Hamlet.[44] Sexuality is connected with temporality, memory and futurity in two essays on *Hamlet* by the influential queer theorist Lee Edelman, one of them published in a cluster of three essays in *Shakespeare Quarterly* in 2011, Carla Freccero and Kathryn Schwarz offering responses to and critiques of Edelman's work via their own engagement with *Hamlet*.[45] Other approaches to same-sex relationships are offered by recent essays by James

Kuzner and Michael Neill on friendship in the play.[46] While *Hamlet* studies has traditionally been preoccupied with the representation of disordered subjectivity and mental illness, scholars working with early modern and disability studies have offered new insights, not least into what Sonya Freeman Loftis and Lisa Ulevich sardonically term 'Hamlet's position as a melancholy supercrip'.[47] A range of ecocritical approaches to *Hamlet* have recently been offered by Randall Martin, who notes Hamlet's 'willed strategy of existential and ecological discovery', activated by his disquisition on worms, Karen Raber, who suggests that '*Hamlet* is fundamentally about parasitism', and Rebecca Laroche, who reads Ophelia through the herbs that she wields.[48]

In their different ways, all of these essays offer fresh thinking on *Hamlet*. Our collection picks up some of these approaches, while also presenting its own distinctive takes on questions of gender, race, history, performance, text and adaptation. The collection opens with essays by Kaara L. Peterson and Kathryn M. Moncrief that offer materialist approaches to *Hamlet*. Peterson's essay examines the workings of Shakespeare's visual imagination, suggesting that two traditions of early modern portrait painting – the 'citizen portrait' and portraits of melancholy young men in outdoor settings – exercised a shaping influence on his development of the figure of the prince in the graveyard. Moncrief's essay also begins with a painting, *The Judde Memorial*, which depicts 'unsmiling newlyweds contemplating a corpse' (51). She sees painting and play as belonging to the same early modern tradition of coupling memory and mortality, and expressing that connection in material form. Her essay examines in detail the stage properties of 3.1, in which Ophelia seeks to 'redeliver' a set of 'remembrances' to Hamlet (3.1.92–3), and the floral gifts that she distributes in 4.5, looking at their early modern contexts and their treatment across a wide range of stage and screen performances.

The next two essays, by Kelly Stage and David Sterling Brown, deal in various ways with masculinity in *Hamlet* and its relationship with early modern modes of thought around culture and race. Stage views Hamlet as 'an urbanite in exile at Elsinore' (82), a cosmopolitan who cannot ultimately survive in Demark, studying in detail the workings of the global and local in the play. In doing so, she connects the play with debates about whether young men should be educated at home or abroad, and resituates the ways in which it makes use of references to the contemporary London theatre scene. In his important intervention in the study of race in *Hamlet*, Brown returns to Erickson's question, 'Can we talk about race in *Hamlet*?', answering it with an unequivocal 'yes'. His analysis of this 'white-centric' play focuses on the workings of unmanliness, which he sees as one element of a 'triangulated relationship between whiteness, unmanliness and blackness' (103–4). By 'cloaking rotting, and rotten, white Danish masculinity in literal and figurative blackness', Shakespeare both abjects and elevates blackness as 'a symbolically dominant force used as a support beam to stabilize notions of the ideal white self' (104).

Questions about the nature of character in *Hamlet*, which have been implicit in many of the opening essays of the collection, are brought to the fore in Jay Farness's essay, which analyses in detail the character-making, or 'character-fictionalizing', in which Shakespeare's characters engage, setting it in the context of acting and, especially, clowning in the play. Hamlet's 'antic' behaviour should facilitate his revenge plot, but, as Furness puts it, 'he appears to be performing for more localized theatre effects that cannot be described as either ambitious "self-fashioning" or purposeful "role-playing"' (134).

The next two essays included in our collection focus on the peculiar features and possible provenance of Q1. Q1 has recently received sustained critical attention, as mentioned above. The level of attention attracted by Q1 is justified by the significant impact that Q1 has had in the way in which we understand the longer and better-known versions of the play preserved in Q2/F1. Unlike all other early printed editions of Shakespeare's plays, whose existence was well known to all early editors of Shakespeare from the early eighteenth-century onwards, Q1 was only discovered, or recovered, in 1823, two hundred years after the publication of F1. As Lesser explains, the copy discovered by Sir Henry Bunbury at his manor house in Great Barton, Suffolk, predictably caused a literary sensation. This copy happened to lack the last page, so Hamlet speaks his final line, followed by the stage direction, '*Ham. dies*', and the catchword '*Enter*' (sig. I3v). Readers of this previously unknown version of the play were therefore left wondering who enters after Hamlet dies or how Q1 ended.

However, in another spectacular twist in the history of the rediscovery of Q1, another copy surfaced when a student from Trinity College Dublin, wanting to sell an old playbook, approached local bookseller M. W. Rooney. No one up to this point, neither the student nor the bookseller, had realized that this playbook was the only other extant copy of Q1, because this copy lacked the title page! Crucially, though, it included the final page, so by sheer good luck, we have since then been able to read and enjoy theatre revivals of a full and radically different version of the play, which has kept Shakespeare scholars debating its provenance since its original discovery.

William Dodd's essay provides new evidence to prove that the text of the play as preserved in Q1 reflects its use in performance. By identifying and analysing pragmatic markers, that is local interjections instinctively added by the actors to clarify or modulate the dialogue, as normal speakers do in everyday conversation, Dodd offers an exciting set of fresh insights into how Shakespeare's actors may have inflected his lines with their own understanding of the characters they played. Charles Kelly and Dayna Plehn, on the other hand, offer a wide range of textual and bibliographical evidence to argue that Q1 is more likely to have predated the longer versions of the text of the play preserved in Q2/F1, thus departing from an older theory according to which Q1 was set from an unauthorized, memorially reconstructed copy of the play as abridged (and/or toured) by Shakespeare's company, after the premiere of the longer version on the Globe stage around 1600.

The last two essays included in our collection shift its focus from the textual transmission of *Hamlet* into print to its transmission across art forms. The play has often been revived on stage. Besides the recent landmark productions mentioned above and those discussed in Moncrief's essay, *Hamlet* has also continued to inspire artists across different art forms. We therefore chose to include two essays that reflect the play's afterlife beyond the stage. In her essay about Bhardwaj's film adaptation, *Haider*, which relocates *Hamlet* to Kashmir, in the midst of the violent territorial conflict that has plagued the region since the Indo-Pakistani War of 1947, Pompa Banerjee analyses the productive interplay between Shakespeare's Gertrude and Bhardwaj's Ghazala, questioning both our understanding of this character and the figure of the Hindu Sati. This 'rearticulated' *Hamlet*, Banerjee argues, speaks not merely to the 'loss and violence' of contemporary Kashmir but transforms the play into 'a witness and participant' in India's 'own ritualized cultural violence against women' (201).

The final essay by Neil Taylor and Ann Thompson considers the eclectic text of Matthew Jocelyn's libretto for Brett Dean's *Hamlet*, which opened at Glyndebourne on 12 June 2017. In his libretto, Jocelyn draws on all three early versions of the play, as preserved in Q1, Q2 and F1, and not necessarily in the order in which these lines appear in their original editions. In this respect, Jocelyn's libretto represents an intriguing departure from the play and from earlier operas inspired by it. According to Taylor and Thompson, Jocelyn's approach thus speaks to recent developments in the editorial tradition, with recent editors, including Taylor and Thompson, valuing Q1, Q2 and F1 in their own right, as opposed to largely ignoring Q1 and conflating Q2 and F1 in single-text editions, as earlier editors had done from the rise of the editorial tradition in the early eighteenth century to the late twentieth century.

This collection therefore offers its readers a representative snapshot of the 'state of play' of critical and creative responses to *Hamlet* in our time, while also redressing some of the gaps and lacunae that characterize any scholarly field of enquiry, no matter how expansive, as indeed '*Hamlet* Studies' is, as a major area of research interest in its own right. The essays gathered in this collection encourage its readers to continue to think of *Hamlet* as a key platform, or 'cultural field', within which gaps in our own way of thinking not only about this play but also about the diversity of position-takings of those who engage with it, critically or creatively, become to emerge, telling us as much about the play as the assumptions, world views and expectations that we bring to it.[49]

Notes

1 We are very grateful to Yihang Qin for telling us about this saying, of which we were previously unaware.

2 Laura Estill, 'Was Shakespeare as Popular in his own Time as he is now?', *British Council Voices Magazine*, 9 June 2015, https://www.britishcouncil.org/voices-magazine/was-shakespeare-popular-his-own-time-he-now.

3 William Shakespeare, *The Tragicall Historie of Hamlet Prince of Denmarke* (London, 1603).

4 This early reference to *Hamlet* comes from a set of annotations that scholar and author Gabriel Harvey added to the margins of his copy of Thomas Speght's 1598 edition of Chaucer's *Works* (BL Add. MS 42518, fol. 394v).

5 William Shakespeare, *The Tragicall Historie of Hamlet, Prince of Demarke . . . Newly Imprinted and Enlarged* (London, 1604/5).

6 See Dodd, 175–97, and Kelly and Plehn, 151–74.

7 See, for example, Eric Rasmussen, 'The Date of Q4 *Hamlet*', *Papers of the Bibliographical Society of America*, 95(1) (2001): 21–9.

8 Edward Arber, *A Transcript of the Registers of the Company of Stationers, 1554–1640*, 5 vols. (London: Privately Printed, 1875–94), 3: 212.

9 See Peterson, 27–50.

10 Thomas Middleton, *The Revenger's Tragedy*, in *Thomas Middleton: The Collected Works*, ed. Gary Taylor and John Lavagnino (Oxford: Oxford University Press, 2007). All subsequent quotations from *The Revenger's Tragedy* in the Introduction are from this edition.

11 Thomas Nashe, 'To the Gentleman Students of Both Vniversities', in Robert Greene, *Menaphon* (London, 1589), sig. **3r.

12 Thomas Lodge, *Wits Miserie* (London, 1596), sig. H4v.

13 *The Tragedy of Hamlet, Prince of Denmark. As it is now Acted at his Highness the Duke of York's Theatre* (London, 1676).

14 'Mr Greenhat' (Richard Steele), in *Tatler*, 1, 22 September 1709.

15 Francis Bacon, *The Essayes or Counsels, Civill and Morall* (London, 1625), sig. D2r.

16 Tony Howard, *Women as Hamlet: Performance and Interpretation in Theatre, Film and Fiction* (Cambridge: Cambridge University Press, 2007), 1.

17 On Smith and other Black actors' performances up to the 1980s, see Errol Hill, *Shakespeare in Sable: A History of Black Shakespearean Actors* (Amherst: University of Massachusetts Press, 1986).

18 T. S. Eliot, 'Hamlet and his Problems', in *The Sacred Wood: Essays on Poetry and Criticism* (London: Methuen, 1920), 95–103 (101).

19 Please note, though, that Q1 includes an exchange between Gertrude and Horatio, which is not present in Q2 and F1, the longer versions of the play, and which exonerates Gertrude from being Claudius's accomplice in murdering Old Hamlet.

20 Margaret Atwood, 'Gertrude Talks Back', in *Good Bones* (London: Bloomsbury, 1992), 15–18 (18).

21 David Bevington, *Murder Most Foul: Hamlet Through the Ages* (Oxford: Oxford University Press, 2011), 4.

22 Paul Menzer, *The Hamlets: Cues, Qs, and Remembered Texts* (Newark: University of Delaware Press, 2008); Terri Bouros, *Young Shakespeare's Young Hamlet: Print, Piracy, and Performance* (New York: Palgrave Macmillan, 2014); Zachary

Lesser, '*Hamlet' After Q1: An Uncanny History of the Shakespearean Text* (Philadelphia: University of Pennsylvania Press, 2015). Bouros has also edited a special issue on 'Canonizing Q1 Hamlet', *Critical Survey*, 31(1–2) (2019).

23 Sonya Freeman Loftis, Allison Kellar and Lisa Ulevich, eds, *Shakespeare's Hamlet in an Era of Textual Exhaustion* (New York and Abingdon: Routledge, 2018).

24 Stanley Wells, 'The Play's the Thing – In Triplicate', *Observer*, 9 July 2006, https://www.theguardian.com/books/2006/jul/09/classics.features

25 Elaine Showalter, 'Representing Ophelia: Women, Madness and the Responsibilities of Feminist Criticism', in *Shakespeare and the Question of Theory*, ed. Patricia Parker and Geoffrey Hartman (New York and London: Routledge, 1985), 77–94; Carol Thomas Neely, 'Documents in Madness: Reading Madness and Gender in Shakespeare's Tragedies and Early Modern Culture', *Shakespeare Quarterly*, 42(3) (Autumn 1991): 315–38; Carol Chillington Rutter, 'Snatched Bodies: Ophelia in the Grave', *Shakespeare Quarterly* 49(3) (Autumn 1998): 299–319.

26 Kaara L. Peterson and Deanne Williams, eds, *The Afterlife of Ophelia* (New York: Palgrave Macmillan, 2012), 2.

27 Patrick J. Cook, *Cinematic Hamlet: The Films of Olivier, Zeffirelli, Branagh, and Almereyda* (Athens, OH: Ohio University Press, 2011); Mark Thornton Burnett, '*Hamlet' and World Cinema* (Cambridge: Cambridge University Press, 2019).

28 Alan R. Young, *Hamlet and the Visual Arts, 1709–1800* (Newark: University of Delaware Press, 2002).

29 Tzachi Zamir, 'Introduction', in *Shakespeare's Hamlet: Philosophical Perspectives* (Oxford: Oxford University Press, 2018), 1.

30 Alexander Welsh, *Hamlet in his Modern Guises* (Princeton: Princeton University Press, 2001), ix.

31 Stephen Greenblatt, *Hamlet in Purgatory* (Princeton: Princeton University Press, 2001).

32 John Lee, *Shakespeare's Hamlet and the Controversies of Self* (Oxford: Clarendon Press, 2000), 1. On *Hamlet*'s role in controversies over selfhood and periodization, see David Aers, 'A

Whisper in the Ear of Early Modernists; or, Reflections on Literary Critics Writing the "History of the Subject"', in *Culture and History, 1350–1600: Essays on English Communities, Identities and Writing*, ed. David Aers (Hemel Hempstead: Harvester Wheatsheaf, 1992), 177–202.

33 Linda Charnes, *Hamlet's Heirs: Shakespeare and the Politics of a New Millennium* (London: Routledge, 2006), 47.

34 Margreta de Grazia, *'Hamlet' Without Hamlet* (Cambridge: Cambridge University Press, 2007), 1.

35 Rhodri Lewis, *Hamlet and the Vision of Darkness* (Princeton: Princeton University Press, 2017), 5.

36 Ibid., 6.

37 András Kiséry, *Hamlet's Moment: Drama and Political Knowledge in Early Modern England* (Oxford: Oxford University Press, 2016).

38 For an overview, see Julia Reinhard Lupton and Kenneth Reinhard, *After Oedipus: Shakespeare in Psychoanalysis* (Ithaca: Cornell University Press, 1993), 11–118.

39 Ayanna Thompson, 'Suture, Shakespeare, and Race: Or, What Is Our Cultural Debt to the Bard?', in *Almost Shakespeare: Reinventing His Works for Cinema and Television*, ed. James R. Keller and Leslie Stratyner (Jefferson, NC: McFarland & Company, 2004), 57–72 (67).

40 Peter Erickson, 'Can We Talk About Race in *Hamlet*?', in *Hamlet: New Critical Essays*, ed. Arthur F. Kinney (New York: Routledge, 2002), 207–13; Goran Stanivukovic, 'Introduction: Queer Shakespeare – Desire and Sexuality', in *Queer Shakespeare: Desire and Sexuality*, ed. Goran Stanivukovic (London: Bloomsbury Arden Shakespeare, 2017), 1–29 (8).

41 Urvashi Chakravarty, 'More Than Kin, Less Than Kind: Similitude, Strangeness, and Early Modern English Homonationalisms', *Shakespeare Quarterly* 67(1) (Spring 2016): 14–29; Emily C. Bartels, 'Identifying "the Dane": Gender and Race in *Hamlet*', in *The Oxford Handbook of Shakespeare and Embodiment: Gender, Sexuality, and Race*, ed. Valerie Traub (Oxford: Oxford University Press, 2016), 197–210.

42 Jami Rogers, 'Talawa and Black Theatre Live: "Creating the Ira Aldridges That Are Remembered" – Live Theatre Broadcast and

the Historical Record', in *Shakespeare and the 'Live' Theatre Broadcast Experience*, ed. Pascale Aebischer, Susanne Greenhalgh, Laurie E. Osborne and Rachael Nicholas (Arden Shakespeare, 2018), 147–60; Hill.

43 Pompa Banerjee, '"Accents Yet Unknown": *Haider* and *Hamlet* in Kashmir', *Shakespeare Survey* 71 (2018): 18–25, and her essay in our collection; Abhishek Sarkar, '*Hariraj* and *Haider*: Popular Entertainment and the Nation in Two Indian Adaptations of *Hamlet*', *Literature Compass* 14, no. 11 (November 2017); Amrita Sen, 'Locating *Hamlet* in Kashmir: *Haider*, Terrorism, and Shakespearean Transmission', in *Shakespeare's Hamlet in an Era of Textual Exhaustion*, 87–100; Jyotsna G. Singh, *Shakespeare and Postcolonial Theory* (London: Bloomsbury Arden Shakespeare, 2019), 177–94; Sandra Young, 'Beyond Indigenisation: *Hamlet*, *Haider*, and the Pain of the Kashmiri People', *Shakespeare*, 14 (2018): 374–89.

44 Bettina Bildhauer, 'Queer Medieval Time in *Hamlet* (1921)', in *Sex, Gender and Time in Fiction and Culture*, ed. Ben Davies and Jana Funke (Houndmills: Palgrave Macmillan, 2011), 19–37.

45 Lee Edelman, 'Against Survival: Queerness in a Time That's Out of Joint', *Shakespeare Quarterly*, 62(2) (Summer 2011): 148–69, and '*Hamlet*: Hamlet's Wounded Name', in *Shakesqueer: A Queer Companion to the Complete Works of Shakespeare*, ed. Madhavi Menon (Durham, NC: Duke University Press, 2011), 97–105; Carla Freccero, 'Forget Hamlet', *Shakespeare Quarterly*, 62(2) (Summer 2011): 170–3; Kathryn Schwarz, '*Hamlet* Without Us', *Shakespeare Quarterly*, 62(2) (Summer 2011): 174–9.

46 James Kuzner, 'Hamlet and the Truth About Friendship', in *This Distracted Globe: Worldmaking in Early Modern Literature*, ed. Marcie Frank, Jonathan Goldberg and Karen Newman (New York: Fordham University Press, 2016), 100–120; Michael Neill, '"He That Thou Knowest Thine": Friendship and Service in *Hamlet*', in *A Companion to Shakespeare's Works, Volume I: The Tragedies*, ed. Richard Dutton and Jean E. Howard (Oxford: Blackwell Publishing, 2006), 319–38.

47 Sonya Freeman Loftis and Lisa Ulevich, 'Obsession/Rationality/Agency: Autistic Shakespeare', in *Disability, Health, and*

Happiness in the Shakespearean Body, ed. Sujata Iyengar (Abingdon: Routledge, 2015), 58–75 (63).

48 Randall Martin, *Shakespeare and Ecology* (Oxford: Oxford University Press, 2015), 134; Karen Raber, 'Vermin and Parasites: Shakespeare's Animal Architectures', in *Ecocritical Shakespeare*, ed. Lynne Bruckner, Dan Brayton, Greg Garrard and Simon C. Estok (Abingdon: Routledge, 2011), 13–32 (27); Rebecca Laroche, 'Ophelia's Plants and the Death of Violets' in *Ecocritical Shakespeare*, 211–21.

49 We adopt the term 'cultural field' from Pierre Bourdieu's *The Field of Cultural Production* (New York: Columbia University Press, 1993).

1

Hamlet's Touch of Picture

Kaara L. Peterson

When Hamlet is presented with Yorick's skull in the play's famous graveyard scene in Act 5, audiences reflexively expect to see the melancholy Dane holding the skull aloft in thoughtful reflection, as performed by innumerable actors famous and obscure. The evocative setting sums up in a single gesture *the* quintessential picture of Hamlet's melancholy character and, arguably, even the play's, as well as Shakespeare's, singular place in the Western canon. After all, the scene subsequently inspired myriad artistic representations, from Thomas Lawrence's 1801 rendering of the commanding John Philip Kemble in the role, possibly the first such painted depiction, to Eugène Delacroix's multiple early nineteenth-century illustrations; Stratford-upon-Avon's Victorian-era statue commemorating the play in Bancroft Gardens (1888); and the famous film still of Olivier in the role (1948), not to mention countless parodies.[1] Erroneously long believed to be of Shakespeare himself, the Ashbourne portrait (1612) of Sir Hugh Hamersley hanging in the Folger Shakespeare Library (Fig. 1.1) was in fact altered, apparently to suggest that Shakespeare the man could be identified with his character Hamlet were the playwright merely accessorized with Yorick's skull.[2] These works tell us a great deal about how the play's graveyard scene has gradually distilled into a visual representation of Shakespeare's original genius.

FIGURE 1.1 Ashbourne Portrait, *1612. Courtesy of the Folger Shakespeare Library.*

But would the early modern playgoing public have viewed the scene this way when they attended a performance of *Hamlet c.* 1600? And what prevailing aesthetic currents might have led Shakespeare to picture the graveyard scene in the particular fashion that he does? While it is not new to observe that the famed scene draws on contemporaneous visual arts examples for its composition, namely familiar memento mori images, less well noted is Shakespeare's debt to more than one strain of pictorial influence.[3] Accordingly, this essay explores what examples from period portraiture likely help shape Shakespeare's visual imagination as he composes the graveyard scene, how he combines several genres of portrait painting fashionable in the late sixteenth and early seventeenth centuries to inform his own 'picture' of the scene. Even if it is difficult to identify conclusively the very *first* in a catalogue of images to depict Hamlet in the manner to which we have been become so accustomed since the character's subsequent representation in a long history of visual art, it is possible to trace the aesthetic influences exerted on Shakespeare's artistry in the quintessential scene to the genre of domestic 'citizen portraits', with their distinct memento mori elements, as well as to the English portrait miniature's depictions of melancholy males set in rustic outdoor or country garden settings. In bringing these two genres of visual representation to life in the form of kinetic performance by actors on a stage, arguably Shakespeare's graveyard scene is identifiable as a very early example of a *tableau vivant*, or living picture, a theatrical presentation by re-enactors whose poses mirror those represented in two-dimensional works of art. Seen in this light, this essay explores how *Hamlet*'s scene not only records the contemporary visual influences brought to bear on a playwright's imagination but also documents how these influences translate into novel performance practices on stage. Appropriately enough, Shakespeare's iconic scene has a significant afterlife of its own and seems to have also widely influenced other artists' compositions since its appearance, from Middleton's staging of his *Revenger's Tragedy* to a portrait of Queen Elizabeth in a melancholy pose, which I will turn to at the essay's close.

Staged portraits

What did Shakespeare's scene look like to playgoing audiences? Unlike some artistic representations of scenes in Shakespeare's canon that interpolate what is only off-stage action (Ophelia's drowning, for instance), the actor's lines in Act 5 would seem to indicate that Hamlet does indeed take Yorick's skull from the gravedigger's grip and poise it in his hand in the signature contemplative gesture, performed on stage:

> FIRST CLOWN This same skull, sir, was
> Yorick's skull, the King's jester.
>
> HAMLET
> This?
>
> FIRST CLOWN
> E'en that.
>
> HAMLET
> Let me see.
>
> [*He takes the skull*]
>
> Alas, poor Yorick.
>
> (5.1.166–71)[4]

It is important to establish what early modern audiences apparently would have seen – Hamlet grasping the property of the skull after he asks to view it – and his subsequently spoken observations would also authorize further indexical gestures by the actor: '*Here* hung those lips that I have kissed I know not how oft' (178–9; my italics). It also seems likely, in line with the longstanding custom of the play's theatrical performance, that audiences see the gravedigger enter and perform standing from within the trapdoor or 'hell' recess below, a useful means of realistically evoking a grave in early modern staging practice, which typically evokes the setting of a scene through dialogue alone. If the trapdoor recess represents the open grave where the gravedigger stands, it is just as unlikely, then, that seventeenth-century viewers of *Hamlet*'s stage would see anything resembling a naturalistic representation of an outdoor exterior, such as a graveyard, the location instead established imaginatively for the audience by the gravedigger's exchange with Hamlet and the stage property of Yorick's skull. Taking the skull aloft in his hand, the melancholy prince then muses on the quintessence of dust, certain inspiration for the many subsequent artistic representations that have taken the imprint of this scene and left it to posterity as Shakespeare's most iconic.

Yet already by the time of Hamlet's creation, Shakespeare's scene's 'picture' is just as much a visual arts cliché as the play is thought to be an innovation in the revenge tragedy canon. Rather than be seen as the wholly original mark of Shakespeare's genius, the play's visual tableau of Hamlet holding Yorick's skull might more promisingly be seen instead as inspired by a large catalogue of period portraits, the popular 'citizen portrait' identified by National Gallery curator Tarnya Cooper.[5] In her monograph *Citizen Portrait*: *Portrait Painting and the Urban Elite of Tudor and Jacobean England and Wales* (2012), Cooper explores the rise of the memento mori portrait as a popular mode of self-depiction for urban middle-elite citizens. The portrait genre has escaped much extended commentary, thus 'creating the false impression that portraiture was only employed by, and socially acceptable for, the nobility and gentry as the hereditary elite'; rather, 'it is now clear that in the latter half of the sixteenth century the employment of portraiture became an increasingly useful strategy of distinction for new types of patrons, broadly categorized here as the urban elite'.[6] Commissioning artworks to testify to their worldly success, these pious English citizens temper celebrations of their wealth and stature with a recognition that all is passing show. Fairly sober compositions display the sitter at usually three-quarters' length, often dressed in the expensive black textiles favoured by the merchant class and aristocrats; the depicted personages might stand beside a table where a skull sits merely as an accessory, or, more intimately, rest their hands atop the skull.[7]

A survey of Cooper's catalogue reveals the skull portrait genre is certainly popular, proliferating with examples ranging from renowned painters such as Hans Eworth's work *Unknown Man in a Red Doublet* (*c.* 1546) and John de Critz's portraits of wealthy individuals and aristocrats, to portrayals of the merchant classes, to the portrait of the commercially successful embroiderer William Brodric (1614).[8] The 1612 Ashbourne portrait of Hamersley – the same portrait later repainted to suggest not Hamersley's but Shakespeare's likeness, paired with the iconic skull and conflated with his character Hamlet – was also the model for Brodric's depiction. In an odd recapitulation, then, Hamersley's real-life image inspired Brodric's memento mori portrait before Hamersley's own portrait metamorphosed into a painterly, biographical fiction of Shakespeare as Hamlet.

Given the prevalence of urban elite citizen portraiture in the sixteenth century, it seems unlikely Shakespeare would *not* have encountered several or even many of these artworks in his lifetime and he may have owned portraits himself. Susan Foister observes that while 'a lack of evidence' in documentary records 'has long made it difficult to arrive at an accurate assessment of the extent of picture owning in sixteenth-century England', some public records of extant household inventories do document merchants' and everyday citizens' ownership of august personages' portraits, including those of Elizabeth I, revealing some information about non-elite domestic habits and patterns of 'picture' collecting in the period.[9]

The most significant example of merchants' portraiture Cooper highlights is of Thomas Gresham, founder of the Royal Exchange (opened by Queen Elizabeth in 1571). Dated 1544, the portrait commemorates the year Gresham joined the Mercers' Company. Unusual for its 'full-length format' that is 'principally reserved for portraits of royal sitters', it is equally 'rare' and 'audacious', its style apparently borrowed for later merchant portraits.[10] As Cooper observes, 'Gresham's portrait would have been considered an exceptional sight hanging within a mercantile context in London'.[11] Cooper elaborates, 'Where Thomas Gresham's portrait hung for the remainder of his life is not clear, but it is probable that it came back to England soon after completion'.[12] Despite these uncertainties, Gresham's portrait offers, regardless, a compelling real-life example of mercantile professional success in Shakespeare's day immortalized in art, a testament to outsize aspiration and ambition left to future viewers not unlike Shakespeare's oeuvre.

It seems likely, therefore, that the playwright himself would have seen just such an example of a London merchant's portrait in a domestic interior or, less likely, even Gresham's own imposing life-size portrait.[13] Shakespeare need not have seen any particular portrait, of course, to have been cognizant of the artform's general vogue, a point made by many other scholars about popular forms of visual art or illustrations that influenced him. The conventions of portraiture were also current enough to urban playgoing audiences generally, Cooper points out, such that John Marston's contemporaneous

FIGURE 1.2 Portrait of Thomas Gresham, *1544. Courtesy of the Mercers' Company.*

Antonio and Mellida (*c.* 1599) expected viewers 'to understand the joke being played out on stage when an idiotic character discusses a portrait with a painter and misunderstands the Latin inscription'.[14]

Later altered by the artist to emphasize the visual, indexical line between Gresham's gloves and the skull, the rendering of the portrait's skull is, however, memorably unconventional, distinctive amongst its peers.[15] The skull's perspective tilts back to the right, looking upwards into the cavity from its base, with a top row of teeth and the nasal and spinal column cavities visible.[16] With its odd perspectival angle, the skull once again distinguishes Gresham's memento mori portrait from orthodoxy. It is also notably 'quite chapfallen', in Hamlet's phrase (182) or, put more precisely, missing its lower jawbone. This anatomical stylistic element does appear in many other citizen portraits, with slight variations. A work by an unattributed English artist of Gawen Goodman of Ruthin, dated around 1582, also depicts a prominent skull without a lower jawbone and bearing a single top dental row. Unusually, this skull is placed in a trompe l'oeil recess at the sitter's right, bearing the motto 'Cogita mori'.[17] Is the contemplative 'goodman' Shakespeare's pensive Hamlet? Could any of these striking images of real historical personalities, each with its distinctive theme, have been the actual models for Shakespeare's staging of the graveyard scene? These are, of course, speculative queries. Nonetheless it is true that Gresham's and Goodman's – or other mercers' and merchants' – portraits are not lesser examples of the widely available visual material that inspired the urban London playwright's imagination when he limned the play's iconic scene.

Setting the scene

Precisely because the staging unfolds at the site of an open grave, it is interesting that the dialogue between Hamlet and the gravedigger focuses solely on the cranial remains of the grave's inhabitants rather than on the more fully complete skeletons associated with common memento mori, those 'dance of death' skeletal images that decorate tombs and other sites in Shakespeare's England.[18] It is therefore distinctly possible that the attention paid to Yorick's skull is instead directly attributable to the scene's origins in the fashionable domestic citizen portraiture that concentrates the viewer's attention on the skull. Andrew Sofer notes that the graveyard scene 'is apparently the first known scene in which skulls are used as stage properties', and if Roland Mushat Frye's claim that Shakespeare's use of the skull property is 'a striking innovation on the London stage' is also correct, then it is equally conceivable that this development charts just how the citizen portrait finds particular tribute in *Hamlet*.[19]

We might say that Hamlet's imitative pose is truly a staging or an enactment before his audience of an exceptionally popular form of early modern visual art – the static two-dimensional citizen portrait brought to vivid life through Shakespeare's appropriation, that is, or art imitating art.[20] Sofer discusses Hamlet's holding Yorick's skull with another popular art form of the period, the anamorphic portrait, but we might see *Hamlet*'s scene instead as an early depiction of a *tableau vivant*. The *tableau vivant*, 'A silent and motionless person or group of people posed and attired to represent a well-known character, event, or work of art', or 'a person or group of people forming a striking or picturesque scene', is of course commonly understood to develop as an identifiable art form only in the eighteenth century. The playwright's employment of a familiar citizen portrait genre to illustrate the graveyard scene thus turns one genre of art into another, a living picture, making *Hamlet* a picture for the times. It is also useful to note that the *tableaux vivants* in *Hamlet* – I will return to another later – anticipate by a decade the more celebrated staging of Hermione, the Julio Romano statue, ostensibly animating in *The Winter's Tale* (*c.* 1610), notably the very scene staged as a *tableau vivant* by Gwendolyn Harleth in George Eliot's *Daniel Deronda* (1876). Seen in this light, *Hamlet*'s aesthetic contribution to the history of art may be far more important than previously recognized.

The graveyard scene contains further interesting innovations, revealing Shakespeare's debt to other forms of artistic expression. For many citizen portraits and *vanitas* works, the solitary skull is the primary ornament and focal point, the setting clearly indoors. Occasionally a composition depicts the sitter situated in front of what might be an exterior wall, though most commonly, a curtain or tapestry creates a domestic interior backdrop, along with minimal furniture or ornament, perhaps a clock. Other memento mori paintings, however, do frequently depict interiors resplendent with material objects paying homage to human invention and intellectual achievement, such as those observed in Hans Holbein's famous anamorphic work *The Ambassadors* (1533).[21] When nature is present in *vanitas* paintings, it is often in the form of *nature morte*, with game animals, exotic marine crustacea or shells, and other natural things domesticated, brought indoors.

Yet *Hamlet*'s graveyard scene is unambiguously set outdoors, or at least is imagined to be so by playgoers, in distinct contrast to the static interior settings of the other examples above. If the play pays tribute to the popular citizen portrait then in vogue, then it is also true that the graveyard scene draws on another native English tradition of portraiture, namely miniatures, with their pensive melancholy figures captured in natural settings, gardens and landscapes. This genre includes familiar works ranging from Nicholas Hilliard's *Young Man Among Roses* (1585–95), who leans against a tree, and Isaac Oliver's *Young Man Seated Under a Tree* (1590–5) perched above formal gardens. Other images such as Oliver's *Herbert of Cherbury* (1610–14) and Hilliard's miniature of Henry Percy (*c.* 1594–5) depict each peer in a sylvan landscape, head declining on his open hand in the classic melancholy attitude; Percy appears suited in black with a book beside him.[22] Roy Strong writes that Oliver's *Young Man Seated Under a Tree* 'turns his back on wordly matters in pursuit of a life dedicated to arcane contemplation', though this might describe all of the examples equally well.[23] The ostensibly natural setting where Hamlet considers Yorick's skull animates the character's distinctive yet fashionable melancholy. By dislocating the stock elements of the domestic citizen portrait, then, Shakespeare resituates his picture of Hamlet out of doors, thus achieving a novel effect. Thus it is specifically here in the graveyard scene where the current fashion for urban elite portraiture in Shakespeare's day coalesces with the musings of a pointedly melancholy hero on the English stage.

Hamlet's parodic, antic re-enactment of lovesick melancholy for Ophelia's audience in 2.1 may be said to mirror precisely the familiar affective nature and dishevelled dress of Henry Percy or the other lovesick individuals in Hilliard's and Oliver's miniatures.[24] His melancholy disposition established early in the play through allusions to his 'inky' clothing (1.2.77), Ophelia describes Hamlet's now alarming sartorial appearance, 'with his doublet all unbraced, / No hat upon his head, his stockings fouled, / Ungartered and down-gyved to his ankle, / Pale as his shirt' (2.1.75–8). In her account, Hamlet re-enacts something that must look very much like a portrait of the typical melancholy lover, miming a familiar scene and a character type for Ophelia's private witness. The miniature depiction of the stylized melancholy lover is enacted by Hamlet silently for Ophelia as a *tableau vivant*, in fact, when the 'antic' prince brings an iconic, even clichéd art form to life, though it is only through Ophelia's report that the audience may picture for themselves the off-stage *tableau vivant*, those melancholy lovers in portraits given animation by Hamlet's performance.[25] Later when Hamlet demands that Gertrude compare portraits of Claudius and his brother in order to evince their true character, his albeit brief ekphrastic description of the royal personages must allude to the presence of real, ambulant portrait miniatures, stage properties or costume elements, not merely rhetorical flourishes. While this is a distinctly different theatrical moment from Hamlet's re-enactment of a melancholy lover's portrait, he demonstrates his further cognizance of portrait miniature conventions and, arguably, refers to their material presence on the London stage.[26]

It is thus reasonable to perceive that Shakespeare patterns his Danish prince as a fashionably melancholic character who holds a memento mori skull in his hands in the recognizable manner of a citizen portrait set outdoors. There is no evidence whatsoever, however, that the actor performing Hamlet's role on stage ever mimics the recognizable pose associated so famously with melancholics or, put more precisely, with Albrecht Dürer's *Melencolia I* (1514) – the signature inclining posture achieves iconic status well before the seventeenth century. By 1600, Dürer was an artist current enough for Nicholas Hilliard, the great innovator of the native English miniature tradition, to allude directly to the German artist in his *Treatise Concerning the Arte of Limning* (1600).[27] Whether it was perceived as such or not by London's urban citizenry, Dürer exerts significant influence over English artists' compositions. According to Erwin Panofsky, 'The influence of Dürer's *Melencolia I* . . . extended all over the European continent and lasted for more than three centuries. Its composition was simplified or made even more complicated . . . [and] reinterpreted according to the taste and mental habits of the day'.[28] That Dürer's work was commonly recognized as a visual metaphor for the 'intellectual situation of the artist' raises the compelling notion that Shakespeare may also have had *Melencolia*'s model in mind when he limned the intellectual prince.[29] We cannot know whether the actor playing Hamlet ever struck a melancholy attitude on stage, thereby documenting Dürer's direct influence on Shakespeare. It is similarly impossible to know whether the playwright sought to create yet one further visualization for his audience, one further *tableau vivant*, this time Hamlet enacting *Melencolia*'s iconic pose, with his head in hand. It is not implausible that Shakespeare might have done so, though.

At some juncture in cultural history, the artistic influences that inform Shakespeare's graveyard scene – the citizen portrait, Oliver's and Hilliard's miniature portraits of melancholic heroes, and possibly Dürer's *Melencolia* – do intertwine and form a representational commonplace, setting the pattern for how Hamlet's character is portrayed in the art of later periods.[30] While it may be an impossible task to locate

FIGURE 1.3 *Albrecht Dürer,* Melencolia I, *1514. Courtesy of National Gallery of Art, Washington DC.*

the very first example that conflates the two main compositional elements (the melancholy attitude, the material object of Yorick's skull held by Hamlet) within an artwork that definitively postdates the play, this conflation is entirely orthodox well before the nineteenth century. Frye comments that Franz Hals' earlier painting *Young Man with a Skull* (*c.* 1624–5) 'in the nineteenth and early twentieth centuries was confidently identified as a painting of Shakespeare's Hamlet' too, though Hals' subject is not in a melancholy pose.[31] Not

FIGURE 1.4 *Robert Walker,* Portrait of John Evelyn *(1648–c. 1656). By Permission of the National Portrait Gallery, London.*

explicitly identified with Hamlet at the time of its original composition, a portrait of the writer John Evelyn (*c.* 1648–56) does paint Evelyn in the familiar melancholy attitude, with a skull in hand, accompanied by a quotation about death by Seneca. But if Evelyn's melancholic pose is original to this example, the skull and sententia were only painted over other original elements at some later time; perhaps the point of the revision is not just to imagine that, for Evelyn, the readiness is all, but to cast him pointedly as Hamlet – an echo of the alterations made to the Ashbourne portrait of the playwright, those mentioned above that remade another personage into Shakespeare, cast in the image of his own character of Hamlet.[32] At what point, then, the artistic tradition coalesces and arrives at a demonstrably identifiable Hamlet holding a skull, in the classic melancholy pose, thus remains interestingly elusive.

Hamlet's afterlife

Like Dürer, the artist long recognized for innovations to his medium, Shakespeare sought to craft his pensive Hamlet as a character portrait with novel theatrical aspects. After all, Shakespeare's real innovation in *Hamlet* is to draw his figure with a melancholy intellectual *temperament* – in contradistinction to the cast of typically more bloody, hot-headed revenge tragedy characters (Hieronimo, Titus, Laertes). No scholar has missed that Hamlet is an uncommonly thoughtful revenger, influencing subsequent character portrayals, and while he may well have been a familiar visual arts amalgam of different allusions by the time Shakespeare draws him, this revenger wears his rue with a difference. Accordingly we might say that, in the graveyard scene, Shakespeare gives his Hamlet a touch of picture following the fashions of the day, pairing his novel revenger figure treading the stage with yet-*au courant* visual iconography. As Sofer notes, already by 1604, Thomas Dekker was crafting for *The Honest Whore, Part I*, 'a sandwich of leftovers from *Hamlet*', which included melancholic figures paired with skulls set within domestic scenes.[33] Even more explicitly, by Middleton's penning of *The Revenger's Tragedy* around 1607, the playwrights' public had received the full force of this imagery, for Middleton overtly satirizes *Hamlet*'s scene by opening his play with another arresting visual tableau, namely the revenger Vindice's address to the skull of Gloriana. Vindice's conceit now turns on Gloriana's hollow eye sockets rather than Yorick's lips:

Thou sallow picture of my poisoned love,
My study's ornament, thou shell of death,
Once the bright face of my betrothed lady,
When life and beauty naturally fill'd out
These ragged imperfections,
When two heaven-pointed diamonds were set
In those unsightly rings

(1.1.14–20)[34]

It is not accidental that Middleton's most pointed satirical treatment of *Hamlet* zeroes in on the graveyard scene, making it the opening for his own quixotic revision of the revenge tragedy genre and the memento mori portrait. Perhaps Middleton also wished to parody what he recognized as a familiar image of the citizen portrait by placing Gloriana's skull in the hands of a highly irreverent middling-sort revenger, achieving a send-up of *Hamlet* as well as of the portrait genre Middleton seems to have recognized as the source of the scene's inspiration to begin with.

Several scholars have noted that Gloriana's skull is a grotesque allusion to or even a metonymy for Elizabeth, the head of state and the skull of 'Gloriana' recently deceased.[35] Middleton's reference to Elizabeth through the vehicle of Vindice's 'Hamlet' scene is especially recognizable and memorable for a Gloriana who is 'killed into art',[36] but it is not the only work to associate the English Gloriana with Yorick's skull, or, moreover, with *Hamlet*. *Hamlet*'s visual tableaux performed in theatre seems to have gained enough notoriety to have loosely inspired requotation in subsequent stagecraft as well as more 'Hamlets' in artworks, marking a shift from the original play's aesthetic debts to new depictions of Gloriana, the queen, herself, in visual art.

A remarkable portrait of Queen Elizabeth at Corsham Court (*c.* 1610) represents an early example of two coalescing strains of artistic influence after *Hamlet* treaded the stage.[37] Few even heavily allegorical portraits of individuals contain the number of pronounced memento mori elements crowding the queen's portrait. An exemplar of the Renaissance era's characteristic expression of melancholy, Dürer's *Melencolia* clearly also inspired the Corsham artist's depiction of Elizabeth as a fashionable melancholic prince interrupted in the act of reading, her head resting in her open hand. Elizabeth's portrait is itself apparently an innovation in presenting melancholy female subjects that was not to become popular in court portraits until later depictions of Lucy Harington, Countess of Bedford, and others appear, mimicking Elizabeth's pose but

FIGURE 1.5 Queen Elizabeth I (1538–1603) in Old Age, c. *1610 (oil on panel). Bridgeman Images.*

without any of the other complex compositional detail: the attitude is all.[38] If it is evident that the Corsham portraitist borrows from Dürer's *Melencolia* directly for his limning of Gloriana, the painting's memento mori elements can also be said to reveal the possible influence of *Hamlet's* graveyard scene replete with its memento mori elements, Yorick's skull, and a melancholy prince. Is the Corsham artist's Queen Elizabeth modelled after the Danish prince?

Frye finds a ready correspondence between the two works' memento mori elements: 'executed at about the same time that Shakespeare was completing *Hamlet*, the painting shows the aged Queen Elizabeth with her prayerbook, flanked on the left by the weary figure of Time, and on the right by a menacing skeleton holding an hourglass'.[39] The queen's clearly defined melancholic attitude is perhaps the most striking, given that female melancholy is so inextricably linked to the era's reflexive Galenic belief in the inferiority of female humorality; even Elizabeth herself was documented to have suffered from the prosaic ailment at various points in the course of her reign.[40] Seen in this light, presenting the queen as an intellectual melancholic modelled after Dürer's design merely amplifies the compliment to her paid by the Corsham artist: the melancholy Elizabeth is no mere ordinary woman or urban elite of Shakespeare's or Thomas Gresham's ilk, but a superior melancholy *prince*, a familiar appellation used to describe Elizabeth's person in the uncanny uniting of bodies politic and natural, male and female respectively, that defined her reign.

Like Shakespeare's artful, composite graveyard scene but composed for a different medium, the Corsham tableau seems to execute a grand synthesis of all the available representational material – Dürer's *Melencolia*, *Hamlet*'s graveyard scene, various memento mori portraiture. For the anonymous artists who added the skull to the original portrait of the melancholy John Evelyn and who painted the Corsham's Elizabeth, these works all betray a gradual accretion of visual artistic influences circulating around *Hamlet* that join melancholy attitudes and memento mori imagery in a particular creative fashion.

Middleton's skull of Gloriana brought on stage to shock audiences into recapitulating (somewhat literally speaking) and thus recognizing the satirical jab at *Hamlet*'s graveyard scene it interpellates, then, is just one demonstration of *Hamlet*'s subsequent refraction and broad diffusion through early modern creative artists' imaginations. Of course, as this essay has explored, Shakespeare himself was already drawing from a veritable visual arts catalogue – the citizen portrait, the pensive melancholy figures in Hilliard's and Oliver's sylvan landscapes, and possibly Dürer's *Melencolia* – all to lend his *Hamlet* some colour and a touch of picture.

Notes

Grateful thanks to my colleagues in Miami University's Early Modern Studies group, James Bromley and Anna Klowsowska, and to this volume's editors and readers for providing helpful feedback on the essay at various stages. Grants supporting visits to the Folger Shakespeare Library from Miami University and the Newberry Renaissance Consortium made collections work possible. Special thanks are owed to the archivists at the Mercers' Company, London, especially Donna Marshall, for information about and images provided of Thomas Gresham.

1 Sir Thomas Lawrence's portrait of Kemble is at the Tate Britain, http://www.tate.org.uk/art/artworks/lawrence-john-philip-kemble-as-hamlet-n00142. Several of Eugène Delacroix's depictions from 1827–8, 1839, 1843 and 1859 are in the Louvre, http://cartelen.louvre.fr/cartelen/visite?srv=car_not_frame&idNotice=8209&langue=en.

2 See the Folger's site for a discussion of the painting's transformation from a portrait of Sir Hugh Hamersley to Shakespeare's, http://folgerpedia.folger.edu/The_Ashbourne_portrait. For a more detailed study, see William L. Pressly's 'The Ashbourne Portrait of Shakespeare: Through the Looking Glass', *Shakespeare Quarterly*, 44.1 (Spring 1993): 54–72, esp. 59–60.

3 For scholarship on the resonances of memento mori, *vanitas,* and similar imagery, see Bridget Gellert Lyons, *Voices of Melancholy:*

Studies in Literary Treatments of Melancholy in Renaissance England (New York: Barnes and Noble, 1971); Roland Mushat Frye, *The Renaissance Hamlet: Issues and Responses in 1600* (Princeton: Princeton University Press, 1984); Phoebe S. Spinrad, *The Summons of Death on the Medieval and Renaissance Stage* (Columbus: Ohio State University Press, 1987); Andrew Sofer, *The Stage Life of Props* (Ann Arbor: University of Michigan Press, 2003); Marjorie Garber, '"Remember Me": "Memento Mori" Figures in Shakespeare's Plays', *Renaissance Drama* 12, ns (1981): 3–25. On Shakespeare's 'artful' imagination broadly, see Stuart Sillars' *Shakespeare and the Visual Imagination* (Cambridge: Cambridge University Press, 2015) and Alan R. Young, *Hamlet and the Visual Arts, 1709–1900* (Newark: University of Delaware Press, 2002).

4 Quotation taken from *Hamlet*, *The Norton Shakespeare*, ed. Stephen Greenblatt et al. (New York: Norton, 1997), 1668–1759. Textual variants 'Let me see' derive from F1 and 'I prethee let me see it' from Q1. See *Hamlet*, The Arden Shakespeare, ed. Ann Thompson and Neil Taylor (London: Thomson, 2006), esp. 422, n.172; further quotes are from this edition.

5 Tarnya Cooper, *Citizen Portrait: Portrait Painting and the Urban Elite of Tudor and Jacobean England and Wales* (New Haven: Yale University Press, 2012). Cooper writes, 'The skull or "death's head" was a universally understood device in court culture and more generally across sixteenth-century Europe' and may have come to represent faith-based salvation for a Protestant England (82).

6 Cooper, *Citizen Portrait*, 1. I borrow Cooper's term 'urban elite'.

7 See Cooper, *Citizen Portrait*, esp. chapter 3. Most sitters are male, but Katheryn of Berain is depicted as her male peers are. See Cooper, *Elizabeth I and Her People*, 48.

8 The Eworth painting is located in Besançon. The portrait of William Brodric in Wandsworth is cited in Cooper's *Searching for Shakespeare* 36 and *Citizen Portrait*, 72, 79, where she identifies him as the 'king's embroiderer'.

9 Susan Foister, 'Paintings and other works of art in sixteenth-century English inventories', *The Burlington Magazine* 123.938 (May 1981): 273–82; 273, 274. Foister's analysis of 613 Public

Record Office records largely from 1480–1580 demonstrates that many portraits are owned by non-elite citizens, members of the gentry, merchants, and/or guild members.

10 Cooper, *Citizen Portrait*, 90.

11 Cooper, *Citizen Portrait*, 91. Roy Strong, *Tudor and Jacobean Portraits*, Vol. 1 (London: Her Majesty's Stationery Office, 1969), states that there are three copies of the portrait, one at Titsey Place; the more certain provenance of the Mercers' copy is 'Gresham's house at Hoxne Abbey' (130).

12 Cooper, *Citizen Portrait*, 91.

13 Gresham died in 1579, before Shakespeare's arrival in London following the 'lost years'. The Royal Exchange stood until 1666, however.

14 Cooper, *Citizen Portrait*, 3–4.

15 The National Portrait Gallery, London, notes on the painting's chat card that the gloves were repainted.

16 Cooper comments, 'the skull is not simply an emblem, but seems to play an important role in its composition,' with its unusual 'pure physicality of its crevices' (*Citizen Portrait*, 91).

17 The National Museum of Wales attributes Goodman's portrait (1582) to a 'British School' artist. See https://museum.wales/art/online/?action=show_item&item=160. Cooper writes about Goodman in the exhibition catalogue *Elizabeth I and Her People* (London: National Portrait Gallery, 2013), 146.

18 See Nigel Llewellyn's chapter on the subject, *The Art of Death: Visual Culture in the English Death Ritual c. 1500-c.1800* (London: Reaktion, 1997) 19ff; Frye, 212, 221, and 223; Cooper, *Citizen Portrait* 108–9; Garber; and Keir Elam on Shakespeare's pictorialism, especially in *Hamlet*, in *Shakespeare's Pictures: Visual Objects in the Drama*, the Arden Shakespeare (London and New York: Bloomsbury, 2017).

19 Sofer, 47 and Frye, 206. Marjorie Garber discusses memento mori imagery written into stage performances; alluding to a 'scene in terms of its stage picture' (13), but does not explore the graveyard scene.

20 *The Oxford English Dictionary*, third edition, 2008. The second edition (1989) provides deeper historical contextualization and

further definition, 'A group of persons and accessories, producing a picturesque effect'.

21 See the National Gallery website: http://www.nationalgallery.org.uk/paintings/hans-holbein-the-younger-the-ambassadors

22 Hilliard's *Young Man Among Roses* is in the Victoria & Albert Museum, http://www.vam.ac.uk/content/articles/y/nicholas-hilliards-young-man-among-roses/, and *Harry Percy* is in the Rijksmuseum, https://www.rijksmuseum.nl/en/collection/RP-T-1981-2, while Oliver's *Young Man Seated Under a Tree* is in the Royal Collection, https://www.royalcollection.org.uk/collection/420639/a-young-man-seated-under-a-tree, and *Herbert of Cherbury* is at Powis Castle, https://artuk.org/discover/artworks/sir-edward-herbert-later-1st-lord-herbert-of-cherbury-158115821648-244835. On these works, see Roy C. Strong, *The Cult of Elizabeth: Portraiture and Pageantry* (London: Thames and Hudson, 1977), 56ff and *The Artist and the Garden* (New Haven and London: Yale University Press, 2000) and Laurinda S. Dixon, *The Dark Side of Genius: The Melancholic Persona in Art, ca. 1500–1700* (University Park, PA: Pennsylvania State University Press, 2013).

23 Strong, *The Artist and the Garden*, 95. See also Elam on the melancholy Percy.

24 Strong also notes that Hilliard's lovelorn personage in *Among Roses* and Percy's 'somewhat disheveled' state, 'with shirt and doublet undone' (*Artist*, 96), are some of the many available visual arts models for Hamlet's antic performance and true melancholy. Similarly, Cooper recalls Hamlet's 'customary suits of solemn black' in her discussion of black clothes favored by citizens (*Citizen*, 78) and also Ophelia's observations on Hamlet's garb, noting the typically disheveled clothing of melancholics (193).

25 While the melancholic and sometimes also lovesick males depicted in the miniature art form may be more elite than those individuals typically presented in the citizen portrait, the portrait miniatures limned by Hilliard and Oliver became popular enough with non-elites to support a significant production and workshop. On this subject, see the exhibition catalogue by Catharine MacLeod, ed., *Elizabethan Treasures: Miniatures by Hilliard and Oliver* (London: National Portrait Gallery, 2019).

26 The term 'ambulant' to describe portrait miniatures is Marcia Pointon's; see 'Surrounded with Brilliants, Miniature Portraits in Eighteenth-Century England,' *The Art Bulletin* 83. 1 (2001): 48–71; 51. Elam considers whether the portraits need be miniatures (252ff) but the scene suggests the intimacy of a portrait 'in little'.

27 See Nicholas Hilliard, *A Treatise Concerning the Arte of Limning*, ed. R. K. R. Thornton and T. G. S. Cain (Ashington: Mid-Northumberland Arts Group/Carcanet New Press, 1981), 61, 89. On Dürer's influence on Hilliard see Elizabeth Goldring, *Robert Dudley, Earl of Leicester, and the World of Elizabethan Art* (New Haven and London: Yale University Press, 2014).

28 Erwin Panofsky is the classic authority on Dürer's *Melencolia* and the melancholy 'attitude', *The Life and Art of Albrecht Dürer* (Princeton: Princeton University Press, 1955), 170.

29 See Panofsky, 171 and the Metropolitan Museum's site: '*Melencolia I* is a depiction of the intellectual situation of the artist and is thus, by extension, a spiritual self-portrait of Dürer': http://www.metmuseum.org/toah/works-of-art/43.106.1/. See also more recent scholarship by Drew Daniel, *The Melancholy Assemblage: Affect and Epistemology in the English Renaissance* (New York: Fordham University Press, 2013) and Dixon.

30 Alan R. Young locates the earliest illustrations of *Hamlet* in eighteenth-century printed editions of the play. See *Hamlet and the Visual Arts, 1709–1900*, esp. 246.

31 Frye, 207.

32 For an image of the portrait and also the details about its compositional changes, see http://www.npg.org.uk/collections/search/portrait/mw08141/John-Evelyn. See also Llewellyn, 12 and Frye, 207. Hals' work is at the National Gallery: https://www.nationalgallery.org.uk/paintings/frans-hals-young-man-holding-a-skull-vanitas

33 Sofer, 55.

34 Citation from *The Revenger's Tragedy*, ed. Brian Gibbons, New Mermaids (New York: Norton, 1991).

35 See for instance Steven Mullaney, 'Mourning and Misogyny: *Hamlet*, *The Revenger's Tragedy*, and the Final Progress of Elizabeth I, 1600–1607', *Shakespeare Quarterly* 45.2 (Summer 1994): 139–62, Garber, and Sofer.

36 The term is Laurie Finke's, brought to my attention by Sofer, 63.

37 The Corsham Court painting owned by Lord Methuen is currently unattributed; Methuen-Campbell gives the date as *c.*1610, *Corsham Court* (n.p.: Jarrold, 2004), 12.

38 Lucy Harington's melancholy portrait is in the National Galleries of Scotland, *c.* 1620. There are few examples before the Corsham work, before 1600.

39 Frye, 212.

40 See my longer discussion of Elizabeth's melancholy, 'Picturing Elizabeth I's Triumph of Melancholy', *English Literary Renaissance* 48.1 (2018): 1–40; a footnote in that essay led me to explore Shakespeare's scene further here.

2

Remembering Ophelia

Theatrical Properties and the Performance of Memory in Shakespeare's *Hamlet*

Kathryn M. Moncrief

The Judde Memorial (see Fig. 2.1), a 1560 painting by an unknown English artist, featuring unsmiling newlyweds contemplating a corpse, hands on a skull as they exchange vows, may strike the modern viewer as unusually macabre. In the painting, the close connections between love, marriage and death are clear. It bears several suggestive inscriptions, including 'Thus consumythe our tyme', 'we behowlde ower ende', 'The word of God / Hath knit us twayne / And death shall us / Divide agayne', and, finally, 'Live to dye and dye to lyve eternally'. As Nigel Llewellyn notes, the emblematic

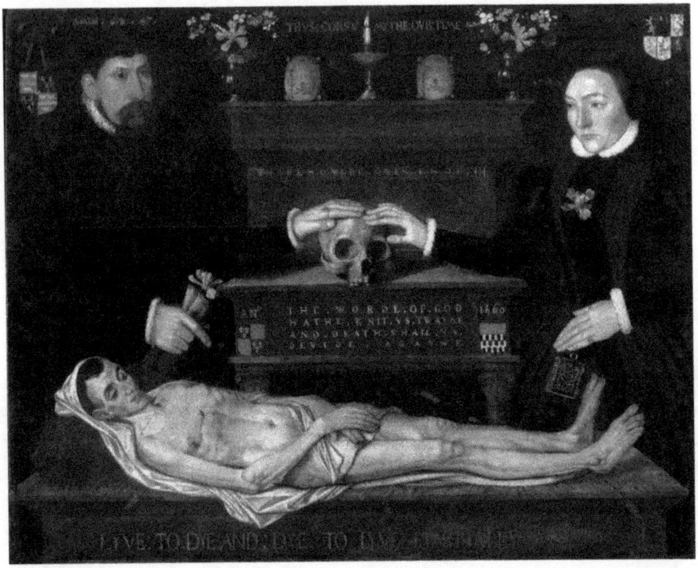

FIGURE 2.1 *British School,* The Judde Memorial, c. *1560, oil on panel, 80 × 102.2 cm, DPG354. Dulwich Picture Gallery, London.*

picture is a visual representation of 'Till death do us part', unsettling to the modern viewer, but familiar in the tradition of *momento mori* artefacts and objects.[1] Marjorie Garber identifies the importance of memento mori themes in Elizabethan portraiture: 'skulls, rotting cadavers, clocks, and watches frequently appeared as part of the composition – in effect moralizing on the time – emphasizing the transitoriness of the sitter and of his station in life'.[2] The couple, even in the present moment of union, must remember to be aware of the fact that life and death are intertwined.

The passage of time and the importance of memory are further enhanced by the inscription on the original frame: 'When we are deade and in owr graves, and all owre bones are rottun, by this shall we rememberd be, when we shuld be forgottyn'.[3] The painting itself, commemorating its long-dead subjects who are themselves as 'rotten' as the corpse with which they are associated, is an object of memory, asking the reader to gaze on and remember the couple while, at the same time, prompting viewers to remember, ponder and confront their own inescapable mortality.

I believe that *Hamlet* belongs to the same tradition, as a play obsessed with both memory and mortality. It opens with the guards interpreting what they have seen by remembering the dead King – 'Such was the very armour he had on / When he the ambitious Norway combated' (1.1.59–60) – and the final scene is bookended with memory.[4] In this scene, Hamlet asks Horatio, 'So much for this, sir. Now shall you see the other: / You do remember all the circumstance?' (5.2.1–2), referencing the letter he had sent Horatio (4.6) that described how he managed to escape from the ship that had been carrying him to England. It ends with Hamlet, as he nears his final breath, imploring his friend to remember him, to 'report me and my cause aright / To the unsatisfied' (5.2.323–4) and 'To tell my story' (5.2.333). Examples of remembering and the consequences of forgetting echo and reverberate throughout the play, from King Claudius's assertion that, though the memory of his brother's death 'be green' (1.2.2), his listeners ought to 'think on him / Together with remembrance of ourselves' (1.2.6–7), to Hamlet's tortured 'Must I remember?' (1.2.143), to Polonius's desire to impart 'these few precepts in thy memory' (1.3.57) before his son departs, to Laertes' insistence that his sister 'remember well / What I have said to you' (1.3.83–4), to the ghost's injunction to his son that he must 'remember me' (1.5.91) and his reminder 'Do not forget!' (3.4.106), to Ophelia's handing out of 'rosemary . . . for remembrance' (4.5.169). The words 'memory', 'remember', 'rememb'red' or 'remembrance(s)' appear twenty-four times in *Hamlet*, more frequently than in any other play by Shakespeare.[5]

The play is also keenly conscious of the connection between material objects and memory. As Peter Stallybrass, Roger Cartier, J. Franklin Mowery and Heather Wolfe have convincingly shown, books are prominent in *Hamlet* and are intricately connected to memory; more specifically, they argue that 'perhaps the most important book in the play, both figuratively and literally, is that of memory' (379).[6] Another prominent material object, Ophelia's rosemary 'for remembrance' (4.5.169), is an obvious object of memory, as is Yorick's skull, which functions as a present and effective *memento mori*. Gail Kern Paster suggests that Yorick's skull functions as a 'cognitive prop'[7] by being both the embodiment of Yorick and of idealized memory. The image of Hamlet holding the skull of 'poor Yorick' (5.1.174), remembering him as a 'fellow of infinite jest' (5.1.175) who 'bore me on his back a thousand times' (5.1.176), is one of the play's most enduring and easily identifiable moments; no promotional materials for a production of the play are complete without a version of this iconic image (see Web Figs 2.2, 2.3, 2.4) as the skull easily triggers visual associations with the play.[8]

Although Yorick's skull is perhaps the most recognizable and widely noted memory object in *Hamlet*, other aspects of the play associated with memory have been neglected. This essay focuses on the stage properties in 3.1 – the so-called 'nunnery scene' – in an effort to understand the significance of Ophelia's lines, 'My lord, I have remembrances of yours / That I have longed long to redeliver. / I pray you now receive them' (3.1.92–4) and Hamlet's response, 'No, not I. / I never gave you aught' (3.1.95).[9] It also explores how memory is embodied in the play, as well as this scene's implications for theatrical performance. Although these lines suggest that Ophelia gives (or attempts to give) something back to Hamlet, what, exactly, she returns to him is unclear. Many other properties used in the play, including weapons (a partisan, foils, daggers), gauntlets, books, writing-tables, recorders, flowers and herbs, a spade, skulls, flagons of wine, cups, and a pearl, are either specified in stage directions or mentioned in the dialogue. That Ophelia's 'remembrances' should remain unidentified is noteworthy, especially in light of the fact that they are associated with memory.

There are many possible options for Ophelia's 'remembrances'. Ann Thompson and Neil Taylor, in their Arden edition of the play, gloss 'remembrances' as 'gifts, mementoes, love-tokens',[10] while Pamela S. Hammonds defines 'love tokens' as 'items exchanged to show affection, love, or desire between romantic lovers, family members, or friends or to express religious devotion'[11] and notes how frequently love poems 'refer to or depict very tangible material items, such as rings, bracelets, necklaces, flowers, lace, body parts and children'.[12] Assuming that Ophelia's remembrances are gifts or love tokens affects how we understand her relationship with Hamlet. As Karen Newman has observed, drawing on the seminal work of Marcel Mauss, 'Gift-giving is significant . . . because it establishes and expresses social bonds between partners of the exchange'.[13] Further, as Diana O'Hara has shown, 'gift-giving was a socially recognised, even psychologically binding custom in a pre-industrial society. . . Attitudes to giving and receiving, to refusing or returning gifts and tokens, demonstrate the constraints imposed, the repercussions experienced and the implicit significatory force behind the practice'.[14] Hamlet's offering of a gift (or gifts), that Ophelia has received, demonstrates that some kind of relationship exists; returning it then, even under duress, shows a break or rupture.

Also pertinent, in the context of this essay, is Jennine Hurl-Eamon's exploration of the significance of love tokens in confirming relationships and as a physical aid for memory, particularly between lovers who are apart (for example, soldiers who are deploying and leaving their wives or sweethearts behind): 'In the absence of such modern memory aids as video, telephone calls, and emails, these love tokens bore an even stronger role in retaining the memory of the giver, and of the relationship that inspired the gift'.[15] Ophelia later refers to the '[r]ich gifts' (3.1.100) she is trying to return, acknowledging that the objects, accompanied by Hamlet's 'words of so sweet breath composed / As made these things more rich' (3.1.97–8), have been made valuable to her by his words. These are not the only relationship-establishing gifts, or powerful words, in the play; the Ghost of Hamlet's father refers to the 'traitorous gifts – / O wicked wit and gifts that have the power / So to seduce' (1.5.43–5) his brother used to win Gertrude, hinting at a courtship that Hamlet (and the audience) were not privy to.

Courtship gifts and love tokens often appear in Shakespeare's plays in exchanges between would-be lovers. In *A Midsummer Night's Dream*, Egeus recounts for Theseus that Lysander has 'interchang'd love-tokens with my child' (1.1.29), then proceeds to name them. They include not only 'verses of feigning love' (1.1.31) but also 'bracelets of thy hair, rings, gawds, conceits, / Knacks, trifles, nosegays, sweetmeats' (1.1.32–3). Other courtship gifts include Desdemona's embroidered handkerchief in *Othello*, a 'token' (3.3.297) which was 'her first remembrance from the Moor' (3.3.295), and the favours of verses, gems, a glove and pearls that the men send to the women in *Love's Labour's Lost*. David Cressy, discussing the significance of gifts in the courtship process, explains that

> [w]hether driven by love or scripted by social convention, courtship required the giving and acceptance of presents and tokens. Coins, rings, ribbons, gloves, girdles, and similar knick-knacks did the trick. Such gifts, usually passed by hand from the man to the woman, signaled the intimate strengthening of their bond. Their monetary value mattered less than their symbolism. Further gifts, most commonly a ring, changed hands when the couple was contracted, betrothed, or 'made sure'.[16]

In addition to the objects listed by Cressy, also popular was the posy or poesy ring, usually a plain or decorative gold band with an exterior or interior inscription (or both), typically given as a token between friends, as love gift, or as a betrothal or wedding ring. As Loreen L. Giese has revealed a study of courtship, men and women exchanged clothing and personal accessories as well as money with rings being the 'third most common gift prior to marriage'.[17]

Touchwood Junior, for example, in Thomas Middleton's *A Chaste Maid in Cheapside*, commissions from the goldsmith father of his sweetheart Moll a posy ring inscribed with the telling 'Love that's wise, binds parents' eyes' (3.1.47).[18] A short pamphlet from 1624, *Loves Garland or Posies for Rings, Hand-kerchers, and Gloves; And such Pretty Tokens that Lovers send their Loves*, both lists common love-gifts which might be inscribed and serves as a guide for selecting a stock inscription appropriate for the occasion and temperament of the giver, including verses for passionate lovers, scornful lovers, those far from their loves, and those who wish to show the 'simplicity and truth of love'.[19] Likewise, *Cupid's Poesie for Bracelets, Handkerchers and Rings, with Scarves, Gloves, and other things* (1642), advertised as written by Cupid, provides short, inscribable verses for a wide range of gifts, occasions and people, including 'young Lovers which have newly discovered their affections'.[20]

Unsurprisingly, inscriptions in rings reference love and faithfulness. Sixteenth- and seventeenth-century examples abound in the ring collection at the Victoria and Albert Museum including 'With all my heart'[21] and 'Continnue Faithfull'.[22] A gold ring with an intricate black letter inscription goes further, adding both joy and desire to the promise: 'my wordely ioye' and 'alle my trust' are separated by a cross and stars and appear on the exterior, while 'hert tought lyfe and lust' adorn the more private interior.[23] Another ring's inscription perhaps references the harder reality of marriage: 'nothing without effort'.[24]

These inscriptions, like the ones on *The Judde Memorial* painting, frequently connect love, faith and death. One ring, for example, admonishes, 'Kepe Fayth Teil Dethe'.[25] A ring with a seemingly simple expression of fidelity, 'A faithful love none can remove',[26] is ornamented with a skull and floral decorations. As Marjorie Garber notes, 'The skull was perhaps the most common of *momento mori* objects appearing often in the form of a watch or personal adornment'.[27] The fleeting nature of love and marriage is contrasted with the finality of death; the inevitability of death in turn reminds the wearer to live a moral life. A gold ring with two pivoted hoops reads 'Accept this gift of honest love which never could nor can remove' (exterior) and 'Hath tide mee sure whilst life doth last' (interior), thus commenting on its own significance as a gift and symbol of the bond.[28] A sixteenth-century English wedding ring, an engraved gold band (see Web Fig. 2.5), is inscribed with 'Observe wedloke' on the outside and the Latin '*momento mori*' ('remember you must die') on the inside.[29] A more elaborate British ring made between 1550 and 1600 (see Fig. 2.6) features a white enamel skull encircled with 'Be hold the end,' and a second inscription, 'Rather death than fals of fayth'[30] around the outer edge. On the back, the entwined initials, 'ML', are connected by a true lover's knot, suggesting that is both a *memento mori* ring and a betrothal or wedding ring. As Anne Ward et al. observe, 'the themes of love and death were so closely identified and intermingled

FIGURE 2.6 *Mourning Ring. England, sixteenth century. © Victoria and Albert Museum, London.*

that it is often difficult to decide whether the primary function of the ring was as a memento-mori or a fede ring'.[31] The intertwining themes of love, faith, memory and death that are so common on posy rings are not only prominent in *Hamlet*, but also in the stage properties associated with Hamlet and Ophelia.

Shakespeare certainly knew of posy rings – which were conventional from the thirteenth through the seventeenth centuries – the importance of a ring as gift between lovers, and their perceived connection to fidelity; he makes significant use of the ring as a symbol of faith in *Romeo and Juliet*, when Juliet sends a ring to Romeo via the nurse, in *Twelfth Night* when Olivia tries to send a ring after Cesario, in *All's Well that Ends Well* as revelatory evidence of the relationship between Helena and Bertram, and in *The Merchant of Venice*. In *Merchant*, Gratiano dismissively describes the ring his wife had given him, as well as its inscription, in his attempt to minimize his loss of it:

> About a hoop of gold, a paltry ring
> That she did give me, whose posy was
> For all the world like cutler's poetry
> Upon a knife, 'Love me, and leave me not'.
>
> (5.1.147–50)

Nerissa's response, however, makes clear its symbolic value, connecting the ring, the poetry, and the substance of his oath:

> What talk you of the posy or the value?
> You swore to me when I did give it you,
> That you would wear it till your hour of death,
> And that it should lie with you in your grave, –
> Though not for me, yet for your vehement oaths,
> You should have been respective and have kept it.
> Gave it a judge's clerk! no – God's my judge –
> The clerk will ne'er wear hair on's face that had it.
>
> (5.1.151–8)

Portia too reinforces the value of the gift in chastising Gratiano's slight care of it:

> You were to blame, – I must be plain with you –
> To part so slightly with your wife's first gift,
> A thing stuck on with oaths upon your finger,
> And so riveted with faith unto your flesh.
>
> (5.1.166–9)

As both Nerissa and Portia emphasize, the ring-token, 'riveted with faith' is, as a representation of fidelity, more important than its monetary value; in giving away their rings so easily, both Gratiano and Bassanio have broken faith. The connection also appears in *Hamlet,* when Hamlet replies to the player's prologue with, 'Is this a prologue or the posy of a ring?' (3.2.145). Ophelia responds ''Tis brief, my lord' (3.2.146). His retort to her – 'As woman's love' (3.2.147) – draws on the significance and length of the posy ring's concise inscription, contrasting the sentiment it is supposed to convey with Hamlet's experience of feminine fidelity, which could, in this case, be his perception of his mother or Ophelia.

Love tokens, including rings and other significant gifts, serve to remind the recipient of the giver's affections and to signify the relationship between the giver and the recipient. As Hammonds writes, 'While love tokens could thus have serious, binding meanings, their symbolic complexity could make them very slippery to interpret'.[32] This would indeed seem to be the case in *Hamlet*. Staging 3.1, however, requires directors and actors to make choices about which properties to use. Andrew Sofer's observation about the importance of stage properties is relevant here:

> while props may seem tangential to written drama, any regular theatergoer knows that objects are often central in performance. This is especially evident in the theater of Shakespeare and his contemporaries, whose absence of illusionistic scenery thrusts objects into unusual prominence.[33]

On a nearly bare stage, individual objects would have increased resonance in both storytelling and character development.

In Shakespeare's play, Hamlet and Ophelia share very little stage time in which they actually interact with each other. While Ophelia reports Hamlet's frightening treatment of her, 'He took me by the wrist, and held me hard' (2.1.84), the audience does not witness this moment. Only 3.1 and their brief conversation before the play-within-the play (3.2) show them together. Given the centrality of their relationship, many questions about the couple remain unanswered: How long have they known each other? How and when might they have communicated? What is their level of intimacy and commitment? Do they have a sexual relationship? Do they have plans for the future? Given this lack, it is common for directors to give Hamlet and Ophelia a brief bit of word-less interaction in 1.2 – a glance across the room, a coming together for the touch of a hand or a kiss – that shows that they have some kind of relationship before the audience sees their intense interaction in 3.1. Kenneth Branagh made a similar choice in his 1996 film to include a flashback of a love scene between the two in 2.2.

The evocative 'remembrances' of 3.1, which are easy to overlook in reading but are vital to the scene in performance, must translate into specific objects on stage. Stage productions and films must, as a practical matter, decide what Ophelia returns (or tries to return) to Hamlet and profitably explore the question of what physical object(s) they are. The choice of objects in production fills a gap, and provides an interpretation, since Shakespeare indicates little about the history of their relationship. The specificity of the choice of props necessarily affects the audience's perception of the relationship, as those choices provide an interpretation of their relationship.

So, what are the 'remembrances'? How many gifts? How personal are they? Selected recent productions and familiar films of *Hamlet* show some of the possibilities. The most common choices are letters (bundled, tied or boxed) and jewellery (necklaces, bracelets and rings), though there are some notable variations. (See the appendix for a list of properties from selected films and productions.)

Kenneth Branagh's 1992 Royal Shakespeare Company Hamlet (see Web Fig. 2.7) gave Joanna Pearce's Ophelia enough tokens and gifts to fill a small suitcase: rehearsal notes indicate 'Ophelia's small suitcase full of love tokens, various momentos [*sic*], photos, dried flowers, letters from Hamlet, and Hamlet's college scarf'.[34] Shakespeare's text does not specify when she receives the gifts, but in this case, the choice of props (like his college scarf), as well as their quantity, tells a story about a relationship conducted over time, perhaps while Hamlet was away at Wittenberg. In this case, the physical objects show that they have had enough time together to accumulate a shared history.

The return of a piece of jewellery (perhaps even a posy ring) might indicate a more intimate or committed relationship with Ophelia than the return of letters only. There is whimsy in a bathtub duck, included with a stack of letters that Julia Stiles' Ophelia tries to return to Ethan Hawke's Hamlet in Michael Almereyda's 2000 film (see Web Fig. 2.8), intensity in an overflowing box of letters, and foreshadowing with flowers given and saved.

Returning to the play in order to establish whether textual clues can shed more light on what 'remembrances' Ophelia returns to Hamlet and what their significance might be, 3.1 begins with Ophelia, at the insistence of her father, returning Hamlet's gifts. Consider here the posy ring inscription that instructs, 'I am a love token, do not give me away'.[35] Her return of his gifts, like Gratiano and Bassanio's loss of their wives' rings, and Desdemona's failure to hold onto Othello's handkerchief, which he 'conjur'd her she should ever keep it' (3.3.294), would have signalled to Hamlet a breaking of whatever bond or pledge they had made. Ophelia, in forsaking his gifts, obeys her father but, in doing so, may be breaking faith with Hamlet. For her, this is an impossible and consequential choice between her father and her beloved, particularly while being observed by both her father and King Claudius; to choose one is to betray the other.

For the purpose of staging the scene, her first lines, 'My lord, I have remembrances of yours / That I have longed long to redeliver. / I pray you now receive them' (3.1.92–4), have an implied stage direction: the adverb 'now' and the pronoun 'them' indicate that she is perhaps extending a hand, or both hands, towards him and that her 'remembrances' might even be within his reach. His line, 'No, not I. I never gave you aught' (3.1.95), shows his initial refusal, for she both corrects him with 'My honoured lord, you know right well you did' (3.1.96) and tries again to return them: 'Take these again, for to the noble mind / Rich gifts wax poor when givers prove unkind. / There, my lord' (3.1.99–101). How anxious, distressed, reluctant, stoic or forceful is Ophelia in her attempt to return the gifts? Does Hamlet continue to refuse them, or does he eventually take them? If the latter, when and how? Does he react in anger, sadness or disbelief? What does he do with the gifts? And what finally becomes of the 'remembrances' at the end of the scene?

Actual examples of production choices are once again helpful in responding to these questions.[36] In the RSC's 1989 production, directed by Ron Daniels, Ophelia (Rebecca Saire) entered reading a book, then removed the necklace and bracelet she was wearing. That Ophelia was wearing the jewellery showed the intimacy of the gifts and their importance to her. Saire tried several times to return them; each time Hamlet (Mark Rylance) refused them. On 'why would thou be a breeder of sinners?' (3.1.120–1), he placed his hand on her stomach, perhaps implying that they had consummated their relationship.[37] Only later in the speech, after 'What should such fellows as I do crawling between earth and heaven?' (3.1.126–7), did he seize the jewellery and her book before throwing them upstage against the back wall. Rylance's Hamlet also violently attacked Ophelia: screamed at her, grabbed her, forced her to the ground and himself on top of her between her legs, and spat on her before rubbing it into her face with his hand. Leaving Ophelia on the ground, crying, he exited without the remembrances, suggesting a total rejection of their relationship.

However, in the RSC's 1985 *Hamlet*, directed by Barry Kyle, Roger Rees's Hamlet exited with the necklace Frances Barber's Ophelia had been wearing and returned to him, perhaps keeping a memory object to cherish. In each production, jewellery, as a recognizable memory object (as with posy rings), showed an established bond between the couple.

Letters are another popular choice. In the RSC's 2008 production, directed by Gregory Doran, Ophelia (Mariah Gale) gave Hamlet (David Tennant) a few letters in envelopes on the line 'Rich gifts wax poor when givers prove unkind. / There, my lord' (3.1.100–1). He took them, but threw them to the ground on 'You should not have believed me . . . I loved you not' (3.1.116, 118), then picked some up, ripped and destroyed them,[38] before throwing them back at Ophelia on 'It hath made me mad. I say we will have no more marriage' (3.1.145–6). After Tennant's exit, Gale was left sitting among the shredded pages which she gathered after 'O woe is me / T'have seen what I have seen, see what I see' (3.1.159–60) (see Fig. 2.9). Similarly, in a 2013 RSC production, directed by David Farr, Pippa Nixon's Ophelia carried letters in a pink shoe box and was, once again, left to retrieve shredded bits of paper that Jonathan Slinger's Hamlet had thrown at her. Slinger exited after aggressively yanking Ophelia's skirt off, leaving her exposed and vulnerable in her tights and a sweater (see Web Fig. 2.10).

Alternatively, in the 2016 RSC production directed by Simon Godwin, Natalie Simpson attempted to return a large box of gifts (decorated with colourful paper and construction paper hearts), including a small teddy bear, graphic print t-shirt, and packet of letters, to Paapa Essiedu's Hamlet, who ignored them. She placed the box on the floor on 'Get thee to a nunnery!' (3.1.120), after which he picked it up, disdainfully punctuating his phrases, including 'better my mother had not borne me' (3.1.122–3) and 'I am very proud' (3.1.123), by tossing objects to the ground, finally hurling the empty box back at her with, 'go thy ways to a nunnery' (3.1.128–9). He then grabbed Ophelia, throwing her onto a mattress on the

FIGURE 2.9 *Mariah Gale (Ophelia) and David Tennant (Hamlet) in the Royal Shakespeare Company's 2008* Hamlet, *directed by Gregory Doran. Photo by Elie Kurttz, ©RSC 2008.*

floor among the discarded objects, before physically assaulting her, pinning her down, his body on top of hers, at 'Go to, I'll no more on't. It hath made me mad' (3.1.145–6), as she struggled to resist him (see Fig. 2.11). After his exit, she knelt during her monologue ('O what a noble mind. . .' [3.1.149ff.]), staying in this position as she rejected her father's offer of a handkerchief on 'You need not tell us what Lord Hamlet said' (3.1.178), before exiting with the box. In the 2017 Colorado Shakespeare Production, directed by Carolyn Howarth, Lenne Klingaman's Hamlet similarly rejected the return of the remembrances by violently emptying the box in a fit of anger (see Fig. 2.12).

A review of selected productions effectively demonstrates the necessity of understanding the significance of courtship gifts in the early modern period and the power, in performance, of this seemingly small but consequential moment of interaction between Hamlet and Ophelia. Gift-giving and memory are linked and freighted with meaning; gifts establish and cement relationship bonds and work to activate memory. Each of these

FIGURE 2.11 *Paapa Essiedu (Hamlet) and Natalie Simpson (Ophelia) in the Royal Shakespeare Company's 2016* Hamlet, *directed by Simon Godwin. Photo by Manuel Harlan, ©RSC 2016.*

FIGURE 2.12 *Lenne Klingaman (Hamlet) and Emelie O'Hara (Ophelia) in the Colorado Shakespeare Festival's 2017* Hamlet, *directed by Carolyn Howarth. Photo by Jennifer Koskinen, ©CSF, 2017.*

productions taps into the power of memory objects and purposely deploys it. The most common production choices for the remembrances (letters, jewellery, flowers), along with less common choices (a bathtub duck, a graphic print t-shirt, a handkerchief, a college scarf), demonstrate the level of intensity and connection in Hamlet and Ophelia's prior relationship and help, from within the context of early modern courtship gift-giving, to make sense of his reaction to her return of them.

Ophelia's return of his gifts signals her rejection of him; this betrayal is then compounded by her response to his question, 'Where's your father?' (3.1.129). 'At home, my lord' (3.1.13), she lies, trapped by the surveillance of both her father and the king.[39] This exchange is also gendered; the 'divided duty' (1.3.181) that Desdemona recognizes when she must choose between her obedience to father and her loyalty to new husband is potently and devastatingly staged in the split-second choice Ophelia must make. Actors playing Hamlet in these productions most often refused or destroyed the objects and displayed extreme physical violence toward Ophelia (shoving her, pushing her to the ground, forcibly climbing on top of her, spitting on her).[40] While it does not excuse Hamlet's behaviour, understanding the cultural significance of love tokens helps contextualize it. His reaction (anger and violence, including sexual violence) must also be understood as gendered – a toxic form of early modern masculinity in a culture that required and valorized his dominance over her. Seeing violence enacted forces the audience to bear witness to and to confront the trauma inflicted on Ophelia's body, which itself becomes the focus of the scenes that follow.

Properties in later scenes also help audiences understand the consequences of Hamlet and Ophelia's interaction in 3.1. In 4.5, Laertes' shocked assessment of his sister's actions, 'A document in madness – thoughts and remembrance fitted!' (4.5.172), connects Ophelia with both memory and all that has been lost. While most interpret her madness as a response to both her grief over her father's death and Hamlet's cruel treatment of her, some production choices also work purposefully to connect the remembrances in 3.1. to her actions in this scene. Many productions include flowers among the remembrances,[41] a choice which powerfully enhances the significance of Ophelia's properties here. If flowers are among the gifts she received from Hamlet, her attempt to give 'pansies' (4.5.170), 'columbines' (4.5.173), 'a daisy . . .' (4.5.176), and 'some violets' (4.5.177) to the onlookers takes on new meaning.[42] In Michael Boyd's RSC 2004 production, for example, the remembrances included love letters of varying sizes and a single dried daisy. Further connecting the two scenes, Ophelia (Meg Fraser) distributed love letters instead of the traditional flowers, thus amplifying the relationship between what happens with the remembrances 3.1 and her subsequent madness. Like Hamlet's skull, Ophelia's 'rosemary . . . for remembrance' (4.5.169) in this scene is perhaps her most famous prop, and the one most remembered by audiences.

In the same scene, a 2019 production of *Hamlet* at the Utah Shakespeare Festival, directed by Brian Vaughn, leaned into the suggestion that Hamlet and Ophelia had had a sexual relationship.[43] Angry about and in grief over her father's death, rather than insane, Emma Geer confronted the king with 'My brother shall know of it' (4.5.70). Dragging the arras, still stained with her father's blood, she balled and compressed it into the shape of a swaddled infant, which she then carried off stage, when she exited for the final time (see Fig. 2.13).[44] The word pregnant does not appear in the text, but this Ophelia, via a potent prop, communicated clearly the relationship she'd had or wished she'd had with Hamlet. In an interview, Geer noted: 'I don't think it matters if she was pregnant but what it shows is that the stakes of their relationship were extremely high. What she could have had with him is the heartbreak, just as much as the dream of having a life and a family with him is tragic'.[45] Even the suggestion of pregnancy, however, heightens the focus on Ophelia's body, with its generative potential. While the right to rule in the Denmark of the play is determined by election, the question of succession would surely have resonated

FIGURE 2.13 *Christopher Peltier (Laertes), Kenna Funk (Waiting Woman) and Emma Geer (Ophelia) in the Utah Shakespeare Festival's 2019* Hamlet, *directed by Brian Vaugh. Photo by Karl Hugh, ©USF, 2019.*

with early modern audiences who understood that the rightful inheritance of titles and property was conveyed via female bodies. Ophelia's death is then possibly a double loss.

Andrew Sofer, in an examination of Ophelia's funeral in the play, suggests that 'Ophelia herself has been used as an object throughout, by both Hamlet and her father'; he notices her body as a 'property', but focuses on how she is upstaged by the disruptive actions of Hamlet and Laertes at her funeral.[46] Carol Chillington Rutter similarly identifies Ophelia's body as 'a "speaking property", an unsettled, unsettling signifier ... challenging spectators onstage and offstage to read it'.[47] Pascale Aebischer goes further: 'Human bodies used as props may become improper properties, objects that challenge their status and may well upstage the living; visual, embodied commentaries that have the potential to undercut the verbal and sideline the play's verbose hero'.[48] I draw on the work of Rutter and Aebischer to suggest that Ophelia's corpse can be a key property, like the skull, the rosemary, and the 'remembrances' of 3.1. Ophelia's body, in other words, functions as an object of remembrance. Its sight is a disruptive spectacle for both on-stage and off-stage audiences. Memory is embodied in and by the display of Ophelia's sullied corpse, one not matching Gertrude's beautiful, elaborate description of her drowning in 4.7. The same 2019 Utah Shakespeare Festival production used this juxtaposition, placing Gertrude upstage right, watching Ophelia's death by drowning at the hands of two of King Claudius's guards, who attacked her at the side of an on-stage pool of water. They pressed her head into the water, as she struggled; then she became still, before they dragged her corpse off stage. In this moment, the body of the actor becomes a stage property (see Web Fig. 2.14).

Similar emphasis was placed on Ophelia's corpse in the 2013 RSC production directed by David Farr. Unshielded by a coffin or shroud (the most common staging choice for this scene), Ophelia's corpse, played by Pippa Nixon (rather than a dummy as is a more common production choice), still wearing the ravaged wedding dress she had worn during her mad scenes, was placed downstage centre in a shallow grave, exposing it to both the on-stage and off-stage audience (see Fig. 2.15). In this production, it was impossible not to focus on the motionless, unprotected body of the actor, which, like Yorick's skull, and the corpse in *The Judde Memorial*, works as powerful memento mori, a reminder, both shocking and familiar, to remember death. Paige Martin Reynolds calls attention to the effect of the exposed body has on the audience: 'This Ophelia is, moreover, vulnerable to the audience's voyeurism for an agonizing amount of time'.[49] In its display, Ophelia's corpse, a potent stage property embodying memory, became a powerful visual representation of a ruined kingdom and a lost dynastic line. Throughout the play, the stage

FIGURE 2.15 *Pippa Nixon (Ophelia) and Charlotte Cornwell (Gertrude) in the Royal Shakespeare Company's 2013* Hamlet, *directed by David Farr. Photo by Keith Pattison, ©RSC 2013.*

properties associated with Hamlet and Ophelia – from the remembrances of 3.1 to Ophelia's corpse itself – are an essential part of the theatrical storytelling, imbued with meanings and possibilities, which reach as far back as the memento mori tradition, an important context, as this essay has argued, for modern re-readings and revivals of the play on stage.

Appendix

Properties used in 3.1 (selected productions and films)

- 1948 (film) directed by Laurence Olivier with Olivier as Hamlet and Jean Simmons as Ophelia): Jewellery.

- 1960 (RSC) directed by Peter Wood with Ian Bannen as Hamlet and Geraldine McEwan as Ophelia: Necklace and a ring, jewels.[50]
- 1965 (RSC) directed by Peter Hall with David Warner as Hamlet and Glenda Jackson as Ophelia: Brooch.
- 1975 (RSC) directed by Buzz Goodbody with Ben Kingsley as Hamlet and Yvonne Nicholson as Ophelia: Flowers and beads.[51]
- 1976 (National Theatre, London) directed by Sir Peter Hall with Albert Finney as Hamlet and Susan Fleetwood as Ophelia: Small trinket box, locket and ring, love letters.[52]
- 1980 (RSC) directed by John Barton with Michael Pennington as Hamlet and Carol Royle as Ophelia: Letters.
- 1986 (RSC) directed by Barry Kyle with Roger Rees as Hamlet and Frances Barber as Ophelia: Necklace.
- 1989 (National Theatre, London) directed by Sir Richard Eyre with Daniel Day-Lewis as Hamlet and Stella Gonet as Ophelia: Locket, handkerchief, jewel box, bundle of letters in ribbon.[53]
- 1989 (RSC) directed by Ron Daniels with Mark Rylance as Hamlet and Rebecca Saire as Ophelia: A small red book of poetry by Shelley, bracelet, and necklace.[54]
- 1990 (film) directed by Franco Zeffirelli with Mel Gibson as Hamlet and Helena Bonham Carter as Ophelia: Necklace/chains.
- 1990 (film) directed by Kevin Kline with Kline as Hamlet and Diana Verona as Ophelia: Letters and dried flowers.
- 1993 (RSC) directed by Adrian Noble with Kenneth Branagh as Hamlet and Joanne Pearce as Ophelia: 'Ophelia's small suitcase full of love tokens, various momentos [*sic*], photos, dried flowers, letters from Hamlet, and Hamlet's college scarf'.[55]

- 1996 (film) directed by Kenneth Branagh with Branagh as Hamlet and Kate Winslet as Ophelia: Bundled stack of letters, tied with ribbon.
- 1997 (RSC) directed by Matthew Warchus with Alex Jennings as Hamlet and Derbhle Crotty as Ophelia: Letter and locket.[56]
- 2000 (film) directed by Michael Almereyda with Ethan Hawke as Hamlet and Julia Stiles as Ophelia: Square box full of letters and yellow bathtub duck.
- 2001 (RSC) directed by Steven Pimlott with Samuel West as Hamlet and Kerry Condon as Ophelia: 'Shoebox with letters + a special letter'.[57]
- 2004 (RSC) directed by Michael Boyd with Toby Stephens as Hamlet and Meg Fraser as Ophelia: Bundle of letters in varying sizes, tied with ribbon and a single dried daisy.[58]
- 2008 (RSC) and 2009 (film) directed by Gregory Doran with David Tennant as Hamlet and Mariah Gale as Ophelia: Letters.[59]
- 2010 (Oregon Shakespeare Festival) directed by Bill Rauch with Dan Donohue as Hamlet and Susannah Flood Ophelia: Letters.[60]
- 2013 (RSC) directed by David Farr with Jonathan Slinger as Hamlet and Pippa Nixon as Ophelia: Letters in a pink shoe box.[61]
- 2015 (Barbican Centre/Sonia Friedman production) directed by Lyndsey Turner with Benedict Cumberbatch as Hamlet and Siân Brooke as Ophelia: grey (shoebox-size) box; contents not revealed.[62]
- 2016 (RSC) directed by Simon Godwin with Paapa Essiedu as Hamlet and Natalie Simpson as Ophelia: Large box covered in coloured wrapping paper, decorated with construction paper hearts, containing a small teddy bear, folded paper notes, a t-shirt printed with a heart and their initials, and tissue paper.[63]

- 2017 Colorado Shakespeare Festival directed by Carolyn Howarth with Lenne Klingaman as Hamlet and Emelie O'Hara as Ophelia: Wooden box, painted with flowers, containing letters, feathers and small toys, and trinkets.[64]
- 2018 Shakespeare Theatre Company (Washington, DC), directed by Michael Kahn with Michael Urie as Hamlet and Oyin Oladejo as Ophelia: A letter.[65]
- 2019 Utah Shakespeare Festival, directed by Brian Vaughn with Quinn Mattfeld as Hamlet and Emma Geer as Ophelia: Letters.[66]

Notes

1 Nigel Llewellyn, *Art of Death: Visual Culture in the English Death Ritual C. 1500-C. 1800* (London: Reaktion, 1991), 11.

2 Marjorie Garber, '"Remember Me": "*Momento Mori*" Figures in Shakespeare's Plays', *Renaissance Drama*, n.s. 12 (1981): 3–25 (6).

3 Quoted in Llewellyn, 11.

4 See Stephen Greenblatt, *Hamlet in Purgatory* (Princeton: Princeton University Press, 2001), 205–57, who reveals that Shakespeare, in contrast to his source materials, introduced the ghost, and the shift from vengeance to remembrance, to the story.

5 'Concordance of Shakespeare's Complete Works', Open Source Shakespeare, https://www.opensourceshakespeare.org/concordance

6 Peter Stallybrass, Roger Chartier, J. Franklin Mowery and Heather Wolfe, 'Hamlet's Tables and the Technologies of Writing in Renaissance England', *Shakespeare Quarterly*, 55(4) (Winter 2004): 379–419 (379). They examine the connection between Hamlet's 'table of my memory' (1.5.98), the literal 'table' he must set down later in the same speech (1.5.107) and the stage property (a 'table-book' or 'writing table') that would have been used.

7 Gail Kern Paster, 'Thinking with Skulls in Holbein, *Hamlet*, Vesalius, and Fuller', in *The Shakespearean International Yearbook: Volume 11: Special Issue, Placing Michael Neill. Issues of Place in Shakespeare and Early Modern Culture*, eds Alexa Alice Joubin, Jonathan Gil Harris, T. G. Bishop, Michael Neill and Graham Bradshaw (Farnham: Routledge, 2011), 41–60 (53).

8 Many scholars have considered the skull in *Hamlet*. See, for example, Andrew Sofer, *The Stage Life of Props* (Ann Arbor: University of Michigan Press, 2003); Pascale Aebischer, *Shakespeare's Violated Bodies: Stage and Screen Performance* (Cambridge: Cambridge University Press, 2004); Paster, 'Thinking with Skulls'; and Elizabeth Williamson, 'Yorick's Afterlives: Skull Properties in Performance', *Borrowers and Lenders*, 6.1 (Spring/Summer 2011), among others. Web images can be found at https://www.bloomsburyonlineresources.com/hamlet-the-state-of-play.

9 The first (or 'bad') quarto of *Hamlet* places this scene in 2.2. Ofelia says, 'My lord, I have sought opportunity, which now I have, to redeliver to your worthy hands a small remembrance – such tokens which I have received of you' (7.138–41).

10 *Hamlet*, The Arden Shakespeare, ed. Ann Thompson and Neil Taylor (London: Thomson, 2006), vol. 1, 3.1.92, commentary note.

11 Pamela S. Hammonds, *Gender, Sexuality, and Material Objects* (Aldershot: Ashgate, 2010), 12.

12 Ibid.

13 Karen Newman, 'Portia's Ring: Unruly Women and Structures of Exchange in *The Merchant of Venice*', *Shakespeare Quarterly*, 38(1) (Spring 1987): 19–33.

14 Diana O'Hara, *Courtship and Constraint: Rethinking the Making of Marriage in Tudor England* (Manchester: Manchester University Press, 2000), 64.

15 Jennine Hurl-Eamon, 'Love Tokens: Objects as Memory for Plebeian Women in Early Modern England', *Early Modern Women: An Interdisciplinary Journal*, 6 (2011): 181–6 (183).

16 David Cressy, *Birth, Marriage, and Death*, 263, quoted in Hammonds, 14.

17 Loreen L. Giese, *Courtship, Marriage Customs, and Shakespeare's Comedies* (New York: Palgrave Macmillan, 2006), 91.

18 Thomas Middleton, *A Chaste Maid in Cheapside*, ed. Alan Brissenden (New York: W.W. Norton, 1991).

19 *Loves Garland or Posies for Rings, Hand-kerchers, and Gloves; And such Pretty Tokens that Lovers send their Loves* (London: John Spencer, 1624), 4.

20 *Cupid's Poesie for Bracelets, Handkerchers and Rings, with Scarves, Gloves, and other things* (London: John Wright, 1642), 6.

21 Victoria and Albert Museum, Museum number 189–1962.

22 Victoria and Albert Museum, Museum number 69–1960.

23 Victoria and Albert Museum, Museum number 895–1871.

24 Victoria and Albert Museum, Museum number 893–1871.

25 Victoria and Albert Museum, Museum number 71–1960.

26 Victoria and Albert Museum, Museum number 78–1660.

27 Garber, 9.

28 Victoria and Albert Museum, Museum number 909–1871.

29 Victoria and Albert Museum, Museum number 905–1871.

30 Victoria and Albert Museum, Museum number 13–1888.

31 Anne Ward, John Cherry, Charlotte Gere, and Barbara Cartlidge, *The Ring from Antiquity to the Twentieth Century* (London: Thames and Hudson, 1981), 97.

32 Hammonds, 17.

33 Sofer, v–vi.

34 Royal Shakespeare Company archives, rehearsal notes 11 November 1992: 'A suitcase is required that will be set on top of the wardrobe. This will be full of various momentos [*sic*], photos, dried flowers and letters from Hamlet. This gets hurled across stage and the contents may well get damaged. Therefore this will need to be a running prop'.

35 Victoria and Albert Museum, Museum number 60–1960.

36 Production details are drawn from prompt books, property lists, and videos from the Royal Shakespeare Company and National Theatre archives as well as personal viewing of productions.

37 Similarly, in the 2001 RSC production directed by Steven Pimlott, Samuel West made the same choice. (RSC archives, promptbook, not dated.)

38 In the 1997 RSC production, directed by Matthew Warchus, Hamlet (Alex Jennings) dropped the locket he had received from Ophelia (Derbhle Crotty) and crushed it under his foot. (Royal Shakespeare Company archives, prompt book, undated.)

39 Whether Hamlet knows they are being observed, when and how he might discover this, and if Ophelia attempts to communicate the situation to him are also important performance choices.

40 Examples from other productions abound but selections include: In the 1970 RSC production, directed by Trevor Nunn, Hamlet (Alan Howard) grabbed Ophelia (Helen Mirren) and held her from behind. In the 1975 RSC production, directed by Buzz Goodbody, Hamlet (Ben Kingsley) dragged Ophelia (Yvonne Nicholson) across the stage and then pushed her to the ground. In the 1989 National Theatre production, directed by Richard Eyre, Hamlet (Daniel Day Lewis) grabbed and shook Ophelia (Stella Gonet) on 'I have heard of your paintings' (3.1.142). In the 1993 RSC production, directed by Adrian Noble, Hamlet (Kenneth Branagh) pushed Ophelia (Joanne Pearce) to floor, got on top of her, and groped under her skirt. In the 2001 RSC production, directed by Steven Pimlott, Hamlet (Samuel West) spit on and pushed Ophelia (Kerry Condon). In the 2004 RSC production, directed by Michael Boyd, Hamlet (Toby Stephens) grabbed Ophelia (Meg Fraser) by the head, choking her. (National Theatre and RSC archives, promptbooks.)

41 1975 RSC directed by Buzz Goodbody, 1993 RSC directed by Adrian Nobel, 2017 Colorado Shakespeare Festival directed by Carolyn Howarth, among others. See Appendix for details.

42 Thompson and Taylor, *Hamlet*, vol. 1, 4.5.169–78, commentary note, identify columbines, violets, and daisies as symbols of, respectively infidelity, fidelity and unrequited love.

43 Kenneth Branagh's film also suggested the Hamlet and Ophelia had consummated their relationship. During one of her songs, 'Before you tumbled me / You promised me to wed . . . An thou hadst not come to my bed' (4.5.62–3, 66), Kate Winslet's Ophelia was on her back on the ground, as she thrust her pelvis

upward (as if during intercourse); at the same time, two memory flashbacks showed her in bed with Hamlet, embracing and kissing.

44 Ophelia's songs, including her song about woman whose lover 'tumbled me' (4.5.62) and would not 'come to my bed' (4.5.66) may be interpreted as evidence of a possible sexual relationship. Some speculate that the 'rue' (4.5.176) Ophelia offers, while traditionally associated with repentance, was also known to be an abortive herb and may indicate that Ophelia could be pregnant. See Lucile F. Newman, 'Ophelia's Herbal', *Economic Botany*, 33.2 (1979): 227–32.

45 Emma Geer, personal interview, 12 December 2019.

46 Sofer, 100, 99.

47 See Carol Chillington Rutter's careful and extended analysis of the scene in *Enter the Body: Women and Representation on Shakespeare's Stage* (London: Routledge, 2001), 41.

48 Aebischer, 63.

49 Paige Martin Reynolds, *Performing Shakespeare's Women: Playing Dead* (London: Arden Shakespeare, 2019), 5.

50 Royal Shakespeare Company archives, prompt book, undated.

51 Royal Shakespeare Company archives, prompt book, undated. Provisional prop setting list notes '1 necklace' and 'Dried Blue Bells/Buttercups'.

52 National Theatre archives, scene to scene prop list, 4 November 1975.

53 National Theatre archives, preliminary prop list, not dated.

54 Royal Shakespeare Company archives, rehearsal notes 15 February 1989: 'One of the things Ophelia is returning to Hamlet in Block 5A is a small book of poetry by Shelley. Are all the books still red in colour?' and rehearsal notes 1 March 1980: 'Ophelia's remembrances that she returns to Hamlet in Block 5A, II Sc II, are a bracelet and a necklace – both of which need to slip off easily without any catches. These are new props'.

55 Royal Shakespeare Company archives, rehearsal notes 11 November 1992.

56 Royal Shakespeare Company archives, props list, not dated.

57 Royal Shakespeare Company archives, props list, not dated.

58 Royal Shakespeare Company archives, rehearsal notes: 'Ophelia's bundle of letters will be untied and some of the letters ripped. The bundle will also contain a single daisy' (7 June 2004) and 'Ophelia's daisy needs to be dried so she can crumble it. It needs to be about the size of a cornflower' (21 June 2004).

59 Assistant stage manager script (undated) indicates: 'Ophelia re-enters DSR with prayer book & letters again'.

60 Notes on production, 9 October 2010.

61 Notes on production, 11 July 2013

62 Notes on production, 11 August 2015.

63 Notes on production, 6 June 2016.

64 Notes on production, 29 July 2017.

65 Notes on production, 27 January 2018.

66 Notes on production, 28 June 2019.

3

'Tragedians of the City' *Hamlet* and Urban Exile

Kelly Stage

In 1586, Shakespeare's contemporaries Will Kemp, George Bryan and Thomas Pope performed at Elsinore. English players had visited in 1585, and were invited back to perform at Kronborg Castle, the fortress at the tip of Zealand (Denmark) overlooking the Sound (*Øresund*).[1] Shakespeare was possibly not yet in London, let alone writing, but we might call these players the first 'tragedians of the city' (Q2, 2.2.292) welcomed to Elsinore.[2] The association of *Hamlet* with the castle has brought many *Hamlets* to Kronborg, including Laurence Olivier's Old Vic production in 1937, and the penultimate performances of the Globe to Globe *Hamlet* Tour (2014–16).[3] *Hamlet* is also a marketing tool for tourism of the castle; the UNESCO World Heritage website for Kronborg proudly boasts, 'It is world-renowned as Elsinore, the setting of Shakespeare's *Hamlet*'.[4] For all of Elsinore's magnificence and iconic presence, however, it is the place that defines Hamlet's placelessness. By tracking Hamlet's relationship to his home, to his sense of the wider world, and to the imagined places of theatrical presentation, I show how *Hamlet*'s struggle to find his place depends upon his own mediation of Elsinore.

I reorient Hamlet by thinking of him as an urbanite in exile at Elsinore, rather than as a son who has returned home. Hamlet and the other young, male characters in the play long for their university communities or their city lives. The older generation demonstrate scepticism; Claudius and Polonius favour courtly lifestyles, and Polonius explicitly invokes the belief that cities corrupt young men. But the play challenges that supposition through Claudius's installation at Elsinore contrasted to Hamlet's obsession with Elsinore's unhomeliness. The new king's first speech immediately emphasizes his interest in demonstrative rhetoric and neatly constructed isocolonic phrases of political propriety, built – as we later learn – to prop up a stolen title (Q2, 1.2.1–39). His court ends up an equally empty shell around a morally bankrupt ruler.

The monumentality of Claudius's court is frequently emphasized by settings used in stage performances and film adaptations (beyond those mentioned above that call on Kronborg itself). For example, Grigori Kozintsev's 1964 *Hamlet* presents an expansive Elsinore – actually Estonia's Ivangorod Fortress – which emphasizes empty spaces, towering drawbridges, iron gates, massive stone battlements and throngs of supporters bowing or curtseying in unison while in full Elizabethan costumes. Branagh's 1996 *Hamlet* offers a remarkable, iconic shot of Claudius and Gertrude parading up the centre aisle of a great hall, surrounded by a massive crowd as brightly coloured confetti rain down from above. Still occupying the foreground, however, the back of black-suited Hamlet remains a human silhouette on an empty dais. Even with New York City as a setting, Michael Almereyda's *Hamlet* (2000) crafts a clever division between the pedestrian reality of the city – in which the Manhattan backdrop buzzes and Hamlet treads the streets (and a Blockbuster Video store) – and Claudius takes refuge in his towering Hotel Elsinore – a skyscraper that quarters the Denmark Corporation and physically elevates Claudius over the city.[5] In these examples, Hamlet's claim, 'Denmark's a prison' (F, 2.2.242), contrasts the restriction of place with Hamlet's cosmopolitanism, not just personal distaste for Claudius. His melancholic uncertainty is a manifestation of his relationship to a home and nation that is literally lost to him. To reclaim it, however, Hamlet must become a casualty of the state.

Urbanitas

The global and local – the urban and the hinterland – reverberate through Hamlet's struggle to find his place. Furthermore, Hamlet's dire end ultimately positions his cosmopolitanism as impossible, at least in Denmark. From his first appearance, Hamlet's alienation from Elsinore is clear. He wishes to return to school in Wittenberg, but he agrees to stay when Claudius insists that his absence would be 'most retrograde to our desire' (Q2, 1.2.114). His mother adds pressure: 'Let not thy mother lose her prayers, Hamlet. / I pray thee stay with us, go not to Wittenberg' (Q2, 1.2.118–19). In obeying Claudius and Gertrude, Hamlet enters an ironic state of exile at home: he is captive in a place he considers backwards – largely because of Claudius. His disdain for Elsinore is clear when he greets his schoolmate, Horatio, who has come to Elsinore for Old Hamlet's funeral. The prince assures Horatio of his visit's benefits: 'We'll teach you for to drink ere you depart' (Q2, 1.2.174). Claudius's love of Rhenish supports the national and local pastime, and Hamlet later ruefully states that other nations 'clepe us drunkards' (Q2, 1.4.19). Having been *away* from court feeds Hamlet's estrangement from his 'native' (Q2, 1.4.14) land.[6] The prince cannot leave, and yet he cannot take his proper place – Claudius '[p]opped in between th'election and [his] hopes' (Q2, 5.2.64) for the crown. Hamlet is stuck by the end of Act 1: nothing is left for him in Denmark but impossible revenge, and he cannot go back to the places he prefers – Wittenberg and beyond.

The play associates youth with urbanity and European expansiveness, and isolation and tradition with the elder generation. The divide was current; in the late sixteenth century, English parents debated whether to embrace European trends to educate young gentlemen in cities or abroad. Advocates argued that cities were centres for intellectual and philosophical activity. As Gail Kern Paster explains in *The Idea of the City in the Age of Shakespeare*, Renaissance humanists regarded the city as the source of human achievement: 'Italian urban theorists identified the city with the creative, civilized life free from molestation and with a historical record of renewed importance'.[7] As Lawrence Manley has discussed, some Renaissance moralists looked back consciously to the need to foster '*urbanitas*' and to create shared commitments to larger communities. Enthusiasm for manners and social skills was also inspired by Baldassare Castiglione's popular *The Book of the Courtier*, which encouraged cultivating sophistication.[8] Manley notes as well that Erasmus praised London as the very bedrock of English humanism, and argues that he 'was implicitly reinforcing the common connection between the literary and pedagogical ideals of humanism and its civic aims and bias – a connection underlined in his recollection of the Socratic dictum that "it is not the fields and trees which can teach me, but men who live in towns"'.[9] For Erasmus, life in a country manor cannot teach civic understanding. Education can be complete only with civil exchange and community engagement provided by an expansive city like London.

In England, the journey from country to city – hinterland to London – could compare to a modest version of the European tour. While Italian urban planners designed cities with utopic ideas in mind, the city of London grew rapidly and without effective regulation. Young men frequently migrated from the country to London and back again in concert with the law terms. For some young men, studying at the Inns of Court or even simply living in London, as well as going abroad to foreign cities, served as a finishing school before they would return to the country to run an estate or enter government. However, overcrowding, poverty, crime and disease were also persistent problems. These conditions led some writers to address London with encomiastic praise and others to excoriate it in satire and complaint.[10]

A generation before the composition of *Hamlet*, texts like *Civil and Uncivil Life* (1579), rehearsed the country–city divide as Englishmen debated the best way to live. 'Valentine' argues for the court and city, and 'Vincent' argues for the country. In a passage that offers the gist of the urban argument, Valentine explains that men must experience city living to be educated:

> My meaning is not to entice them all to Court, or to Cittie from their naturall shier: But that such (as would not doo them selues that great good) that at the least they would some times, & cheefely in their youth, abide in their cheefe towne or cittie of their countrey, where they may conuerse with a people more ciuill, then the poore villaines, and bee notwithstanding at hand to take office (if it be layed on them:) Also if they bee in office already, they dwell there fitly enough to exercise the same. But by this you haue saide, it seemeth you are, or faine would bee an Officer in your countrey.[11]

Exposure and circulation are key. Participating in a more 'civil' community instructs the 'good officer', so that he fosters shared community in his return to the country.[12]

While the likes of Valentine argue for urban exposure, sceptics abound. Advice literature alerted visitors and denizens alike to the parasitical aspects of the city.[13] For example, Thomas Lodge's *An Alaram for Usurers* (1584) or Robert Greene's *Greene's Groatsworth of Wit* (1592) depict such fears and portray urban life as plagued by tricksters, whores and conmen, who victimize young, 'innocent' gentlemen through gaming, drinking and extravagance. These dangers inevitably lead to debt and impoverishment, a fate common in satires, city comedies, broadside ballads and pamphlets throughout the late sixteenth and early seventeenth centuries.[14]

In *Hamlet*, Polonius demonstrates both perspectives. He first plays the part of the moralizing humanist father, and he tosses platitudes at Laertes – 'Neither a borrower nor a lender, boy . . . / to thine own self be true' (Q2 1.3.74, 77) – as he prepares to leave for Paris. His advice is mild compared to that of Henry Percy, ninth Earl of Northumberland. In a 1609 letter, Percy warns his son of urban gallants' parasitical behaviour:

> if they be gallants that are delighted with the pretty contentments of this town, as with love of pleasures, I will not say whoring; or gay clothes, I dare not say wastings of their estates; . . . or to see plays, which must not be named idleness in them whose hours seem wearisome and heavy because they know not what to do with themselves. . . . These kind of men will tell you that a country life is tedious, where your conversation will be but among peasants; . . . when there end is but to pass their times here by help of your expense[.][15]

Polonius too has in mind similar dangers for young men, he just does not offer such advice directly to Laertes. Instead, his conversation with Reynaldo[16] shows fatherly suspicion of Laertes' urban persona. Reynaldo is to track down Laertes by inquiring 'what Danskers are in Paris' (Q2, 2.1.7), to investigate whether Laertes participates in typical urban vices: 'drinking, fencing, swearing, / Quarrelling, drabbing' (2.2.25–6). Polonius's instructions require Reynaldo to commit subterfuge, and the father even encourages Reynaldo to offer 'forgeries' (2.2.20) of Laertes' behaviour to gather information. In public, Polonius acts as a cautious, but permissive, father, but in private, he suspects his son of all the ills Percy mentions.

Polonius and Laertes' relationship offers the clearest articulation of the generational debate over urban education, but Hamlet's student status is more than just a list of bad behaviours. Shakespeare casts his young men as students, and all of them spend their time abroad: Hamlet, Horatio, Rosencrantz and Guildenstern study at Wittenberg, and Laertes studies in Paris. Shakespeare's source texts – the medieval Saxo Grammaticus tale of Amleth in *Historia Danica* and the 1570 popularization by Francoise Belleforest in *Histoires Tragiques* – do not include these details. So, it bears asking: 'Why did Shakespeare send Hamlet to Wittenberg?' Alfred Westfall asked this question more than fifty years ago, and noted the university's popularity as a centre of Reformation learning and Wittenberg's ubiquity in contemporary Renaissance texts – most notably, *Doctor Faustus* – as key reasons to send Hamlet to Wittenberg.[17] Despite the city's small size, it was also accessible for Danes on the continent, and as Suzanne H. Stein offers, 'the epicentre of Northern humanism'.[18] Philip Melanchthon's stewardship of Wittenberg dictated the university's embrace of Erasmian humanism, and its rejection of 'just war' and welcome of worldly citizenship. The cosmopolitanism that Stein identifies with Wittenberg fits Hamlet well.[19] Yet, cosmopolitanism is also part of Hamlet's problem. As Russell Jacoby writes, with Diogenes in mind: 'To be a cosmopolitan means setting oneself against certain local beliefs and mores – to become, perhaps, an outsider or a permanent stranger'.[20] Hamlet has embraced his estrangement, but his need to also belong – formulated most simply in the quest for his father's revenge, and more complexly in his connection to the political world – makes Denmark his prison.

Local-London-exile

I contend that the play offers two key complications for Hamlet's struggle between embracing cosmopolitan estrangement and accepting his local embodiment. The first is the mediation of place that is provided through the visit of the 'tragedians of the city' and the text's invocation of London and its theatrical culture. The second is the reorientation provided by Hamlet's banishment to England and Fortinbras's presence in Denmark. In this section, I discuss the texts' explicit references to contemporary London theatre. The episode in the texts is brief, but it values the connections of shared experience and local knowledge: being in place does matter. As well, the insertion of these references indicates how Shakespeare's text creates shared experience and interpellates playgoers. They are swept into Hamlet's experience and community, while they are provided with a doubled vision of the theatre in Hamlet's 'city' (Q1, 7.264; Q2, 2.2.298; F, 2.2.333) and their own.

The London references in question are a part of the play's complex textual history.[21] Critics, editors, bibliographers and theatre historians have long debated the relationship of the three *Hamlet* texts to each other, and critical consensus on key aspects is still lacking.[22] The sections I will look at here – Hamlet's first conversation with Rosencrantz and Guildenstern in Q1, scene 7; Q2, 2.2; and F1, 2.2 – are among the most fraught. In the three versions of the scenes, the textual details work as indices that reflect Hamlet's rumination on place, as they call on local knowledge of London without naming it. The scenes discussed here call back to the constraints of London performance and the competition between theatre companies, and especially boys' companies, in the early seventeenth century. By slipping these references into Hamlet's questions about the city that he misses while at Elsinore, the play briefly offers an uncanny commentary on London practices through Hamlet, overlaying Shakespeare's theatrical cityscape onto Hamlet's Wittenberg.

Rosencrantz and Guildenstern are not Hamlet's best friends, but the texts carefully establish connections which tie Hamlet and his visitors to shared urban experiences. In Q2, Hamlet explicitly names them as 'my two schoolfellows' (Q2, 3.4.200), even when he is announcing their betrayal – and links the men to his time in Wittenberg.[23] In all three texts, the conversation indicates that London looms, albeit unspoken, in the idea of 'the city'. After Rosencrantz announces that the 'tragedians of the city' (Q1, 7.264; Q2, 2.2.292; F, 2.2.327) – Hamlet's favourite theatre company – are coming to Elsinore, playgoers are left to fill in the specific 'city'. Even though the conversation in Q1 loosely correlates 'city' with Wittenberg, that identification is not absolute. The Q2 and F texts do not provide any definite antecedent. As a result, 'city' is a floating signifier, and simultaneously may imply multiple shared places for the characters and the playgoers, London among them.

The first piece of local theatrical knowledge comes from Hamlet questioning the role of touring. In Q1, Hamlet asks: 'How comes it that they travel? Do they grow resty?' (Q1, 7.266–7). In Q2 and in F, he questions, 'How chances it they travel? Their residence, both in reputation and profit, was better both ways' (Q2, 2.2.293–4; F, 2.2.328–9). Hamlet cannot imagine that touring would be a good choice; however, his disbelief does not change the fact that touring was profitable or that the Chamberlain's Men/King's Men toured widely between 1598 and 1610.[24] The prince is surprised at seeing the players come to Elsinore; he asks what has been happening in 'the city' since he has been away. In this regard, the conversation shows Hamlet's apparent fear that he is uninformed because he is no longer an insider: he misses his place.

Variations across the three texts show differences in the depiction of some of London's theatrical controversies from the early seventeenth century. For example, in Q2, the scene's discussion of playing limitations is significant even though it is cryptic:

HAMLET
How chances it they travel? Their residence, both in reputation and profit, was better both ways.

ROSENCRANTZ
I think their inhibition comes by the means of the late innovation.

HAMLET
Do they hold the same estimation they did when I was in the city? Are they so followed?

ROSENCRANTZ
No, indeed they are not.

(Q2, 2.2.293–9)

In 'I think their inhibition comes by the means of the late innovation' (295–6), Q2 implies that an external condition has forced the company out of the city. Critics have not come to a consensus about the line's reference, but the play's viewers were expected to understand the line's implications.[25] Playgoers had a frame of reference and assigned meaning even if critics today argue over it. The text affirms itself as a product of a specific place and time – London theatre before 1604–5, when Q2 was published.

The re-emergence of the boys' theatre companies depicted in Q1 and F is a richer touchstone for examining the text's insertion of London details. Q1 and F both imply that the boys' popularity has cut into the tragedians' commercial success. In Q1, 'Gilderstone' confirms the players' reputation, but also says 'I'faith, my lord, novelty carries it away. For the principal public audience that came to them are turned to private plays, and to the humour of children' (Q1, 7.271–3). The specification of 'novelty' is telling; companies of boy actors were active in the 1580s, but they were shut down for most of the 1590s.[26] But before 1603, the boys companies' return was novel: in 1599, the Children of Paul's restarted, and by 1600, so had the Children of the Chapel Royal, later the Children of the Queen's Revels. In January 1601, the Children of the Chapel began playing at court, which, as Lucy Munro has argued, showed their near-immediate popularity.[27] These local details paste the text into a specific window of performance and competition in the early seventeenth century, and they praise the audience of *Hamlet* indirectly. The 'public audience' have avoided 'novelty' and chosen an adult tragedy (*Hamlet*).

The children's companies are discussed again in F, which tackles their reputations and recklessness at length. 'Rosincrance' explains that the tragedians'

> endeavour keeps in the wonted pace. But there is, sir, an eyrie of children, little eyases that cry out on the top of question and are most tyrannically clapped for't. These are now the fashion, and so berattle the common stages

> (so they call them) that many wearing rapiers are afraid of goose quills and dare scarce come thither.
>
> (F, 2.2.336–42)

Such performances are nearly monstrous, and Rosencrantz questions the boys' repertory: cutting satires that targeted individuals, put writers in prison, and sometimes resulted in a play's suppression. Hamlet can't believe what he hears, asking:

> What, are they children? Who maintains 'em? How are they escotted? Will they pursue the quality no longer than they can sing? Will they not say afterwards if they should grow themselves to common players – as it is most like if their means are no better – their writers do them wrong to make them exclaim against their own succession?
>
> (F, 2.2.343–9)

Hamlet registers concern over these city boys' possible exploitation, and his suggestions that the companies are unethical may trigger playgoers' memories of past scandal. Henry Evans, the leader of the Children of the Chapel, was accused of abducting a boy, Thomas Clifton, and taking him into the acting company. Henry Clifton, the boy's father, filed a complaint in the Star Chamber in 1601, and the case was heard in 1602, resulting in the censure of Evans. In light of such controversy, as James Bednarz notes, the Chamberlain's Men could offer an oblique question and bring this ugly episode back to attention for playgoers, swiping at the boys' companies. However, Andrew Gurr also notes that the text could *advertise* the children's company, which played on the Blackfriars stage – the property of *Hamlet*-actor and Chamberlain's company sharer Richard Burbage – and paid Burbage rent.[28]

Given that the scene in F is so detailed, critics have often contended that F documents a history of competition between playhouses and writers. For example, the exposition from Rosincrance has been tied to the so-called 'War of the Theatres' of 1598–1602. Bednarz supports this connection convincingly, pointing out Rosencrantz's assertions that 'there has been much to-do on both sides' (F, 2.2.350–1) and '[t]here was for a while no money bid for argument unless the poet and player went to cuffs in the question' (352–4) as evidence of the skirmish's unsettling effects.[29]

However, F could represent a later period in the Children of the Queen's Revels' company history, 1603–8. Following Roslyn Knutson's argument that F is a post-Q2 revision of *Hamlet*, the passages may refer to the scandalous behaviour of the company and the consequences thereof. The company was frequently at odds with the nobles and the king for offensive material. In 1604, Samuel Daniel's *Philotas* (printed 1605) was interpreted as referring to the Essex rebellion and Daniel was fired from his position as master of the revels for the company (formerly a special arrangement).[30] *Eastward Ho* (1605) offended Scottish nobles as well as King James, and landed George Chapman and Ben Jonson in prison for an extended period, while their co-writer John Marston went into hiding. In 1606, John Day's *The Isle of Gulls* was so offensive to Scots that the Queen apparently revoked her patronage of the company.[31] By 1608, Thomas Heywood's *Apology for Actors* expressed concerns similar to Hamlet's about exploitation in such scandalous work.[32] Finally, in 1608, James was so angered by a Children of the Revels play – Chapman's *The Conspiracy and Tragedy of Byron* – that he shut down all playing in London.[33] The assertion that theatres were not paying for plays –'no money bid for argument' – could refer to this ban.

With all of these possible references swirling, *Hamlet* uses such self-aware moments to discuss the pressures on theatre performers and the desire for an audience member to be 'in the know'. It also mirrors such desire as the company's need for the audience's patronage. In each account, viewers are praised for having attended the show. Furthermore, the scene shows a disruption in Hamlet's attention, previously focused exclusively on the court and his isolation. When Hamlet is drawn into the discussion, he finally cares about something other than himself. Almost as soon as it seemingly invites audience identification with Hamlet's world, however, the text twists the identifying impulse. At the end of the exchange, Hamlet asks if the boys 'carry it away' (F, 2.2.358). The answer is yes, with 'Hercules and his load too' (359–60), which references the Globe's sign. In F, the exchange implies that the 'tragedians of the city' are the players that will arrive shortly at 'Elsinore' *and* the players already on the stage. As the play moves forward, theatrical creation of place and Hamlet's *urbanitas* are intertwined. Because of his access to 'the city', Hamlet knows the players and their condition, and the play has shown that the theatre can stage a dual sense of place, in which both places impinge on each other. Shakespeare's playgoers have already been a part of such an exchange, while watching Hamlet ruminate over the controversies of theatrical culture even while participating in it. Hamlet's reconstruction of *The Murder of Gonzago* works in the same way, as the play world challenges Claudius' Elsinore and questions who holds the true story of Old Hamlet's death.

Hamlet the Dane

In this final section, I explore how Hamlet's shedding of his status as an exile exposes the fact that Elsinore cannot be the cosmopolitan world of civility for which he longs. This transformation is made possible by Hamlet's partnership with the tragedians of the city and his realizations from 2.2. In the performance of *The Murder of Gonzago*, theatre comes to Elsinore, and Hamlet's additions to the play work exactly as he anticipates. Claudius indicts himself by shutting down the production when he finds it seditious. In this regard, Hamlet recalls the dangers of playing that are described in both Q2 and F: first, his 'innovation' meets with 'inhibition' (Q2, 2.2.295–6). Second, his production shows – especially if one accepts a post-Q2 composition of F – that Hamlet intellectually rejects the boys' companies, but he steals their modus operandi. Hamlet finally has the urgency to act, but his murder of Polonius rather than Claudius ends Hamlet's ironic Elsinore imprisonment and replaces it with true banishment.

In all three texts, Hamlet's would-be trip to England coincides with Fortinbras's arrival in Denmark on his way to Poland. But in Q2, Hamlet is afforded time to process the enormity of Fortinbras's endeavour, and in Act Four, Scene Four, Hamlet must confront the difference of local and national concerns. Though impressed by the commitment of military men, he marvels at the Norwegians on their way to die over 'a little patch of ground / That hath in it no profit but the name' (Q2, 4.4.17–18). The philosophy student and worldly citizen still struggles with what he sees: 'This is th'impostume of much wealth and peace / That inward breaks and shows no cause without / Why the man dies' (Q2, 4.4.26–8), unable to find justification for war. At first, he cannot believe that the Poles would defend a useless piece of land. Yet, by the end of his soliloquy, he sheds his attitude of indifference and declares: 'O, from this time forth / My thoughts be bloody or be nothing worth' (Q2, 4.4.64–5).

Bloody thoughts may signify determination, but Hamlet must resolve his emotional and physical alienation in order to compete with Claudius. By becoming an actual exile – being sent to England – Hamlet is able to return again to Elsinore with the intent to claim it. In his skirmish with Laertes at Ophelia's funeral, he finally declares his place through his name: 'This is I, / Hamlet the Dane' (Q2, 5.1.246–7, F, 5.1.253–4).[34] Hamlet makes this declaration over Ophelia's open grave and he signals his willingness to divest himself of any other identity: surrendering to national impetus will also mean surrendering his individualism in favour of finally making his claim. At this point, it could seem possible for the play to balance the local, the national and the cosmopolitan, but Claudius's corruption of the fencing match prevents a 'civil' and symbolic fight – a challenge of *urbanitas* – between Laertes and

Hamlet. Instead, interference of family place and a bid for national control (for Laertes and Claudius) guaranteed through cheating undo the fight's theatrical purpose and make it wild, uncivil and unruly.[35]

The final scene provides a last rebuke of Hamlet's attempts to reconcile his desire for place and his urbane attitude. When Fortinbras stumbles upon the bloody scene of 5.2, he compares the palace to a battlefield. It is as filled with pointless death as the Polish plot that Hamlet imagined in Act Four. The play's ending offers the Norwegian taking his place in Denmark, and in his triumph, he brings foreign power to occupy a small, but meaningful, patch of ground. Fortinbras attempts to correct the indignities of the scene he enters, and he orders Hamlet's body be borne 'like a soldier to the stage' (Q2, 5.2.380). While finally Hamlet has a proper place, Fortinbras assigns him the wrong role. Hamlet's end in this bloody tale, told 'while men's minds are wild' (Q2, 5.2.378), affirms that he was impossibly caught between his supposed home as the prince of Denmark and his civilized, urbane life abroad.

Still, Hamlet's story – as told by Horatio, and ultimately, by the tragedians of the city – illustrates the difficulty of translating the civil world, education or philosophy into control of local power and problems. Horatio insists he must tell the events that define the scene:

> Of carnal, bloody and unnatural acts,
> Of accidental judgements, casual slaughters,
> Of deaths put on by cunning, and for no cause,
> And in this upshot purposes mistook
> Fallen on th'inventors' heads.
>
> (Q2 5.2.365–9)

But what of Horatio's performance? The question remains: will this story bring together a community through the passion of performance, and bring *urbanitas* to Elsinore? Or, will the communication of bloody, unnatural acts and cruelty merely inspire more of the same?

Finally committing to place ended Hamlet's exile, but it also ended his life. Identifying the key changes to Hamlet's place relationships charts his attempts to reconcile local knowledge, national control and cosmopolitan sensibilities. However, as Hamlet finds the mechanisms to act – in theatrical doubleness, in national fervour, in the false promise of civilized ritual – Elsinore strips away any chance for reconciling Hamlet's divergent desires for place and no-place, city and hinterland, local and global, until it pins him down permanently. Ironically, the bloody tale and its global reach haunt Elsinore even now. One can tour the castle today, 'In Hamlet's Footsteps' where 'Horatio' guides visitors through a tour.[36] Such is the power of place and stories: a fictional tale will still bring would-be cosmopolitans to Kronborg, 400 years later, eager to walk in footsteps that never existed, to lay some small claim to *Hamlet*.

Notes

1 Ralph Berry, 'Hamlet's Elsinore Revisited', *Contemporary Review*, 279(1631) (Dec. 2001): 362. Alfred Westfall, 'Why did Shakespeare send Hamlet to Wittenberg?', *The Western Humanities Review*, 6(3) (summer 1952): 230.

2 'Q2' refers to the second quarto of *Hamlet, The Tragicall Historie of Hamlet, Prince of* Denmark (London: John Roberts for Nicholas Ling, 1604–5). All references to Q2 are from *Hamlet*, The Arden Shakespeare, ed. Ann Thompson and Neil Taylor (London: Thomson, 2006), vol. 1. I use Q2 as a default when textual variation is not noted. The other key editions are the first quarto (Q1), and the first folio (F). Q1 was commissioned by Nicholas Ling (with John Trundle) and printed by Valentine Simmes in 1603. The first folio edition, *The Tragedie of Hamlet, Prince of Denmark*, appears in *Mr. William Shakespeare's Comedies, Histories & Tragedies*, the collected works edited by John Heminges and Henry Condell and printed by William Jaggard in 1623. On this printing history, see *Hamlet*, ed. Thompson and Taylor, vol. 1, 76–81. All references to Q1 and to F are from *Hamlet*, ed. Thompson and Taylor, vol. 2.

3 See Remedios Perni, 'The Globe to Globe *Hamlet* Tour: A Celebratory Performance in Elsinore. Elsinore Conference 2016 Shakespeare: The Next 400 Years. Kronborg Castle, Helsingør 21 April 2016', *SEDERI: Yearbook of the Spanish and Portuguese Society for English Renaissance Studies*, 27 (2017): 273–4. Kronborg Hamlets include: John Gielgud (1939), Michael Redgrave (1950), Richard Burton (1954), Derek Jacobi (1979), David Threlfall (1986), Kenneth Branagh (1988), Simon Russell Beale (2000) and Richard McCabe (2001). See Berry, 363–4.

4 'Kronborg Castle', *UNESCO World Heritage List* (2019), https://whc.unesco.org/en/list/696. The 'Visit North Sealand' website offers, 'Kronborg is and will always be the Home of Hamlet.' The site has recently included a Shakespeare festival and, an interactive Shakespeare experience. 'Visit Denmark, 2019' and 'Kronborg Castle', *Visit North Sealand*, https://www.visitnorthsealand.com/north-sealand/plan-your-trip/kronborg-castle-unesco-world-heritage-gdk1077722. The 'Danish Riviera' in Helsingør also offers the chance to visit Hamlet's grave, a memorial stone placed in 1926 for Helsingør's 500 year jubilee, the most recent of four such sites since the seventeenth century. See: 'Hamlet's Grave,' *The Danish Riviera*, *Visit Denmark* (2020) https://www.thedanishriviera.com/tourist/plan-your-trip/hamlets-grave-gdk620721.

5 See *Hamlet*, directed by Grigori Kozintsev (1964; Soviet Union: Facets Video, 2006) DVD. *Hamlet*, directed by Kenneth Branagh (1996; Warner Bros. Entertainment Co. and BBC and Turner Entertainment Co., 2007) DVD. *Hamlet*, directed by Michael Almereyda (2000; Sundance: Miramax/Lionsgate, 2001) DVD.

6 This exchange is also present – with some minor variations – in Q1, Q2 and F.

7 Gail Kern Paster, *The Idea of the City in the Age of Shakespeare* (Athens: University of George Press, 1985), 21.

8 Lawrence Manley, ed., *London in the Age of Shakespeare: An Anthology* (London: Croom Helm, 1986), 193–4.

9 Manley, *Literature and Culture in Early Modern London* (Cambridge: Cambridge University Press, 1995), 28.

10 Manley, *Literature and Culture*, 126–31.

11 Anonymous, *Civil and Uncivil Life* (London, 1579), sig. H1v.

12 In frustration, Valentine at one point insists, 'Then *(Maister Vincent,)* sith you encounter mee with mockes, I will speake no more of Court, but as I haue oft tolde, wish you to peruse the booke of the Courtier' (sig. L3v).

13 Manley, *London*, 195; Paster, 150–77.

14 See for example, Thomas Dekker, *The Gull's Horn-book; or, Fashions to Please All Sorts of Gulls*, in *Thomas Dekker*, ed. E. D. Pendry (London: Edward Arnold, 1967), 65–109; Everard Guilpen, 'Satire V', in *The Penguin Book of Renaissance Verse*, ed. H. R. Woudhuysen and David Norbrook (New York: Penguin Books, 1993), 408–9; George Chapman, Ben Jonson and John Marston, *Eastward Ho*, ed. R. W. Van Fossen (Manchester: Manchester University Press, 1999); Anonymous, 'A Merry Progress to London to see Fashions', Magdalene College-Pepys, EBBA 20088.

15 Quoted in Manley, *London*, 201.

16 In Q1, the conversation is a bit different but has the same gist. One difference is that Q1, Scene 2 names France but not Paris.

17 Westfall also conjectures that an 'ur-*Hamlet*' may have introduced Wittenberg to the story, and speculates that Thomas Kyd may have been responsible (233–4).

18 Suzanne H. Stein, 'Hamlet in Melanchthon's Wittenberg', *Notes and Queries*, 56(1) (March 2009): 55–7 (56).

19 Stein, 56.

20 Russell Jacoby, 'Cosmopolitanism and Place', in *Why Place Matters: Geography, Identity, and Civic Life in Modern America*, ed. Wilfred M. McClay and Ted V. McAllister (New York: New Atlantis Books, 2014), 71.

21 There are important differences between Q1, Q2 and F in the exchanges I examine. For opinions on the status of the different texts, see: Terri Bourus, *Young Shakespeare's Young Hamlet: Print, Piracy and Performance* (New York: Palgrave Macmillan, 2014); Zachary Lesser, *Hamlet after Q1* (Philadelphia: University of Pennsylvania Press, 2015); Paul Menzer, *The Hamlets: Cues, Qs, and Remembered Texts* (Newark: University

of Delaware Press, 2008); *Hamlet*, ed. Thompson and Taylor, vol. 1, 76–97, 504–37; and Roslyn Lander Knutson, *Playing Companies and Commerce in Shakespeare's Time* (Cambridge: Cambridge University Press, 2001), 103–26.

22 See *Hamlet*, ed. Thompson and Taylor, vol. 1, 8–13, 92–6; Bourus, 1–10.

23 Because in Q2 and F, Claudius also adds that they were 'brought up with [Hamlet]' (Q2, F 2.2.11) it is less clear what schooling Hamlet might mean, but Wittenberg still seems likely. In Q1, Hamlet addresses both men as his 'kind schoolfellows' (7.237), and they note that Hamlet seemed different 'when we were at Wittenberg' (7.239). In the Folio, the references to a shared past are less clear – Wittenberg is not mentioned – but their conversation in 2.2 still names 'the city' (F, 2.2.331).

24 See Records of Early English Drama (REED) online: 'Patrons and Players', https://reed.library.utoronto.ca/content/kings-players, to trace the travels of the Chamberlain's/King's Men. James Bednarz argues that touring after 1599 was extremely unlikely: 'The company's return to the road was an anxious joke rather than a current event' (*Shakespeare and the Poets' War* [New York: Columbia University Press, 2001], 241). Knutson argues that companies toured to make extra income, or when theatres were forced to close, or if patrons requested performances. See *The Repertory of Shakespeare's Companies, 1594–1613* (Fayetteville: University of Arkansas Press, 1991), 104–7. Andrew Gurr also notes that Shakespeare's company did tour, especially before 1599 and after 1602: see *The Shakespeare Company, 1594–1642* (Cambridge: Cambridge University Press, 2004), 54–63. Barbara D. Palmer observes that critics fail to understand that touring by respectable troupes was carried out across England throughout the early modern period. She also points out that being turned away a great house might net players as much money as if they had performed. See Palmer, 'Early Modern Mobility: Players, Payments, and Patrons', *Shakespeare Quarterly*, 56(3) (2005), 259–305, esp. 263–75.

25 For example, some argue the line refers to the Essex rebellion, others that it could mean an inhibition because of plague in London 1603–4, and others that it refers to a political situation inside or outside the fictive world of the play. See Knutson,

Playing Companies, 115–18; *Hamlet*, ed. Thompson and Taylor, vol. 1, 52–3; Bednarz, 242–4; Bourus, 185–8.

26 Andrew Gurr, *The Shakespearean Stage: 1574–1642*, Fourth Edition (Cambridge, Cambridge University Press, 2009), 45–6.

27 Lucy Munro, *Children of the Queen's Revels: A Jacobean Theatre Repertory* (Cambridge: Cambridge University Press, 2005), 17.

28 See Gurr, *Shakespearean Stage*, 64.

29 A conflict supposedly between Ben Jonson, Thomas Dekker and John Marston in plays that savaged each other. The plays might include: Marston's *Histriomastix* (1599), *Jack Drum's Entertainment* (1600), and *What You Will* (1600), Jonson's *Every Man Out of his Humour* (1599), *Cynthia's Revels* (1600), and *Poetaster* (1601), and Dekker's *Satiromastix* (1601). Marston's plays were mostly performed by the Children of Paul's; Jonson's by the Chamberlain's Men (*Every Man Out*) and the Children of the Chapel, and Dekker's by the Chamberlain's Men and the Children of Paul's together. See Bednarz, 9–13; Thompson and Taylor, vol. 1, 52–3.

30 See Gurr, *Shakespearean Stage*, 68–9.

31 See Andrew Gurr, *The Shakespearian Playing Companies* (Oxford: Clarendon Press, 1996), 350–2; Knutson, *Playing Companies*, 121–3. Gurr attests to constant scandal as well, concluding that '[i]t seems very likely that the Blackfriars plays written between 1601 and 1607 were the most radical ever staged in London between 1574 and 1642' (*Shakespearean Stage*, 71).

32 There are plausible and divergent possibilities for dating the F lines, as Munro has noted. Knutson (*Playing Companies*, 119) and Munro (13–15) both point to Heywood's text.

33 See Gurr, *Shakespearean Playing Companies*, 354–5.

34 In Q1: 'Behold, 'tis I – Hamlet the Dane' (16.147).

35 On 'wild' revenge, see Francis Bacon, *The Essayes or Counsels, Civill and Morall* (London, 1625), sig. D2r.

36 'In Hamlet's Footsteps', *Kronborg*, https://kongeligeslotte.dk/en/palaces-and-gardens/kronborg-castle/whats-on-at-kronborg-castle/in-hamlets-footsteps.html

4

Code Black Whiteness and Unmanliness in *Hamlet*

David Sterling Brown

In 2002, Peter Erickson titled an essay with what undoubtedly was a provocative and productive question: 'Can We Talk about Race in *Hamlet*?' There, he asserted that 'the scope of inquiry [in the study of race in Shakespeare] should be expanded to include the broader sphere of rhetoric and imagery' that make it possible to discuss race in plays such as *Hamlet*.[1] Because of Erickson's essay, and other works like it that examine race beyond the 'so-called "race" plays', it is clear we can talk about race in *Hamlet* (*c.* 1601).[2] And as I will suggest below, it is clear *Hamlet*'s engagement with race, particularly with respect to gender construction, is strong and not quite as 'oblique' and 'latent' as Erickson implies in his reading of the play's male dynamics and its depiction of women;[3] thus, in this chapter I want to build on Erickson's claims, especially those articulated about 'whiteness and weakness'.[4] And I also want to examine how black imagery gets mapped onto white bodies in ways that add to Kim F. Hall's arguments regarding the early modern usage of 'tropes of blackness' in relationship to 'gender differentiation' and to Patricia Parker's ideas about *Hamlet*'s 'preoccupation with blackness, soiling, sullying, and dulling' – for example, through unmanliness.[5]

The work of these critics, and others like Patricia Akhimie, Lisa M. Anderson, Ayanna Thompson and Scott Newstok, to name a few, reveal how strides have been made to scrutinize not what early modern critical race studies scholars are bringing to Shakespeare studies but what Shakespeare's work has brought to early modern race studies scholars.[6] In other words, this essay rejects the field's 'pathological averseness to thinking about race', as Erickson and Hall put it, by showcasing how race cannot be ignored in the premodern context – even in what may appear to be one of Shakespeare's whitest plays.[7] The scholarship of the abovementioned critics, who have examined race in Shakespeare plays that centre on white characters, endorses an underlying desire to expand fully the race play concept, and the early modern critical race studies discussion, through the concentration on race in one of what we might consider Shakespeare's traditionally white plays.[8] When we conceive of Shakespeare's 'race plays', a phrase I hesitate to call a misnomer given its relevance and past utility in the majority of scholarship that has examined Shakespeare and race to date, we can delude ourselves into believing it is only these few plays that centre on race and enable us to have the most fruitful conversations on the subject. Other Shakespeare plays are just as racially rich and critically generative.

For example, *Hamlet* is a dramatic work whose dominant white male characters remind us to 'reassess the presumption that race is, fundamentally, about the faraway rather than about the familiar'.[9] A specific focus on the proximate, on similarity,[10] reveals how Shakespeare raced *Hamlet* and, to borrow language from Ian Smith, used 'language as a racial marker' to generate important socio-cultural distinctions between acceptable manliness – represented in its desired form by whiteness – and unacceptable manliness – represented by blackness, a colour that was stigmatized negatively and linked to African identity in the period.[11] *Hamlet* is replete with discourse that aligns blackness with 'unman[lines]' and fashions the ideal white self-image in relationship to what I view as a white Other who is blackened and also signifies intra-canonically (1.2.92).[12] In other words, examining how *Hamlet* grapples with racialized gender construction opens up possibilities for understanding the more crucial, strained relationship between whiteness and unmanliness beyond the confines of this popular white-centric Shakespeare play.

As such, I want to address *how* this play does that work, focusing on at least one way of what I believe are many, and outline what unmanliness is and does in this tragedy.[13] So, how can we talk about race in *Hamlet* and how can we use its characters to talk about race? Through the play's references to unmanliness that function as a rhetorical device, through the way unmanliness serves 'as a perversion of a code of manly virtue', *Hamlet* dramatizes Denmark's deterioration through the decomposition of white masculinity and, in so doing, codes *un*manliness as black, thereby offering insight into the formation of the (un)manly subject.[14] Aligned with Sky Gilbert, Bernhard Frank and others, I contend that Hamlet exhibits qualities and behaviours that call into question how manly he really is, especially in comparison to his deceased father and Young Fortinbras.[15] As Hall reminds us, black, a negative signifier opposed to whiteness, connotes many things within and outside of Shakespeare's canon (sin, evil, death, melancholy, etc.), and in early modern England,[16] and to the list I would add unmanliness, a quality embodied by other white male Shakespeare characters such as Macbeth and Richard III whose masculinity appears conflicted in their respective plays.[17]

Although *Hamlet* does not contain somatically Black figures, I assert that it is precisely this physical lack of black that allows the play to enrich, though less obviously so at first glance, the Shakespearean canonical discourse regarding the triangulated relationship between whiteness, unmanliness and blackness – and how it may even impact contemporary perceptions of Black men. As Rebecca Ann Bach notes, 'In texts of the English Renaissance many people whom we would see as men – including boys, men who violate their duty, cowards, Catholics (and atheists and Puritans), Frenchmen (and Italians, black men, Jews, and other non-English people), and men of low status – are depicted as more like women than they are like men'.[18] Bach adds that 'they are effeminate because they act like women – i.e. they are frail, unable or unwilling to fight, or subordinate – and also because they desire women'.[19] Through *Hamlet*, then, we might enhance our understanding of Shakespeare's positioning of blackness as base – as in foundational and strong – given that attitudes toward whiteness get mediated through blackness, a symbolically dominant force used as a support beam to stabilize notions of the ideal white self.[20]

Canonical figures associated with unmanliness – Macbeth, Richard III, Hamlet and Othello, for example – enable the following syllogistic reasoning, reasoning that allows the recognition of discourses about 'the failures of masculine performance'[21] to relate to discourses about race in Shakespeare's race plays and his other plays:[22] If questioned masculinity is a marker of blackness, then we must also appreciate the potential for critiqued masculinity, understood as behaviour that 'does not conform to traditional codes of masculinity', to be a social stain, a symbol of blackness that transmits a negative stigma about black(ened) manhood.[23] By cloaking rotting, and rotten, white Danish masculinity in literal and figurative blackness, Hamlet's and Claudius's in particular, Shakespeare calls attention to the white masculine crisis that is the crux of what 'is rotten in the state of Denmark' (1.4.65).

The play shows how the blackening of white men is dangerous and conflicts with the goals of patriarchy; and the play enables blackness to be about and transcend skin colour by depicting unmanliness as a kind of monstrous blackness one can embody, leading a character like Hamlet to 'act black' or be black in a visual or performative sense.[24] Much like villainy and evil-doing, metaphorically black conduct too is black, thus rendering it, as I argue, an underexamined subcategory of difference within Shakespeare's work, one that necessitates racialization, especially given how race and racism, in the past and now, depend on hierarchically imbalanced power dynamics. While critics have questioned Hamlet's masculinity before because of his bond with Horatio and because of his madness and murderous indecision, I contend that his unmanliness becomes more complicated and critically interesting when we consider how blackness, symbolized by the night and the 'inky cloak', among other things, enshrouds this tragic hero and this play (1.2.75).[25]

In *Hamlet*, and even in Hamlet the character, ideal Danish masculinity is dead, as the play makes it challenging for any living Dane to epitomize stereotypical masculine strength without appearing weak; and this reality has disastrous implications for the Danes. This reality, in part, adds to the play's tragic generic qualities since Hamlet's unmanliness contributes to his character flaws. Beginning in medias res, with an acknowledgement of Old Hamlet's recent death, the play reminds us that somewhere in Denmark's landscape the dead king's body is going through the decomposition process. All that the King *was* is no more, as Hamlet's lamentation to Horatio proves: 'He was a man, take him for all in all: / I shall not look upon his like again' (1.2.184–5). Indeed, there are no 'heroic' men like Old Hamlet in Denmark.[26] In having been 'all', including the Danish exemplar of courtliness, patriarchy and 'manhood embodied',[27] the dead king leaves a void in his kingdom. There is no successor to maintain the martial, masculine ideals of Old Hamlet,[28] who is called 'majestical' by Marcellus (1.1.124) and twice referred to as 'valiant' for his defeat of Old Fortinbras and for his military prowess (1.1.83, 1.2.25).[29] Moreover, as a ghost, Old Hamlet's 'armed' appearance, with his military apparel evoking 'a medieval ethos of violence', offers a comparatively hypermasculine image that appears again in the play only through the non-Danish figure Young Fortinbras,[30] whose military strength exists in the play's background. Critics such as Jennifer Low and others have acknowledged, '*Hamlet* is framed by the deeds of Fortinbras'.[31] For the Danes, the idealized Old Hamlet represents an unattainable height of masculinity and majesty. Hamlet insinuates this when he berates his mother in the closet scene for leaving the 'fair mountain,' the highland, to 'feed and batten on [the] moor,' the lowland (3.4.66–7).[32]

The racialized comparison between Old Hamlet and Claudius – between ideal white masculinity and the play's presentation of tainted, blackened masculinity – destabilizes notions about what the dead and living can represent. Through 'fair', a term that appears in F1 and Q2, Hamlet reminds us of his deceased father's whiteness; and through 'moor', which puns on blackamoor, the Prince directs our attention to Claudius's emblematic blackness, his degenerate state of being that Q1's language reaffirms with its reference to Vulcan, the Roman god of fire (11.34). As Parker asserts, the Roman god allusion conjures up the devil and 'explicitly invokes an infernal blackness for this second husband'.[33] In the context of decomposition and dead masculinity, then, an inversion occurs: the paternal juxtaposition revives and raises the dead father, the fair mountain, repositioning his once healthy, majestic embodiment of whiteness above the blackened living stepfather, whom Hamlet puts into the ground, so to speak, later on in the play. Despite the rhetorical variations among the *Hamlet* texts – Q1, Q2 and F1 – one point of intersection among them is how Shakespeare depicts ideal and compromised whiteness by repeatedly evoking and invoking blackness to stabilize racial meaning.[34] Furthermore, as I will discuss in more detail later, the textual variants in the *Hamlet* texts help illuminate the need to locate an image of ideal white masculinity beyond Denmark via references to, and the inclusion of, Young Fortinbras.

Thus, the loss of 'Hamlet, / King, father, royal Dane' is a loss Denmark cannot recover from, hence the state's rapid deterioration under Claudius's rule (1.4.23–4). Through unlikely figures, the minor characters Rosencrantz and Guildenstern, we learn that kingly death has corrosive potential for the nation. Rosencrantz astutely explains: 'The cease of majesty / Dies not alone, but like a gulf doth draw / What's near it with it' (3.3.15–17). This simile would explain why unmanliness swells as the play progresses, for if kingly greatness can die then it can subsequently decompose, metaphorically speaking, like the royal body, and negatively impact everything that 'live[s] and feed[s] upon' it, as Guildenstern warns (3.3.10).

The King's dead body, and the seeming death of masculinity, represents a crisis that darkens the play, as the invisible background image of the rotting human corpse, with its foul odour emissions and visual evidence of decay, denotes a physical blackening of the white body.[35] Images of the human decomposition process, for example, show how the body changes after death, becoming discoloured, darkly spotted and blackened over time during a decay stage called 'black putrefaction'.[36] Even the Ghost's own words point in this direction when he conveys to Hamlet the immediate effect the poison had on his body: 'A most instant tetter baked about / Most lazar-like with vile and loathsome crust / All my smooth body' (1.5.71–3). Through the development of sores, Old Hamlet's white body transforms into something that resembles tree bark, which is usually some shade of brown. The reference to leprosy scabs and the 'crust' that overtake the body create a contrast between the newfound roughness of Old Hamlet's skin and deteriorating stature and the natural smoothness of his once healthy white body.[37] Claudius's evil deed, his choice to poison his brother with 'juice of cursed hebenon', introduces blackness, or blackening, to Denmark through sin and immorality, through Old Hamlet's body's physical response to the poison and through the King's death and the initiation of his decomposition process (1.5.62).

Claudius literally taints Denmark's masculinity through the murder and through *how* he murders since poison was thought to be a feminine and passive way to kill, as *Othello* reminds us when the General suggests he will poison Desdemona. The Ghost's repeated description of the murder as 'foul' (1.5.25, 27, 28) and 'unnatural' (1.5.25, 28) provides commentary on Claudius's unmanliness and emblematic blackness, which we cannot help but notice throughout the remainder of the play. The murder is unnatural and foul, as in corrupt, because the murder*er* is unnatural and foul, as in spiritually soiled with sin. The Ghost describes Claudius as: a 'serpent' (1.5.36); 'incestuous' (1.5.42); and an 'adulterate beast' (1.5.42). The snake image links the new King to the devil and blackens him morally, as does his monstrous sexuality, the characterization of which aligns him with figures such as Aaron and Othello and distances him from his brother who represents white male propriety.[38] Moreover, the Ghost allies Claudius with 'witchcraft' and consequently a stereotype linked to Black sexuality (1.5.43);[39] furthermore, he accuses Claudius of containing 'shameful lust' (1.5.45) and having 'wicked wits and gifts, that have the power / So to seduce!' (1.5.44–5). As seducer, Claudius plays the woman's role, standing in for the play's absent Black seductress. He is a Cleopatra, so to speak. Directly and indirectly, the Ghost paints Claudius as his dark evil foil whose personhood pales in comparison to the Ghost's now dead white masculinity and magnificence. The brotherly dynamic is represented by familiar binaries such as good and evil, white and black, masculine and feminine, and even the language of high and low, which emphasizes the negative stigmas about blackness and unmanliness as undesirable characteristics. According to the Ghost, Gertrude, like Eve, began existing in a fallen state once she chose to sin and 'decline / Upon a wretch whose natural gifts were poor' in comparison to Old Hamlet's (1.5.50–1). The latter possesses the richer natural qualities that represent what is right or socially desirable. Therefore, Gertrude's marital move is reductive for the reasons the Ghost explicitly states and for reasons implied in the subtext that presents the new King as womanish and as having more in common with his spouse than his late brother. The decline from a presumably healthy marriage to one that is incestuous and therefore spiritually unhealthy parallels the deteriorating health of the state; Claudius's rotten masculinity touches the institutions of marriage and family, spoiling and soiling them, too.

Characters recognize Hamlet's changed state, as I will soon discuss, but most of them do not recognize Claudius's transformation – perhaps with the exception of the perceptive Hamlet, who aims to 'catch the conscience of the King' (2.2.600). When Hamlet reduces the King's manliness before he departs for England, he only reinforces what the play has already articulated as a possibility: that the new monarch is a dysfunctional amalgamation of social roles and a cancerous head of state who severely weakens the body politic. Hamlet's intensified disrespect toward Claudius, observed in his resistance to their having a legitimate father–son dynamic, is a manifestation of the tension that exists between both of these unmanly figures. In catty ways, they call out each other's flawed masculinity. By refusing to refer to Claudius as 'father' when leaving for England, for example, Hamlet takes a rhetorical stand that attributes feminine characteristics to his uncle. Their farewell exchange in this pivotal domestic scene reaffirms the new King's failure to solidify himself as a surrogate father and patriarch. The Prince defines Claudius's position with his ambiguous goodbye:

HAMLET Farewell, dear mother.
KING
Thy loving father, Hamlet.
HAMLET
My mother. Father and mother is man and wife.
Man and wife is one flesh, and so – my mother.
Come, for England!

(3.6.46–50)

The one flesh that is Gertrude and Claudius is notably feminine; this should not surprise us given the decomposition of white masculinity, which makes it impossible for Claudius to be seen, like Old Hamlet, as 'King, father, royal Dane' by Hamlet. In her comments on the above exchange, Janet Adelman argues that 'in this fantasy, it does not matter whether Hamlet is thinking of his father or his incestuous stand-in'.[40] On the contrary, I propose that it matters greatly, for the erasure of masculinity heightens Claudius's feminization. Hamlet's clever and dismissive farewell address blackens Claudius through its identification of the King with the incestuous mother figure who, prior to this scene, looks 'into [her] very soul / And there . . . see[s] such black and grained spots / As will not leave their tinct' (3.4.80–2).

By the time we truly discover something is rotten in the state of Denmark, ideal Danish masculinity has been compromised by white unmanliness, which is put on display by the play's two most central male figures. Hamlet's own masculine defects are reflected in his misogynistic language toward Ophelia that personifies 'frailty' and creates an inextricable link between it and 'woman' (1.2.144). According to Hamlet, weakness is a womanly trait. Yet, the male characters' conduct contradicts this logic by underscoring the possibilities for male fragility at various points in the drama. In displaying signs of weakness, the play's men exude what was understood in the period as feminine behaviour: Upon learning about Ophelia's death, for instance, Laertes displays emotion by shedding uncontrollable tears, acknowledging that '[w]hen these [tears] are gone / The woman will be out' (4.3.160–1). In other words, when frailty is in men then so, too, is the woman, for the metaphorical *she* engages men in an internal power struggle that is understood, according to Andrew D. McCarthy, 'as a physical assault on their bodies (i.e. "women's weapons")'.[41] This suggests, especially since gender is a social construct, that it is always possible for men to succumb to the influence of femininity at any given moment.[42]

As Hamlet manages the emotional effects of his father's death, Claudius condemns the Prince's 'unmanly grief' with a critique containing racial undertones and challenging Hamlet's masculinity. He codes Hamlet's black mood as wrong (1.2.92).[43] By shaming the Prince, Claudius aims to police Hamlet's metaphorical blackness, his emotions, perhaps so they become manlier and devoid of prolonged grief.[44] In fact, Claudius's criticism is loaded with meaning that helps us see Hamlet's tarnished whiteness. Those rhetorical moments are worth highlighting here because they document the play's developing discourse surrounding Hamlet's compromised state. Even the Queen takes note of Hamlet's blackness when she orders him to 'cast [his] nightly colour off / And let [his] eye look like a friend on Denmark' (1.2.66–7); in not looking like a friend, Hamlet looks like an enemy. This has negative implications for his relationship with his family and the state, as his nightly colour reflects the blackness that overtakes him. Following Gertrude, the new King specifies how Hamlet's attitude is an affront to Denmark: 'It shows a will most incorrect to heaven', he explains, and he reiterates and expands on that assertion by saying that Hamlet's unyielding unmanly grief is 'a fault to heaven, / A fault against the dead, a fault to nature, / To reason most absurd' (1.2.99–101). Invoking religion, Claudius implies Hamlet's behaviour violates God's will and, in so doing, comes close to being a kind of sin because it is a dereliction of his duty to God. Moreover, Claudius emphasizes that one also has a duty to the dead and to nature. In being unmanly through his incessant grief, Hamlet rejects the rigid boundaries of white masculinity and exhibits feminine behaviour. All of this, as Claudius concludes, is evidence of Hamlet's irrationality and unsound judgement that contribute to his wrongly coloured mood.

But it is not just Hamlet's temperament that is coloured black and therefore wrong; it is also Hamlet himself that is the wrong colour. Not white enough, he is a character who: defines himself as 'too much i'th' sun' (1.2.65);[45] wears an 'inky cloak' (1.2.75) and 'customary suits of solemn black' (1.2.76); and opts to be the 'darkest night' that lets Laertes' star '[s]tick fiery off' (5.2.203–4). All of these descriptions point to an undeniable physical, or external, blackness that complements the internal blackness signalled by Hamlet's melancholy and anger. The play contains a few moments that indicate it is possible for white to be black(ened) internally or externally: Hamlet's allusion to the Greek Pyrrhus' 'sable arms' (2.2.449), or armour, and black 'purpose' (2.2.450) and 'black complexion' (2.2.452) echoes the Prince of Denmark's own disposition and provides another example of blackness consuming a being who is not somatically Black.[46] When Hamlet notes that Pyrrhus 'did the night resemble', he reminds the audience of his own dark appearance at the play's onset and the fact that even a white man can be a Black-like figure (2.2.450). Beyond the Pyrrhus scene, blackness emerges as defining of Hamlet's overall identity in Polonius's assertion that 'the apparel oft proclaims the man', that one's fashion choices are central to how one is perceived, to the judgements others might make and also to one's perception of self (1.3.72).[47] Sartorial choices can convey status, broadly speaking (class, ethnicity, race, gender, etc.), and clothes can be an outward manifestation of one's internal state.[48] Clothing, as Polonius theorizes, speaks for the wearer. As such, Hamlet's initial messages in the play are black and loud, and they are a prelude to his volatile black emotional state that eventually oscillates between melancholy and revenge/anger, what Claudius labels Hamlet's 'dangerous lunacy', a phrase that feminizes him given that women were stereotyped in the period as being predisposed to hysteria and madness (3.1.4).

In this dramatic work that thrives on surveillance, it should be expected that Claudius is not alone in recognizing 'Hamlet's transformation' (2.2.5); the change is best defined by the relationship between Hamlet's whiteness and compromised manliness. Gertrude laments her 'too much changed son' (2.2.35); Polonius wants to find 'the cause of this defect' in Hamlet (2.2.102); and Claudius claims, regarding Hamlet, 'th'exterior nor the inward man / Resembles that it was' (2.2.7–8). Gertrude is concerned with how much the Prince has changed: to the point where he is on the verge of possibly losing himself in her eyes. Somehow, Hamlet's black makeover alarms the play's other main characters – it makes them uneasy. I propose that his 'defect' is his deficient white masculinity that the play associates with blackness.[49] Ironically, the defect revelation is made by Claudius, a white man who is also defective. While these key characters assess Hamlet, they highlight aspects of his rotten masculinity, which the play itself calls attention to just one scene earlier when Hamlet enters Ophelia's closet in 2.1 and displays physical aggression toward her. Paradoxically, his aggression is a symptom of his masculine fragility, which makes him have more in common with a female such as Ophelia and less in common with his valiant deceased father. This dynamic is similar to how Claudius's hypersexuality links him to Gertrude, to the play's other woman. Figuratively speaking, the rot on Hamlet's masculinity tarnishes it in ways that underscore his unmanliness. As the play progresses, not even Hamlet can deny the irreversible deteriorating condition of his masculinity, for which death is the only remedy. Death is the only way the woman will be out, since only the play's catastrophic conclusion can erase the most significant representations of white unmanliness and blackened femininity.

As I argued above, Hamlet's transformation, his defectiveness, links him to blackness and femininity, sometimes independently of one another but often in conjunction. When Polonius comments, 'How pregnant sometimes [Hamlet's] replies are', he feminizes the fruitfulness and complexity of the Prince's intellect and wit in a metaphor that amplifies Hamlet's dramatic emasculation (2.2.206–7). This might explain why Hamlet says, 'My wit's dis- / eased', for he is so troubled with unmanliness (3.2.312–13): For Hamlet's replies to be pregnant, in theory, they must be impregnated; and if we allow for a literal interpretation of 'pregnant', as Tanya Pollard does, then we can observe the homo-hypersexual undertone here through Hamlet's 'potential maternity'.[50] Since only women can become pregnant among humans, the implication is that Hamlet's replies have occasionally copulated – with a man – to be as generative as they are.[51] This occasional copulation conveys a sense of casual fornication, linking the Prince to the concept of whoredom, a type of conduct stemming from stereotypical monstrous blackened female sexuality, which he directly associates with himself later in this scene.[52] He, too, serves as a Cleopatra-like figure. And if Hamlet's replies are pregnant, then so, too, is Hamlet since he generates or births those ideas.

Conversely, when Hamlet's replies are not pregnant, indicated by Polonius's use of 'sometimes', we might say they are barren. Still, such replies showcase the multiplicity of meaning found in the term 'pregnant'. Whenever Hamlet makes loaded statements that give us pause and make us and his dramatic counterparts think, he taps into his unmanly self, which solidifies him as a character who is 'unpregnant of [his] cause' since he is quick to talk and slow to act (2.2.562). I believe Laertes' previously cited line, 'the woman will be out', is even more fascinating when we consider it an extension of how men in this play can be pregnant. To expel the woman from the body is, in a way, to give birth to her so that she exists as a feminine self that is distinct from one's masculine self. When the woman is out, in terms of what *Hamlet* proposes, with her go tears, inconstancy, frailty, fear, monstrous sexuality, hysteria, madness and so many other qualities that the valiant Norwegian Young Fortinbras does not seem to possess because, as an outsider, he has not been touched by the corrosive power of white Danish masculinity. From beginning to end, it is the Danish white men who are pregnant with the woman; they represent well feminine excess through their metaphorically grotesque male bodies.[53]

Hamlet best articulates his own embodiment of unmanliness through self-deprecating behaviour that immediately follows Polonius's indirect critique of the Prince's masculinity. After the Pyrrhus episode, one in which Hamlet's reaction parallels his later response to Young Fortinbras in his 4.4 soliloquy appearing in Q2, but not in F1, Hamlet berates himself for being 'a dull and muddy-mettled rascal', phrasing that acknowledges his weakness (2.2.561). Although it is part of a hyphenated term, the dark, racialized implications of 'muddy' cannot go unnoticed, for 'muddy' connects Hamlet to Ophelia, who dies a 'muddy death' (a darkening of the white body) and is stained by the speculation surrounding whether or not her death was a suicide and therefore a sin (4.3.155). Hamlet's doubts about his masculinity, particularly apparent when he asks himself, 'Am I a coward?' remind us that up to this point he has remained a man of no action (2.2.565). His masculine insecurity overwhelms him, and the audience as well: In a span of about 30 lines in act 2, Hamlet declares he is 'pigeon-livered', as in meek, and 'lack[s] gall / To make oppression bitter' (2.2.571). He chastises himself for being an 'ass' (2.2.577). He self-identifies his 'weakness and my melancholy', qualities that reflect his unmanliness and internal blackness, respectively (2.2.596). And most strikingly, Hamlet criticizes his delayed action with figurative language that repeats the now familiar idea that there is some resonance between the Danish Prince and morally corrupt, hypersexual women. Accordingly, he expresses his frustration with the fact that he 'must, like a whore, unpack [his] heart with words / And fall a-cursing like a very drab, / A scullion!' (2.2.581–2). Claudius also uses similar language when he compares his evil deed to the 'harlot's [ugly] cheek beautied with plastering art' (3.1.51). 'Whore', 'drab' and 'harlot', derogatory terms to describe women with monstrous sexuality – women like Gertrude, who has been 'whored' by Claudius according to her son (5.2.64) – reveal how 'Hamlet pinpoints his own effeminacy, characterizing himself as more like a boy or woman than a man ... Shakespeare could not be clearer that Hamlet is emasculated by his own lack of action', as Gilbert argues.[54]

The types of women Hamlet compares himself to reveal his own masculine insecurities that stem from his misogyny and sexism.[55] Moreover, his alignment with women, or even their abstract image, reminds us of how he is not a reflection of his father's heroic white image, despite bearing the same name. He is, indeed, his own person, but this does not bode well for Denmark since he is a weak white man. When Claudius pronounces that Hamlet is '[f]rom fashion of himself', indicating that the Prince's melancholy has drastically altered his personality, he builds on his previous remark that Hamlet is not what he once was (3.1.176). The Prince is still not in what one might recognize as his usual form, much like Ophelia is not herself after Polonius's death, because something steps in between Hamlet and himself. Identified as the causes of his much-altered state, his 'grief' (3.1.178, 184) and 'melancholy' (3.1.166), feelings spawned by his father's murder, allow yet another parallel between the Prince and Ophelia to emerge since we see her in 'deep grief' over her father's murder in 4.1 (line 74). Just as Hamlet is from fashion of himself, 'poor Ophelia [is] / Divided from herself and her fair judgment, / Without the which we are pictures or mere beasts' (4.1.82–4). She, too, is out of fashion. And it is through this connection that the unmanly construction develops further since grief and melancholy blacken Ophelia's aura in the play, literally separating her from the white-coloured 'fair judgment', and lead her to the kind of deadly madness to which Hamlet arguably succumbs. The possibility of Ophelia being beast-like is an allusion to Hamlet's own bestial state, as foregrounded in Q2, which I will soon explore.

The play's myriad instances of masculine fragility repeatedly remind us that ideal Danish masculinity no longer has a pulse, as signalled by Old Hamlet's dead, decomposing body.[56] Interestingly, when the human body shuts down, and the cells die and release their energy, the body's temperature drops rapidly. As we think of what physically remains of Old Hamlet in the grave, we should envision his body as blackened by the decomposition process and we should also imagine it as cold. The coldness is reflected in the atmosphere of the body politic and Denmark; and it reinforces how much the old King's suspicious death influences the play's tone and setting that support my reading of the play's dead masculinity: In the opening scene, Francisco, a member of the watch, remarks that it is 'bitter cold' (1.1.6); Hamlet begins 1.4 by observing, 'The air bites shrewdly; is it very cold' (line 1); when Ophelia grieves her father's death, she says, 'I cannot choose but weep to think they would lay him i'th' cold ground' (4.1.68–9); and during Hamlet's comical exchange with Osric the former reiterates, "'Tis very cold; the wind is northerly', and the latter concurs, even after he initially claimed it was hot (5.2.97–8). I am not suggesting Old Hamlet's death caused things to be chilly in Denmark, though one could potentially make that argument regarding Hamlet and Claudius's icy relationship. What I am proposing, however, is that there exists a correlation between the King's dead body and the drama's cold atmosphere, which taken together indicate how white masculinity lacks dynamism and life, an argument that *Hamlet*'s sustained frosty climate supports.

It is, after all, in this cold landscape where we find the Danish men who need to let some form of the woman out. While I will not analyse in depth all such examples from the play, I will note some of them here to offer a sense of how unmanliness, attached to blackness or not, is presented as linked to the white Danes. Early on, Claudius mentions that Young Fortinbras '[h]old[s] a weak supposal of our worth'; the possessive form of the royal *we* makes this moment about Claudius and the general Danish population (1.2.18). Ironically, the Player Queen argues in the climactic act that women express weakness and 'fear', but apparently so, too, do men in *Hamlet* (3.2.163, 166). Marcellus and Bernardo watched the Ghost of Hamlet with 'fear-surprised eyes' (1.2.200) as they 'bestilled / Almost to jelly with the act of fear' (1.2.201–2). In discussion with Polonius, Hamlet asserts that old men have 'weak hams', insulting the alleged physical deficiency of elderly men (2.2.198). In a metadramatic fashion, Rosencrantz claims, 'many wearing rapiers are afraid of goose quills and dare scare come thither' (2.2.341–2). Guildenstern and Rosencrantz display moral frailty as they 'soa[k] up the King's countenance' and betray their friend Hamlet in the process (3.5.17). Laertes 'weeps', as the stage directions make clear in 4.3 (line 160). And before Hamlet stops him, Horatio rebuffs his own ethnic identity when he declares he is 'more an antique Roman than a Dane' as he contemplates drinking what is left in the poisoned cup (5.2.295). In the context of suicide, Horatio imagines getting closer to ideal masculine whiteness, albeit rhetorically; the desired adoption of Roman identity contrasts with his unmanly Danish identity. In the Danish white men, unmanliness lives; and it lives on through Horatio and through the tragic story he must recount.

Contrastingly, Norwegian Young Fortinbras's masculine air redirects the play's focus through his leadership and seemingly uncompromised masculinity as he commands the play's concluding action (5.2.341–5, 350–8). Even though we do not hear much from Norway's Prince in the play's last scene, his valiant presence, which counters Hamlet's feebleness (literalized by his dying and death), is apparent, so much so that it forces us to reflect on Hamlet's own inaction that betrays his masculine deficiency. Rather than revenge the Ghost's murder, which is his primary charge from Act 1, Hamlet thinks and talks, and even puts on an 'antic disposition' (1.5.171). Indeed, he acts but he does not act like Young Fortinbras, as his 4.4 soliloquy in Q2 makes clear. The play's opening foreshadows Hamlet's contrasting passivity given that Horatio describes Young Fortinbras as 'hot and full' of manly aggression and strength (1.1.95). Distracted by his unmanliness, Hamlet's questionable revenge is slow. The Q2 language indicates that his revenge is 'dull' and in the process of being activated, as he reflects on Fortinbras's Norwegian soldiers willingly '[g]o[ing] to their graves like beds' (4.4.65). It takes witnessing Fortinbras's steadfastness to compel Hamlet to get back on course, albeit passively, for he notes his 'thoughts [will] be bloody', but conveys nothing about what his actions will be (4.4.65).[57] With his father murdered and his mother whored, the Danish Prince has more than enough reason to enact finally his revenge. Yet instead, he defines for us what inaction means, how it makes a human being indistinguishable from a beast, a previously cited term he uses in reference to Claudius in 1.5 when he calls him an 'adulterate beast' (line 42). Hamlet's passivity, and his inability to be manly or prove consistently 'what is a man', shows us how he and his uncle have more in common with women than they may recognize (4.4.35).[58]

In the play's final act, Young Fortinbras returns to avenge his father's murder, to remind us and the Danes what an ideal masculine white man is and to re-establish order, through violent means if necessary.[59] I contend that in Young Fortinbras is one answer to Hamlet's 'what is a man?' question, an answer that reminds us the Prince of Denmark has yet to prove his manhood, something he never gets to do, especially in light of reading him as a failed avenger. Quite possibly, Hamlet fails because he was 'rotten before he die[d]', as the Gravedigger comically suggests a man can be – rotten because, like Macbeth, he has 'diseased manliness' (5.1.162).[60] If ideal white masculinity died with Old Hamlet, then I propose that unmanliness dies in this play through the purging of Hamlet (and Claudius and the women), as Fortinbras's assuming the Danish throne revives the image of ideal white masculinity that represents strength, valour, rationality and the potential for aggressiveness.[61] The focus on Hamlet's dead body in the end, and therefore the beginning of his corporeal decomposition, recalls his father's body; in so doing, Young Fortinbras creates a contrast between the two dead Danes through his treatment of Hamlet's corpse. Norway's Prince orders his captains to: 'Bear Hamlet, like a soldier, to the stage / For he was likely, had he been put on, / To have proved most royally' (5.2.351–3). 'Like' means Hamlet is, in fact, not a soldier, a social role that might have imbued him with masculine strength. Moreover, the speculation about what Hamlet could have been further solidifies what he never proved himself as – *most* royal, most manly, most valiant like his father.[62]

When Horatio commits to telling the story of *Hamlet*, the 'unnatural acts', he resigns himself to recounting the story of whiteness, Denmark's deterioration and the decomposition of masculinity since, in reciting the play's events, he must focus on the play's two main white male characters to whom Shakespeare attached blackness and unmanliness (5.2.335). Given that a man can be rotten before he dies, as the

Gravedigger explains to Hamlet, it makes sense that we can witness the decomposition of the blackened Hamlet and Claudius before they physically die. Until the end, Hamlet and Claudius are focal points; they are the most socially and politically prominent men. Similar to *Titus Andronicus*'s Aaron, whose highly visible Black body emerges as a vehicle for carrying fundamental messages about fatherhood and domestic ideals, Claudius's and Hamlet's royal white bodies are used to articulate messages about whiteness, blackness, masculinity and femininity in this Shakespearean tragedy.[63]

The concluding entrance of Norwegian Young Fortinbras, an ethnically different kind of white man, and the presence of myriad dead bodies on the stage, is a restorative measure that reaffirms the play's detachment from unmanliness by returning us to the 'esteemed ethnic features' of white maleness that remind us of Old Hamlet.[64] The play reinforces this point by constantly highlighting how it is not somatic difference but Hamlet's sullied whiteness (as in his black mood, fashion, behaviour, etc.), coupled with his unmanliness, that makes him fail to meet the expectations one might have of him based on the precedent set by his heroic father. Thus, how this dramatic work codes unmanliness as black, specifically by stigmatizing it as an inferior category of difference in relation to ideal masculine whiteness – and therefore styling unmanliness as undesirable, even though it may not actually be so given that Claudius and Hamlet are still desired by Gertrude and Ophelia, respectively – serves to enlighten our conceptions of race, racial/gender construction, racial power dynamics and racial subjectivity. Moreover, it serves to open our eyes to the various ways race, because it is everywhere, intersects with, and is relevant to, discourse on everything;[65] not just gender, class and sexuality but also science, politics, religion, nature and, of course, all of Shakespeare's plays that centre on white characters. Despite continued overt and covert resistance to 'premodern *critical* race studies',[66] we must talk about race in *Hamlet* and all of Shakespeare's plays. We must talk about race, especially whiteness, more broadly and more consistently in Shakespeare and early modern English studies if we are to be thoroughly informed, and informative, critics. Shakespeare's canon wills it so.

Notes

I am especially grateful to Arthur Little for allowing me to begin slow cooking these *Hamlet* ideas in his California kitchen in 2018, and for the feedback he provided on a draft of this work. Additionally, I thank Melissa Shields Jenkins and John Michael Archer for reviewing a very early draft of this piece. And many thanks to the volume editors – Sonia Massai and Lucy Munro – for their thought-provoking feedback.

1 Peter Erickson, 'Can we Talk about Race in *Hamlet*?', in *Hamlet: Critical Essays*, ed. Arthur Kinney (New York: Routledge, 2002), 212.

2 Ayanna Thompson, 'What Is a "Weyward" *Macbeth*?', in *Weyward Macbeth: Intersections of Race and Performance*, ed. Scott Newstok and Ayanna Thompson (New York: Palgrave MacMillan, 2010), 3.

3 Erickson, 209.

4 Ibid., 210–11.

5 Kim F. Hall, *Things of Darkness: Economies of Race and Gender in Early Modern England* (Ithaca: Cornell University Press, 1995), 2, 6–7, 23, 53; Patricia Parker, 'Black *Hamlet*: Battening on the Moor', *Shakespeare Studies*, 31 (2003): 127–64 (129).

6 See Patricia Akhimie, *Shakespeare and the Cultivation of Difference: Race and Conduct in the Early Modern World* (New York: Routledge, 2018); Lisa M. Anderson, 'When Race Matters: Reading Race in *Richard III* and *Macbeth*', in *Colorblind Shakespeare: New Perspectives on Race and Performance*, ed. Ayanna Thompson (New York: Routledge, 2006), 89–102; Newstok and Thompson, eds, *Weyward Macbeth*.

7 Peter Erickson and Kim F. Hall, '"A New Scholarly Song": Rereading Early Modern Race', *Shakespeare Quarterly*, 67(1) (Spring 2016): 1–13 (2).

8 I discussed the importance of making whiteness visible during a plenary talk – 'Looking Forward: New Directions in Early Modern Race Studies' – at the 2019 Shakespeare Association of America conference. My talk, 'White Hands: Gesturing toward Shakespeare's *Other* Race Plays', is available as audio and begins at the 43-minute mark: https://youtu.be/szUlxHjUCOg

9 Urvashi Chakravarty, 'More Than Kin, Less Than Kind: Similitude, Strangeness, and Early Modern English Homonationalisms', *Shakespeare Quarterly*, 67(1) (Spring 2016): 14–29 (15).

10 Chakravarty, 15.

11 Ian Smith, *Race and Rhetoric in the Renaissance: Barbarian Errors* (New York: Palgrave Macmillan, 2009), 4, 9.

12 On self-fashioning, whiteness and the Other, see Arthur L. Little Jr., 'Re-Historicizing Race, White Melancholia, and the Shakespearean Property', *Shakespeare Quarterly*, 67(1) (Spring 2016): 84–103 (92). Unless otherwise stated, all *Hamlet* references come from Thompson and Taylor's edition of the 1623 first folio text, in *Hamlet*, The Arden Shakespeare, ed. Ann Thompson and Neil Taylor (London: Thomson, 2006), vol. 2.

13 Emily C. Bartels offers a discussion of *Hamlet*, specifically on ethnicity and gender, as opposed to a detailed discussion of race (whiteness/blackness); as a result, she does not address what is significant about the play's engagement with and critiques of whiteness. See 'Identifying "the Dane": Gender and Race in *Hamlet*', in *Shakespeare and Embodiment: Gender, Sexuality, and Race*, ed. Valerie Traub (Oxford: Oxford University Press, 2016), 197–210.

14 Jarold Ramsey, 'The Perversion of Manliness in *Macbeth*', *Studies in English Literature*, 13(2) (Spring 1973): 285–300 (285).

15 Sky Gilbert, 'A Sparrow Falls: Olivier's Feminine Hamlet', *Brief Chronicles*, 1 (2009): 237–52. Also see Bernhard Frank, '"The Rest is Silence": *Hamlet*, A Closet Case', *Hamlet Studies*, 20(1–2) (Summer and Winter 1998): 94–7.

16 On black/white opposition, see Hall, *Things of Darkness*, 9.

17 Macbeth, whose wife questions his manliness, is referred to as 'black Macbeth' by Malcolm (4.3.52) and Richard III, who is depicted as less than a man because of his deformity, and for other reasons, is referred to as 'hell's black intelligencer' (4.4.71).

18 Rebecca Ann Bach, 'Manliness Before Individualism: Masculinity, Effeminacy, and Homoerotics in Shakespeare's History Plays', in *A Companion to Shakespeare's Works, Volume II: The Histories*, ed. Richard Dutton and Jean E. Howard (Malden, MA: Blackwell, 2003), 220–45 (220).

19 Bach, 221.

20 For more on this interpretation of black as 'base', see David Sterling Brown, '"Is Black so Base a Hue?": Black Life Matters in Shakespeare's *Titus Andronicus*', in *Early Modern Black Diaspora Studies, A Critical Anthology*, ed. Cassander L. Smith, Nicholas R. Jones and Miles Grier (New York: Palgrave Macmillan, 2018), esp. 143–4. Also see Erickson, 212.

21 Jennifer Feather, 'Shakespeare and Masculinity', *Literature Compass*, 12.4 (2015): 134–45 (136).

22 While *Richard III* and *Macbeth* are not plays I analyse thoroughly in this essay, I do recognize their potential to do the kind of work regarding whiteness and unmanliness that *Hamlet* does given the associations made between the protagonists and blackness. For a black Macbeth analysis example, see David Sterling Brown, '(Early) Modern Literature: Crossing the Color-Line', *Radical Teacher*, 105 (Summer 2016): 69–77 (74).

23 Feather, 136.

24 Feather (137) also observes that 'work on racial difference has emphasized the performed and constructed nature of both race and gender in the period'. See Chakravarty, 21; and Brown, '"Is Black so Base a Hue"', 140–2.

25 Guo De-yan claims, '30-year-old Hamlet sometimes acts as if he were a child. In words, he is a man of intellect, is a philosopher and a thinker. In deeds, however, he is dominated by feminine emotions'. See 'Hamlet's Femininity', *Canadian Social Science*, 5(5) (2009), 89–95 (92). Also see Gilbert, 196.

26 Guo, 94.

27 Jennifer Low, 'Manhood and the Duel: Enacting Masculinity in *Hamlet*', *The Centennial Review*, 43(3) (Fall 1999): 501–12 (502, 503).

28 See Robert I. Lublin, '"Apparel oft proclaims the man": Visualizing Hamlet on the Early Modern Stage', *Shakespeare Bulletin*, 32(4) (Winter 2014): 629–47 (635, 638).

29 'Valiant' seems reserved for Old Hamlet, as these are the only usages of the term in the play.

30 Lublin, 632–3. Regarding the play's relationship to the medieval, Reta A. Terry asserts, 'Shakespeare creates characters in *Hamlet* that represent various stages in the evolution of a changing system of honor'. Terry suggests Hamlet reflects the tension between these evolving codes while a character like Laertes adheres to the old code. See '"Vows to the Blackest Devil": Hamlet and the Evolving Code of Honor in Early Modern England', *Renaissance Quarterly*, 52(4) (Winter 1999): 1079–84.

31 Low, 501.

32 For a detailed analysis of the language of blackness in this scene and more detailed *Hamlet* text comparisons, see Parker's 'Black Hamlet' article. The mountain/moor extended analysis can be found on pages 127–9.

33 The Vulcan reference also has cosmetic meaning that refers to "the darkening of a white actor's face with soot." See Parker, 128–9.

34 Parker, 129.

35 Later in the play, Hamlet tells Claudius he shall 'nose' the dead Polonius and find his body.

36 See https://en.wikipedia.org/wiki/Putrefaction.

37 Erickson, 211.

38 For more on Shakespeare and black male sexuality see: David Sterling Brown, 'The "Sonic Color Line": Shakespeare and the Canonization of Sexual Violence Against Black Men', Arizona Center for Medieval and Renaissance Studies, *The Sundial* (August 2019), https://medium.com/the-sundial-acmrs/the-sonic-color-line-shakespeare-and-the-canonization-of-sexual-violence-against-black-men-cb166dca9af8

39 Within Shakespeare's canon, we see a similar association made between blackness and witchcraft in plays such as *The Tempest*, *Othello* and *Antony and Cleopatra* (and characters: Sycorax, Othello and Cleopatra).

40 Janet Adelman, *Suffocating Mothers: Fantasies of Maternal Origin in Shakespeare's Plays, from Hamlet to the Tempest* (New York: Routledge, 1992), 28.

41 Andrew D. McCarthy, '*King Lear*'s Violent Grief', in *Violent Masculinities: Male Aggression in Early Modern Texts and Culture*, ed. Jennifer Feather and Catherine E. Thomas (New York: Palgrave MacMillan, 2013), 151–68 (154). See Gilbert, 197.

42 Guo, 95.

43 For more on the relationship between excessive grief and religion, see Lublin, 635.

44 McCarthy, 154.

45 Parker, 132–3.

46 Other features of a white person can be black according to the play: 'thoughts black' (3.2.253), 'bosom black' (3.3.67) and black 'soul' (3.3.94), for instance.

47 Lublin, 636.

48 See Ross Knecht, '"Shapes of Grief": Hamlet's Grammar School Passions', *ELH*, 82(1) (Spring 2015): 35–58 (45).

49 Hamlet constantly highlights his 'lack'. See Margreta de Grazia, '*Hamlet*' *without Hamlet* (Cambridge: Cambridge University Press, 2007), 2.

50 Tanya Pollard, 'What's Hecuba to Shakespeare?', *Renaissance Quarterly*, 65(4) (Winter 2012): 1060–93 (1063).

51 I am aware that it is possible for transgender men to experience pregnancy. However, exploring that subject further is outside the scope of this essay.

52 Valerie Traub, 'Jewels, Statues, and Corpses: Containment of Female Erotic Power in Shakespeare's Plays', in *Shakespeare and Gender*, ed. Deborah Barker and Ivo Kamps (New York: Verso, 1995), 120–41 (123).

53 Pollard, 1081.

54 Gilbert, 197.

55 I thank Arthur Little for redirecting and pushing my thinking here.

56 As Mia Korpiola and Anu Lahtinen explain, there was a premodern understanding that the physical body started to decompose 'at the moment of death'. See 'Cultures of Death and Dying in Medieval and Early Modern Europe: An Introduction', *COLLeGIUM*, 18 (2015): 1–31 (13).

57 This speech, which appears in Q2 and not in the Folio, has also been read as Hamlet critiquing Young Fortinbras' willingness to sacrifice the lives of thousands of men for land that is not worth much. Even so, that critique does not negate Fortinbras' being a man of action.

58 In the beginning of his Q2 4.4 soliloquy, Hamlet asks, 'What is a man / If his chief good and market of his time / Be but to sleep and feed? A beast – no more' (35–7). Gilbert posits that 'Shakespeare was a man who, through what is arguably his greatest character, dared to valorize the feminine' (203). I would push this point further by indicating that it is through the racialized association of the feminine with the masculine, specifically blackened unmanliness, that Shakespeare valorizes the feminine with a play on contrasts: white with black and masculine with feminine.

59 McCarthy, 154.

60 Ramsey, 295.

61 Guo, 90.

62 Low (503–4) expounds on Hamlet's goal and failure regarding the performance of masculinity.

63 Elsewhere, I have argued how Shakespeare uses his characters' racialized bodies to convey important social, cultural and political messages. See 'Remixing the Family: Blackness and Domesticity in *Titus Andronicus*', in *Titus Andronicus: The State of Play*, ed. Farah Karim-Cooper (London: The Arden Shakespeare, 2019), 111–33; and '"Shake thou to look on 't": Shakespeare's White Hands', in *White People in Shakespeare*, ed. Arthur L. Little, Jr. (forthcoming).

64 Smith, 6.

65 Akhimie, 11.

66 I emphasize 'critical' here because at the Arizona Center for Medieval and Renaissance Studies Race Before Race 2 conference, held in Washington, D.C. at the Folger Shakespeare Library in September 2019, Margo Hendricks made an important distinction between 'premodern race studies' and 'premodern critical race studies', both of which include attention to the early modern period. My work belongs to the latter. In her talk titled 'Coloring the Past, Rewriting our Future: RaceB4Race',

Hendricks boldly declared: 'There is, however, a problematic rupture that is worth examining. In this talk, I'm going to refer to it as "white settler colonizing" of "premodern critical race studies". I want to briefly offer a distinction between "premodern race studies" (PRS) and "premodern critical race studies" (PCRS). PRS is the practice of attempting race studies as if "you discovered the land". Practitioners ignore the pre-existing inhabitants of the land, or if these PRS scholars deign to acknowledge the inhabitants it is with a citation. Nowhere do you truly find recognition of the work done to nurture the land . . . What truly distinguishes PRS from PCRS, of course, is the bi-directional gaze: the one that looks inward even as it looks outward. As bell hooks observed, "spaces of agency exist . . . wherein we can both interrogate the gaze of the Other but also look back, and at one another, naming what we see. The gaze has been and is a site of resistance for colonized . . . people globally" (bell hooks, "The Oppositional Gaze: Black Female Spectators," [in *The Feminist and Visual Culture Reader*, ed. Amelia Jones (New York: Routledge, 2003), 94–105,] 95)'.

5

Character Fictions in *Hamlet*

Jay Farness

In his second soliloquy, Hamlet envies the Player's grief for Hecuba, then he vividly imagines himself vilified by some other who breaks his pate, wrings his nose or plucks his beard and blows it in his face; then he tries the lines of a ranting avenger ('bloody, bawdy villain, / Remorseless, treacherous, lecherous, kindless villain', 2.2.515–16); then, finally, he mocks his own braving. Next he turns – 'About, my brains' (2.2.522) – for a sober preview of the command performance of *The Murder of Gonzago* that he has just requested.

> Hum, I have heard
> That guilty creatures sitting at a play
> Have by the very cunning of the scene
> Been struck so to the soul that presently
> They have proclaimed their malefactions.
> For murder, though it have no tongue, will speak
> With most miraculous organ. I'll have these players
> Play something like the murder of my father
> Before mine uncle. I'll observe his looks,

I'll tent him to the quick. If 'a do blench
I know my course.

(2.2.523–33)

This conclusion to the soliloquy renders its early browbeating histrionics beside the point and perhaps unwarranted. Hamlet does have a plan of action informing his wild behaviour. And playgoers might now expect an exquisitely layered climax of the *Spanish Tragedy* kind to make good on the Prince's two months' idling about the castle. True, the plan sounds wildly hopeful: in one move to test the ghost's accusation against Claudius's murder of Old Hamlet, elicit a public confession from Claudius, and justify an instant revenge. What follows almost answers this hope, except for the fact that Claudius's confession occurs later in private, apparently unheard by Hamlet, and Hamlet talks himself out of seizing his chance for fear of how it might be 'scanned' (3.3.75) (*OED v.* 4).

I begin with a passage giving prominence to 'Hamlet the player', energetically performing in his imaginary theatre for an audience of one, who is in this case unusually supplanted by a glimpse of Hamlet as a plotter, reining in his personal acting-out for the sake of acting in a 'necessary question of the play' (3.2.40–1). Like many, I am intrigued by the Prince's relapsing from plotter to habitual player glimpsed here in condensed form.

In a famous sequence in the *Poetics,* Aristotle puts character second to story, and *ethos* second to *mythos*. This *ethos* is not character in the literary sense: Aristotle is saying that something like a *moral* in the work comes second to plot. In fact, one could skip the *ethos* and still have a *mythos,* in the way that one can have a pleasing picture without colours. Characters in the literary sense do rustle through these pages as 'agents' (*prattontes*) but their impact is limited by the architecture of the scheme: '"character" [*ethos*] is that which determines [for us] the quality of the agents'.[1] Aristotle's *Rhetoric* contributes an important amplification by suggesting that *ethos*, the quality of an agent and 'the most effective means of proof', is a rhetorical effect of a 'speech delivered in such a manner as to render [the orator] worthy of confidence' and not a result of 'any preconceived idea of the speaker's character'.[2] As a function of rhetorical performance, this *ethos* is subject to art – and artful simulation, a fact emphasized in Plato and the rhetoricians who precede him, if you recall concerns of participants in the *Gorgias* or *Republic* about unjust people who might cunningly pass as just.

Hence the rhetorician is potentially a maker of fictions of character, of imaginary persons. Similarly, as Shakespeare makes fictions, he also makes characters who make fictions of themselves. These layers of fictional persons are so obvious, so naturalized, that we might overlook them as ordinary social performance represented in the plays, where the plays' social milieus allow people some control over the way they represent themselves to one another, as in our own daily experience. But the hyper-theatrical settings of Shakespeare's plays put particular premium on such social representations. We're never far away from court societies and the elite, stylized behaviours that emulate attractive social exemplars (and consult Renaissance self-help books and their disseminated discourses). In studying Shakespeare, we can to an extent delaminate the *presented* impersonations of the theatrical occasion from impersonations in the fictional theatrical occasions *represented* onstage: by impersonations, I mean the incessant, ephemeral character-making with which these imaginary people address one another, try to impress one another and about which they have a lot to say – and in saying it reveal how self-regarding these characters can be.

Certain discourses can help delaminate these multiplicities and bring them into clearer focus. With *As You Like It*, for example, discourses of love would lend themselves to exploration of character duplicities, particularly in Rosalind/Ganymede's complex portrayals of persons 'in love'. In this play, Rosalind disguised as Ganymede convincingly impersonates a lover while also, so to speak, noticeably looking over the top of her performance in a way congruent to a player's looking over the top of his performance as Rosalind – a phenomenon teasingly reprised in the play's epilogue. The duplicities of lovers' routine performances compose a familiar theme in which, when pressed, basic questions of character (in the more diffuse Aristotelian sense) remain elusive (Does s/he love me? Does s/he love me not?). The idea that Rosalind is actually in love with Orlando would, if true, naturalize some of her/his performance complexities, in effect suppressing lawless possibilities of constructed character, as if 'nature to her bias drew in that' (*Twelfth Night*, 5.1.256). But – to put the case extremely – what if Rosalind were not in love with Orlando, but playing at it (as Ganymede does), as if Rosalind were actually following up on devising 'sports' from her first scene: 'Let me see: what think you of falling in love?' (*As You Like It*, 1.2.25) How would we know the difference? This extreme possibility with Rosalind in love might also apply to Hamlet in madness (is he?) or to Hamlet in mourning the death of his father or the death of Ophelia (does he?).

My efforts to slow down the flow of presented self-representations to better appreciate them have been helped by Harry Berger's slowing them down to the instants of portraiture. In doing so, Berger critiques the incautious use of the now ubiquitous term 'self-fashioning', which unfortunately shades toward total prosthetic replacement of self-consciousness. Stephen Greenblatt has given this term great currency for Renaissance studies in reference to 'increased self-consciousness about the fashioning of human identity as a manipulable, artful process' aiming at the 'achievement of . . . a distinctive personality, a characteristic address to the world, a consistent mode of perceiving and behaving'.[3] The idea of a self-inventing self proves very difficult to parse, however, and, as Berger points out, it gets caught up in the representations implied by 'address', 'perceiving and behaving', and even in the implications of 'fashioning' that emerge in scenes where adornment or costume matters a lot:

> As a work of art, the object of metaphors of shaping and fashioning, the self is made to seem comfortably thinglike.

> But the bounded entity evoked by those metaphors conceals a vague, fluid, and protean potpourri of aspects as hard to pin down as The Old Man of the Sea and perhaps more frustrating because, as Butler puts it in *Gender Trouble*: the 'figure of the interior soul understood as "within" the body is signified through its inscription *on* the body' [and] 'the effect of an internal core or substance' is produced '*on the surface* of the body, through the play of signifying absences that suggest, but never reveal, the organizing principle of identity as a cause' . . . How . . . do we determine whether or not people are engaged in fashioning themselves – or, possibly, their selves – if they don't represent themselves fashioning themselves? And if they do, how can we tell whether the self-fashioning they represent to others is actually going on 'inside' the performers?[4]

In the theatre, 'a vague, fluid, and protean potpourri of aspects' is actually what you get, since theatre as a medium relies precisely on the sort of presented self-representations I mention above. Character fictions are normally stabilized by the consistency of the performers' bodies and voices – one body per character for major roles though fraying at the edges when performers double in supporting parts. But this stability can also be undermined by characters' fickle self-representations, by their resistances to social ascriptions (or to their natural bodies), or by their efforts to install deviant plots that challenge a unified Aristotelian master plot.

The term 'self-fashioning' can be helpful for captioning Malvolio's ambition for a 'characteristic mode of address to the world',[5] or Othello's envy of the apparent polish and sophistication of Cassio's 'address to the world', or Sir Andrew's regretful lost chances for accomplishing 'a structure of bounded desires' ('I would I had bestowed that time in the tongues that I have in fencing, dancing and bear-baiting. O, had I but followed the arts' [*Twelfth Night*, 1.3.89–92]). In each case, the 'fashioned' self occurs as an external, theatrical exemplar to be envied and as if it could be somehow imprinted on one's interior.[6] At the same time, the play is letting us know that Othello is wrong about Cassio: it repeatedly shows us the anxiety with which Cassio sustains, and doubts, the represented Cassio that impresses Othello. Self-fashioning doesn't quite catch the changeable, reflexive aspects of how Cassio is representing his person to himself and to others. Such representing yields speaking, shifting, moving pictures rather than 'a sense of personal order' or assurances of 'a consistent mode of perceiving and behaving'. Cassio – like Othello, for that matter – is a personal fiction sustained more as a makeshift process of theatrical, specular 'selving' than as a product, a 'self', though in either case one might be describing a character fiction.

Such character-fictionalizing moments are not self-fashioning exactly, but they're not exactly role-playing either. Self-fashioning invites thoughts of more permanent makeover – a prosthetic substitute, like an idealizing portrait. Role-playing, a different makeover strategy, pays respects to the Aristotelian preference for plot over character: the role for a Shakespeare role-player is a means to a well-considered end of reversal, recognition, and other people's reckoning with pity and fear. These are the character fictions of Richard II, of Prince Hal, of Kent, of Helen (in *All's Well*), of Iago, of Portia. They typically aim at a wish-fulfilling personal vindication or triumph in stories that at points double as the plots of Shakespeare plays. These stories do not imply self-fashioned personal makeovers, since they envision one-time theatrical impacts – consummations at climaxes offering much anticipated pleasure to their inventors. It's something in between these that I'm imagining – more fleeting, more improvisational performances. As a revenger, Hamlet should be plying his antic role for a revenge plot. Most of the time, he appears to be performing for more localized theatre effects that cannot be described as either ambitious 'self-fashioning' or purposeful 'role-playing'.

With a few *Hamlet* passages, I explore such impersonation as it ranges between two extremes, one inverting the other.

Hamlet, like many of his peers, impersonates the *courtier*. But then in recoil and unlike his peers, at least for this play, he also impersonates the *clown*. Hamlet, '[o]ur chiefest courtier' in the King's phrase (1.2.117), embraces an antic inversion of his former self: 'antic' is 'grotesque' but also 'clown' (*OED adj*. 2; *n*. 4). There are latent theatrical agendas here, too, since the clown epitomizes the popular theatre before *Hamlet*. In contrast is an emerging author's theatre patronized by such gentlemen and courtiers as the Prince lording it over visiting players. We gauge our courtier from an impression he has made on Ophelia.

> O, what a noble mind is here o'erthrown!
> The courtier's, soldier's, scholar's eye, tongue, sword,
> Th'expectation and rose of the fair state,
> The glass of fashion and the mould of form,
> Th'observed of all observers, quite, quite down.
> And I, of ladies most deject and wretched,
> That sucked the honey of his musicked vows,
> Now see what noble and most sovereign reason
> Like sweet bells jangled out of time and harsh –
> That unmatched form and stature of blown youth
> Blasted with ecstasy. O woe is me
> T'have seen what I have seen, see what I see.
>
> (3.1.149–60)

At last allowed a chance for eloquence, Ophelia offers this exquisite lament of her disenchantment. Using idioms more akin to audience response than amorous dismay, she doesn't give her eavesdropping father the Hamlet-in-love he had hoped for, but a Hamlet who, in private, is more than ever the cynosure of gazes, an arrant knave who indeed spies on himself. Ophelia testifies to another Hamlet-in-performance anterior to the one we've been seeing. This is my courtier-Hamlet, the Hamlet from whom the Hamlet we know has fallen off, to the general notice of Denmark. Ophelia's gallery of mirrored images, now broken – 'The glass of fashion and the mould of form, / Th'observed of all observers', 'That unmatched form and stature' – sounds brittle even in the describing. She captures the reflexivities and mirror-abysses that apply in these courts, where agents watch themselves getting watched by others who are watched in turn. And her second line's blazon – about the 'eye, tongue, sword' for multiple Hamlets – likewise conveys a dismantling in word and image of the complete Renaissance man that she tries to evoke. Ophelia has caught up with and finely captioned the kaleidoscope we've been seeing for two acts. Or, as Christy Desmet puts it:

> Hamlet's character . . . appears to be socially constructed. In anthropologist Clifford Geertz's terms, he is a cultural artifact; as Richard Lanham puts it, he is 'rhetorical man.' Ophelia's soliloquy verifies an important lesson of post-modern Shakespearean criticism: because direct portrayal of subjectivity is impossible, the self's integrity or self-presence is revealed as a fiction. Hamlet has ethical character [i.e. consistent, reliable identity] only when he has ceased to be himself, first in madness and finally in death. [Ophelia's] portrait of Hamlet affirms that the self, if not constructed by discourse, becomes comprehensible only through rhetorical representations.[7]

The void of lost ideals that Ophelia feels is the undoing of the illusory self-fashioned self of Renaissance makeovers: as Desmet says, there is no accessible self before the representations to somehow present or *re*make, and so no lost integrity to return to. On the other hand, Ophelia's testimony might tempt one to think that, having lost the bad faith with which such courtiers as Polonius, Laertes, Rosencrantz or Guildenstern more steadily address themselves – *represent* themselves – to onlookers, a more honest Hamlet cannot find that bad faith again. But the nasty fervour of what he has just done to Ophelia, wresting her to his 'frailty thy name is woman' theme centred on Gertrude, shows us probably the most dishonest Hamlet we have yet seen.

Missing from both Ophelia's astute assessment and Desmet's critical analysis is Hamlet's active rejecting of the passive cast of her ethical ascriptions ('o'erthrown', 'blasted'). Instead, Hamlet's antic performance energetically inverts the following performance paradigm from the courtesy book tradition, where one name regularly given to such courtly ethos as Hamlet formerly exemplified is *grazia*, or social 'grace'. In *The Courtier*, the seminal text for sixteenth-century ideas about refined personal makeover, Count Lodovico acknowledges the possibility of natural, unselfconscious *grazia* but then emphasizes its simulation with his concept of *sprezzatura,* studied 'nonchalance':

> But, having thought many times already about how this grace is acquired (leaving aside those who have it from the stars), I have found quite a universal rule which in this matter seems to me valid above all others, and in all human affairs whether in word or deed: and that is to avoid affectation in every way possible as though it were some very rough and dangerous reef; and (to pronounce a new word perhaps) to practice in all things a certain *sprezzatura*, so as to conceal all art and make whatever is done or said appear to be without effort and almost without any thought about it. And I believe much grace comes of this: because everyone knows the difficulty of things that are rare and well done; wherefore facility in such things causes the greatest wonder; whereas, on the other hand, to labor and, as we say, drag forth by the hair of the head, shows an extreme want of grace, and causes everything, no matter how great it may be, to be held in little account.[8]

According to Count Lodovico, the problem of affectation is not art, but too much effort or art of the wrong kind – for example, Malvolio in smiles, or the odd flourish of a Cassio nervously blowing finger-kisses. One infers from this passage and its context the necessity that *sprezzatura* be artful and visible, not entirely concealed, despite what Count Lodovico at first indicates. Cesare Gonzaga provokes this discussion by demanding the 'art', 'discipline' or 'method' by which natural grace can be studiously emulated,[9] and this process of simulation thereafter dominates the discussion. If *grazia* is heaven-sent or innate, moreover, there is nothing difficult about it, and there is no *sprezzatura*, no overcoming of difficulty to admire or to discuss. In court, as in the theatre, everyone is looking, some more knowingly than others, so a spectator responds not only to simple naturalness (as if 'from the stars'), but more often to a pleasing, artificially artless naturalness. This model courtier conveys a *grazia* that is natural, but not quite. It is a performance that imparts an awareness of its performance, that looks over the top of one's first impression. And it's that second impression that appeals to the connoisseur.[10] In this way, Cesario's is a more intriguing performance than Sebastian's (in *Twelfth Night*), Rosalind's or Ganymede's more than Orlando's (in *As You Like It*). Horatio, or Celia, exemplifies the connoisseur's part when Hamlet toys with Osric, or Ganymede with Orlando.

Observe Hamlet, 'observed of all observers', in his first scene where he protests too much his difference from 'actions that a man might play'. His denial of pretence is undercut by his preoccupation with it. The surly wordplay of 'kin', 'kind' and 'son' announces the gracelessness he is keen to display. The framework for Count Lodovico's exposition is competition for the favour of the prince, in whose court the courtier finds himself: 'he who has grace finds grace'[11]. In aiming for an opposite effect, Hamlet plays a natural fool or foil, already hinting at antics to come. His grief is inherent, essential, he claims. But his memorable rejoinder to the Queen's chiding makes a fashion-statement on at least two levels in order to represent himself – to project an ethos – to King, Queen and court. One statement comes with the conventional mourning clothes he wears, the second – an actual statement – is the ekphrastic detailing of the artful figure he cuts.

> 'Seems', madam – nay it is, I know not 'seems'.
> 'Tis not alone my inky cloak, cold mother,

Nor customary suits of solemn black,
Nor windy suspiration of forced breath,
No, nor the fruitful river in the eye,
Nor the dejected haviour of the visage,
Together with all forms, moods, shapes of grief,
That can denote me truly. These indeed 'seem',
For they are actions that a man might play,
But I have that within which passes show,
These but the trappings and the suits of woe.

(1.2.76–86)

Yes, this moment is metatheatrical, though its quick metatheatrical frisson (mine 'are actions that a man might play', intones Master Richard Burbage) doesn't provide ready grist for interpretation, unless we press harder. This moment is also metafictional, inasmuch as Hamlet is making a fiction – a fiction of character, of ethos – and making his making conspicuous. In my case, he explains, my outside is a natural index (like smoke and fire), not only a conventional sign, which cannot 'denote me truly'. Again, his mindfulness of simulation might make a knowing bystander think more of smoke and mirrors than smoke and fire. And his statement's elegant periodic design, built up by anaphoras, sustains a rhetorical performance augmented by timely prosodic effects. 'Windy suspiration of forced breath', for instance, not only reports involuntary heaving, but does so with a soundtrack, in a notably artful, onomatopoetic way – 'windy suspiration' is a cue for a sigh, 'forc'd breath' prompts a plosive exhalation.

It appears that Queen and King have rightly, if ungently, called out his affectation. Like his first words in the scene, this speech feels premeditated, virtually pre-scripted, again maybe metatheatrical, but more trenchantly disclosing something about Hamlet's own interpersonal theatrics. For a man playing these actions – for the self-referencing Burbage – these are obviously pre-scripted lines. But it's not hard to imagine Hamlet, like Burbage, practising his lines, striking poses before a real or mental mirror in real or mental shadow-boxing preparations for the opportune moment: '"Seems", madam – nay it is, I know not "seems"' – as if Hamlet has been waiting, lurking for someone to stumble into the trigger-word *seems* – his cue – and ignite the pleasure of this rejoinder.

Such artful, stagey performance doesn't aim at some durable social self-fashioning as a courtier – he already has that – but at a more fleeting, posturing kind of self-representing, a pleasurable sniping at the King and court to make himself look good, especially to himself, and thereby feel good. Then his speaking moment passes, confronted by another speaker's part in the scene, and the King ends up with the last word: his final, notably false description of Hamlet's 'gentle and unforced accord' (1.2.123) drips unanswerable contempt. For an audience, this sequence might register as momentary disorientation of attempts to bring this peevish, contrarian, would-be scene-stealer into focus. This confusion could use a clarifying soliloquy – something to establish this namesake of the play as a candidate for sympathy. But the character's solidity in the first soliloquy is also illusory and not because it melts into dew. Rather, it luxuriates in dazzling words that begrudge the duel with King and Queen just lost, words that seek solace in self-pity and indignation, that try out insults, and otherwise revert to shadow-boxing, to what he disparages, in a later moment self-critical of his theatrics, as the posture of a 'whore' unpacking 'my heart with words' (2.2.520). And then, shortly after his first soliloquy's all-consuming, suicidal melancholy, we learn that Hamlet has been adroitly courting and winning Ophelia's affections. Who would have suspected the romancing Hamlet evoked in scene three from the despairing Hamlet of scene two? This is our welcome to Hamlet's theatre, in which one man in his time plays many parts.

The details of this sequence show Hamlet-the-courtier tightly winding himself up, as in his angry first soliloquy's reflection of his foiled performance before King and Queen, for elastic recoil into the antic in scene five. But his theatre persists during somewhat awkward interactions with Marcellus and especially Horatio, made uneasy by the Prince's expressions of intimacy. When Hamlet proposes his 'antic disposition' to them, his first thoughts are consumed with the impact of his performance, especially on knowing observers, whom he imagines performing back at him in a manner he then himself performs.

> But come,
> Here as before: never – so help you mercy,
> How strange or odd some'er I bear myself
> (As I perchance hereafter shall think meet
> To put an antic disposition on) –
> That you at such times seeing me never shall,
> With arms encumbered thus, or this headshake,
> Or by pronouncing of some doubtful phrase
> As 'Well, well, we know', or 'We could an if we would',
> Or 'If we list to speak', or 'There be an if they might',
> Or such ambiguous giving out to note
> That you know aught of me.
>
> (1.5.166–77)

In the syntax one might see evidence of the onset of Hamlet's mania, and the verse is in fact irregular. Still, this hectic utterance does hold together, especially with the help of gestures and interjections that, following the cues, accompany it. As remarkable is the theatre that Hamlet imagines: he sees Horatio or Marcellus, or both, seeing him perform the antic Hamlet, as if they are knowing courtiers or gentlemen at court, and he imagines them performing and himself observing their meaningful words and gestures in response, which he performs here and now for them as he imagines it. The utter theatricality of this, not just the daunting twelve-line sentence, is breathtaking. Hamlet's labouring of a conspiratorial conceit through multiple oath-swearings by his companions as he roams the stage and, here, by the extended burlesque interplay of gestures and words shows Hamlet in increasingly exorbitant full-body mode, flouting 'that cool *disinvoltura* [ease]' in the 'matter of bodily movements' that, according to Count Lodovico, also marks courtly *grazia*.[12] Such enactment heralds his mimicry of Laertes, Osric and others and awakens chances for mocking voices, mugging, pantomime, jigging, ambling or nicknaming God's creatures – outlandish behaviours of the 'Renaissance Hamlet', whose return de Grazia urges.[13]

The clown, the anti-courtier here embraced, also enjoys a well-developed discourse and a rhetoric blending the social and the theatrical. As with Castiglione's courtier, with the clown there is also the division of natural and artificial, between heaven-sent, lunatic folly and impersonated folly in the old difference between 'naturals' and those artificial fools who act natural, but not quite. In Hamlet's antics we catch both the acid licence with which Jaques, the disenchanted courtier, envisions his fooling, when he longs to 'cleanse the foul body of th'infected world' (*As You Like It*, 2.7.60), and the more carefully pointed mockery that singles out Polonius in the first antic encounter (2.2.168–214), then Rosencrantz and Guildenstern, Ophelia, Osric, and the King, according to the method in the folly that Cesario admires in Feste:

> He must observe their mood on whom he jests,
> The quality of persons and the time,
> And, like the haggard, check at every feather
> That comes before his eye.
>
> (*Twelfth Night*, 3.1.62–5)

This clown operates with the rhetorician's awareness of audience and of *kairos*, the opportune moment for performance. Almost the same terms could be applied to Count Lodovico's courtiers.

His antic behaviours counter Hamlet's words to the players. There he advocates a performer's self-limiting adherence to a play's *representational* fiction to counter the many crowd-pleasing, show-stealing turns by clowns or ranting tragedians that he has evidently suffered through. His message is clear enough and Aristotelian in two ways—both in its commitment to a kind of plausible mimesis of a unified action and in its fussiness with what sounds like courtly moderation, 'modesty', 'temperance', 'smoothness', with not overstepping or overdoing (3.2.7–8, 19–20). Hamlet's theatrical manner in this lecture, however, is something else again. It follows another offstage Hamlet performance ('Speak the speech, I pray you, as I pronounced it to you', 3.2.1–2). And then with a captive audience, Hamlet goes off on a discourse that is one part professorial self-consciousness – 'I pray you' and 'as I may say' and 'as 'twere' and similar neat rhetorical flourishes – and one part performance envy. As de Grazia points out, Hamlet repeatedly emulates his criticism's targets:

> At the same time that Hamlet urges moderation, he goes quite over-the-top himself, as in his diatribe against bombastic acting: 'O, it offends me to the soul to hear a robustious periwig-pated fellow tear a passion to tatters, to very rags' (3.2.8–10), a mouthful that hardly lends itself to the 'temperance' and 'smoothness' (3.2.7–8) he has just recommended. 'I would have such a fellow whipped' (3.2.13), he histrionically claims.[14]

His hectoring, imperative manner sharply offsets mild responses of players he suspects of not paying enough attention. Could these journeymen be showing impatience for Hamlet's dramaturgical claptrap even when theatrically embellished?

Hamlet concludes this way in Q2 and F:

> and let those that play your clowns speak no more than is set down for them. For there be of them that will themselves laugh to set on some quantity of barren spectators to laugh too, though in the meantime some necessary question of the play be then to be considered. – That's villainous and shows a most pitiful ambition in the fool that uses it.
>
> (3.2.36–42)

This finish seems almost an afterthought, a supplement with no apparent bearing on these players of Hamlet's *Mousetrap*, though we do learn here he has studied clowning. In the sequel, his clown-lore proves integral to Hamlet's own practice. After talking back to the performance, he steps out of the audience to impose ad hoc theatre of his own on the play he authorized.

In David Wiles's view, the clown 'stands at the heart of the Elizabethan debate about acting'.[15] Wiles's treatment of the subject broadens into differential analysis of 'the clown', his successors, and of the idea of Shakespeare's company structurally defined by Will Kemp, on the one hand, and by Robert Armin, on the other:

> The Elizabethan theatre was always in flux, but its underlying history was one of a drift towards characterization/acting based on notions of mimesis, and away from acting based on iconography or non-representational signalling. The replacement of Kemp by Robert Armin was part of a broad drift towards a new type of theatre. The play had to depict a coherent social milieu. Characterization had to be based on careful observation. The actor had to be responsible to the author, and to realize a character possessing an anterior existence in the author's imagination. The rift which took place in 1599 between Kemp and the Chamberlain's company is . . . a significant jolt on the graph of theatrical change.[16]

We confront the discrepancy of a Hamlet who advocates for this 'new type of theatre' while himself performing from the repertoire of the old. This scenario would entail the odd, thrilling, but easy-to-conceive business of Burbage doing Kemp, giving us Hamlet performing in a theatre where, as Michael Bristol puts it,

> [t]he players are not 'actors' – they are the immediate creators of the performances and interludes. Their creativity relies on their capacity to extemporize dramatic texts out of

> 'secondhand' or 'used' plays combined with other materials, including literary and folk narrative, by their own improvisatory skill. This is a form of creativity that favors contingent and ephemeral manifestations over the finished text or work of art. The resulting aesthetics of heterogeneity, crude sensation and parodic mimicry create a situation of maximum intellectual and affective openness, but minimum accountability.[17]

In truth, what major Shakespeare character, imprisoned in the great world, does not dream of 'minimum accountability'? It might be no wonder that antic Hamlet 'favors contingent and ephemeral manifestations' of impromptu ethos over the 'finished text', the Aristotelian whole that would be his revenge-plot mythos.

One more passage will help me reach my ending. I resume Hamlet's theatre lecture where I left off, with the help of *Hamlet*'s First Quarto. This more performance-centred edition shows even more the Prince's clowning strains at the moment when he urges 'temperance' against such antics.[18] After he excoriates the 'pitiful ambition in the fool', he adds,

> And then you have some again that keeps one suit of jests
> – as a man is known by one suit of apparel – and
> gentlemen quotes his jests down in their tables before they
> come to the play, as thus: 'Cannot you stay till I eat my
> porridge?' and 'You owe me a quarter's wages!' and 'My
> coat wants a cullison!' and 'Your beer is sour!' and,
> blabbering with his lips and thus keeping in his cinquepace
> of jests when, God knows, the warm Clown cannot make
> a jest unless by chance – as the blind man catcheth a hare
> – masters, tell him of it.
>
> (9.29–38)

In his mind's eye Hamlet sees a comedian with a limited, predictable routine, whose artless material is funny only by chance, but Hamlet cannot avoid acting out, caught up again in the theatre of the moment. Wiles annotates the passage as follows:

> Hamlet touches on many conventional aspects of the clown's role. The clown-actor plays a character of servant status. The character is not historicized, but earns the standard pay and wears the standard uniform of an Elizabethan serving-man. His needs and aspirations are material, not spiritual. To draw laughter, the clown relies both on verbal gags and on non-verbal techniques. The image of hare-chasing evokes the clown's speed of delivery. The *cinque-pace* metaphor is a reminder that dancing was also part of the clown's repertoire.[19]

Here we also find class contention between gentleman and clown underlying Hamlet's advocacy of gentrified, neo-classical drama.

Double takes in the passage resemble those of the speech in which Hamlet initiates his antics in 1.5. Concluding his lecture with a vivid immersion in an imagined scene, Hamlet is both clown and 'tables'-toting gentleman to the extent that it is not clear whom Hamlet is quoting – performing clown or gentlemen reading from their tables? Sharing the 'elastic gag',[20] he throws in a lame jest of his own at the end (of blindman and hare) to further confound the voices and statuses. Moreover, gentlemen appear to have recorded a supposedly improvising clown's stock or pre-scripted jests in order to outdo or undo the artlessly improvising clown – beating him to a punchline or proving on the spot, with documentation, that the clown is *not* a natural extemporizer. In this moment with the visiting players, we come back to a half-concealed art of a clown's anti-*grazia* played for immediate effect by Hamlet-Burbage, against Hamlet's claim to be a courtly theatre patron.

The Q1 clown lines do not appear in Q2 and F. Instead there is further exposition of the neo-classical purposes of playing, including the 'mirror up to nature' of mimesis, that are implicit in complaints about performer excesses that dominate the parallel Q1 text. But even in Q2 and F, as I've tried to suggest, embedded gestural cues show Hamlet still drawn to self-pleasing histrionics. These interrupt, confuse or defer the purpose of the plot he is pledged to and, of course, set playgoers laughing in the process. This happens for much of the play, but it is particularly remarkable when his wise-cracking commentary first jeopardizes, then spoils the performance of *The Murder of Gonzago* that his notes on the theatre were aimed at guarding. But the offence he takes at the clowns who usurp the noble 'purpose of playing' is probably already compromised when he wrests the play to his own purposes: 'the play's the thing' suggests a high art commitment till Hamlet weaponizes that art to 'catch the conscience of the King' (2.2.539, 540). And then his upstart behaviour at the performance defeats any chance of this prospect, since one couldn't really know whether the king bolts because he's guilty of the crime or because, having attended a play as a favour to Hamlet, he finds Hamlet's behaviour offensive or because the idea of a nephew killing an uncle in the dumb-show and Hamlet's overeager captioning of this act is intolerable. The muddle Hamlet's impetuous clowning makes of all this leaves us with something more intriguing, more complicated, and more weirdly beautiful than anything he could stage by the book.

Finally, I note that, despite the hero's theatre theses, the 'author' of all this design – whoever or whatever that might be – appears to be complicit in the clown's enduring. He/it empowers a Kemp-like gravedigging clown to insult from 'his' grave (5.1.110–12) the condescending gentleman of Act 3 who sought to bury him. Hamlet takes inspiration from this to mock a skull, like a jester trading gags with his bauble-head, and then, playing fool to Horatio's wiseman, to discomfort his confidant with cynical ditties of Alexander's and Caesar's vain ambition. There follow scenes where Hamlet mimics and mocks Laertes and then courtier Osric, before moving off without a plot or plan to improvise an ending that – is this a surprise? – makes no mention of avenging his father. This omission, which I imagine most playgoers overlook or forgive, would have completed a plot, a mythos, of purposeful antic role-playing. In fact, my Hamlet, a courtier-clown virtuoso of scenes and situations, leaves plots or closures to Horatio, who will 'tell my story' (5.2.333) and salvage 'a wounded name' (5.2.328). Another omission seems to follow, however. In previewing the lurid, neo-Senecan drama he will tell (5.2.363–69), Horatio makes no mention of our hero and offers no inkling that the Hamlet-centred show that playgoers have just witnessed will leave its mark on Denmark.

Notes

1 Aristotle, *The Poetics*, trans. W. Hamilton Frye, Loeb Classical Library (Cambridge: Cambridge University Press, 1932), 1050a.

2 Aristotle, *The 'Art' of Rhetoric,* trans. John Henry Freese, Loeb Classical Library (Cambridge: Cambridge University Press, 1932), 17.

3 Stephen Greenblatt, *Renaissance Self-Fashioning: From More to Shakespeare* (University of Chicago Press, 2012), 2.

4 Harry Berger, Jr., *Fictions of the Pose: Rembrandt Against the Italian Renaissance* (Stanford: Stanford University Press, 2000), 19–20.

5 Unattributed quotations in this paragraph come from Greenblatt, 1, 2.

6 In *Julius Caesar*, a play almost contemporary with *Hamlet*, Brutus and Caesar similarly share this self-fashioner's longing: 'It is the dream of every Roman male to be a statue of himself' (Meredith Skura, *Shakespeare the Actor and the Purposes of Playing* [Chicago: University of Chicago Press, 1993], 184).

7 Christy Desmet, *Reading Shakespeare's Characters: Rhetoric, Ethics and Identity* (Amherst: University of Massachusetts Press, 1992), 12–13.

8 Baldassare Castiglione, *The Book of the Courtier*, trans. Charles Singleton (Garden City, NY: Anchor Books, 1959), 43 (Book I, Section 26).

9 Castiglione, 41 (Book I, Section 24).

10 Harry Berger , Jr., *The Absence of Grace: Sprezzatura and Suspicion in Two Renaissance Courtesy Books* (Stanford: Stanford University Press, 2000), 9–25.

11 Castiglione, 41 (Book I, Section 24).

12 Castiglione, 44 (Book I, Section 26).

13 Margreta de Grazia, *'Hamlet' Without Hamlet* (Cambridge: Cambridge University Press, 2007).

14 Ibid., 39.

15 David Wiles, *Shakespeare's Clown: Actor and Text in the Elizabethan Playhouse* (Cambridge: Cambridge University Press, 1987), x.

16 Ibid., x–xi.

17 Michael Bristol, *Carnival and Theater: Plebeian Culture and the Structure of Authority Renaissance England* (New York: Methuen, 1985), 116–17.

18 *Hamlet* Q1 'is fast, plot-driven and far less ruminative than the other texts. Its emotions are raw rather than mediated and it is more of an ensemble piece, not a showcase for a single star performer', in Ann Thompson and Neil Taylor, 'Introduction', *Hamlet*, The Arden Shakespeare, ed. Ann Thompson and Neil Taylor (London: Thomson, 2006), 16. This 'Introduction' offers more information about this *Hamlet*'s staging advantages, as well as about the difficulty in dating Q1 in relation to Q2 and F. See also Dodd's and Kelly and Plehn's essays in this collection.

19 Wiles, viii.

20 De Grazia, 177.

6

Q1 *Hamlet* and the Sequence of Creation of the Texts

Charles Adams Kelly and Dayna Leigh Plehn

Variant texts

The 1623 First Folio (F) is the only source for the texts of half of the thirty-six plays appearing in the iconic volume. The other eighteen plays had been printed individually in the smaller quarto format, and for many of these, the text appearing in the Folio was set in type from an earlier printed quarto. By contrast, the textual circumstances of a handful of other early quartos are more complex, with entire passages unique to each of two (and in a few cases, three) texts. Between the 1880s and the 1980s, it was generally accepted that Shakespeare had written but a single text of each of his plays, and any variant text must have somehow been derived from that single original. By the 1980s, in contrast, it became accepted that the Quarto and

Folio texts of *King Lear,* with the unique passages in each, were both Shakespearean. The other highly variant early quartos continued to be widely regarded as derivative texts.

The textual circumstance of *Hamlet* is vastly more complex. The second Quarto (Q2) of late 1604 has ten passages not to be found in F. F has three passages not to be found in Q2, two of which very much seem to be replacements for two of the passages deleted from Q2. By comparison, the 1603 first Quarto (Q1) is short and irregular. For a century, Q1 *Hamlet* was thought to be somehow derived from the pre-existing Q2 or F. However, there has always been a small group of textual scholars who have questioned the nature of Q1 and the sequence of creation of the texts. Not commonly studied is the enigmatic *Der bestrafte Brudermord* (BB), a fourth text of *Hamlet,* which is available only by way of a German manuscript, which we consider in this essay alongside the short Q1, the fully realized Q2, and the closely related F.

The theory that Q1 *Hamlet* is a pre-Q2 text is becoming more prominent as a variety of recently developed findings are reconciled with the work of several scholars over recent decades. Findings pertaining to printing, publishing and to Shakespeare's fellow players will also play a role. Additionally, the charting of plot elements of the BB text against Q1 and Q2/F will reveal that BB is likely to be a predecessor to both Q1 and Q2/F, with Q1 being an intermediate version between BB and Q2/F. As scholars have consolidated their findings, they have sought *the least obstructed path through the evidence.* Implicit in this idea is that there are a finite number of ways Q1 could have been created and a finite number of possible sources of the text (see Table 6.1).

This essay will formally recognize that the possible creators of the text of Q1 and the possible sources of the text represent *collectively exhaustive* possibilities. By definition, a set of events, such as the outcomes of the tossing of a six-sided die (1, 2, 3, 4, 5, or 6), is collectively exhaustive if it includes all possible outcomes. Thus, if both possible non-Shakespearean types of creators of a theorized reported text can be eliminated, the remaining possibility of the text being a pre-Q2

TABLE 6.1 *Collectively Exhaustive Lists of Possible Creators and Possible Sources of the Text of Q1 Hamlet.*

Possible Creators of the Text of Q1	Possible Sources of the Text
☐ Actor(s) Perhaps by Memory* of a Pre-Existing Text	☐ Pre-Existing Q2 Text
*Memorial Reconstruction frequently theorized	☐ Pre-Existing Intermediate Q2-F Text
☐ Audience Members Noting of a Pre-Existing Text	☐ Pre-Existing Folio Text
	☐ Pre-Existing Post-Folio Text
☐ Author's Earlier Text (Perhaps a Draft)	☐ Author's Earlier Text (Perhaps a Draft)

Shakespearean text becomes a certainty. Likewise, if each possible Q2 and post-Q2 *source* text can be eliminated, only the possibility of Q1 as an earlier text will remain. As this process unfolds, a compelling dual argument (method and source) will emerge for Q1 as a pre-Q2 text. This experience has led us to replace the 'derivative text model', most commonly thought to be by 'memorial reconstruction', with the theory of Q1 *Hamlet* as 'an earlier text in some state' as a more probable general model for several of the irregular early quartos.

The term 'bad quarto' was coined by Alfred W. Pollard in 1909 for five texts he deemed to have been printed without authorization from Shakespeare's company.[1] The original five so-called bad quartos, listed in Table 6.2, are the first Quartos of *Romeo and Juliet, Henry V, Hamlet, Merry Wives of Windsor and Pericles.* The idea that the texts had been created from memory seems to have come into focus in 1910,[2] and since then it has often been assumed that the *good* texts were often published *in response* to the publication of the bad texts of many early quartos.

Since James Roberts filed for the Elizabethan equivalent of copyright for *Hamlet* in 1602, its printing by Valentine Simmes in 1603 was thought by scholars to be 'unauthorized' (not agreeable to Shakespeare's company). Nicholas Ling was publisher of both Q1 and Q2, which, as Pollard noted, 'may well amaze us' (see Table 6.3). Pollard concluded that the assumed dispute was 'settled quietly'.[3] By the early 1990s, the concept of memorial reconstruction had been invoked by

TABLE 6.2 *Printers and Publishers of the 'Bad Quartos' and Their Q2 Successors.*

	Q1	Printers	Publishers	Q2	Printers	Publishers
Romeo and Juliet	1597	Danter		1599	Creed	Burby
Henry V	1600	Creed	Milltn/Busby	1602	Creed	Pavier
Hamlet	1603	Simmes	Ling/Trundel	1604/5	Roberts	Ling
Merry Wives of Windsor	1602	Creed	Johnson			
Pericles	1608	White/Breed	Gosson	1609	White/Breed	Gosson

TABLE 6.3 *Publishing Q1 and Q2 Hamlet – Simmes vs Roberts vs Ling.*

	1602	1603 1st Quarto	1604 2nd Quarto	1607
Registration	Roberts	Timing of Transfer		Ling
Printers		Simmes	Roberts	
Publisher		Ling	Ling	

TABLE 6.4 *Financial Model of Quarto Printing.*

Compositors	18%	100%
Presswork	14%	
Printer's Profit	15%	
Copy & Registration	22%	
Paper	31%	

scholars to account for the irregular early texts of over forty plays by Shakespeare and others. In 1996, however, the entire concept of memorial reconstruction, never universally accepted, came under intense scrutiny.[4]

As mentioned earlier, 'good texts' were assumed to have been printed in response to the bad. However, the financial model of Elizabethan publishing should have been a reminder that the fixed costs of compositors, press work, and paper had to be spread over a large number of copies to be sold over a period of time to produce a profit (see Table 6.4).[5] Therefore, publisher Nicholas Ling must have been absolutely assured that a more desirable text would not be released and printed immediately to eclipse his investment in the 1603 quarto of *Hamlet*. All of the so-called 'bad' quartos should be examined in this light. Perhaps none of them were unauthorized.

This perspective seems to answer the question of why the second Quartos of *Henry V* and *Romeo and Juliet* followed publication of their first Quartos by two years. Q2 *Hamlet* was also probably delayed the better part of two years, as the mix of 1604 and 1605 on the extant title pages suggests they were printed in late 1604. Additionally, the text of the second edition of *Pericles* is not 'better' than the first, and the fact that a good text of *Merry Wives of Windsor* was never printed prior to the Folio of 1623 further suggests that publication of perhaps all five of these early quartos was not offensive to Shakespeare's company.

Another question recently answered is why the printer Roberts did not insist on printing Q1 *Hamlet* himself when he was presumed to own the copy. In 2001, David Scott Kastan revealed that 1603 was the third busiest year in the lengthy career of James Roberts.[6] With a backlog of large-scale, highly profitable book projects, a busy printer would seek to put off quartos and other pamphlet-like publications. Furthermore, the fact that Simmes printed at least four Shakespeare quartos subsequent to Q1 *Hamlet* suggests his printing of Q1 *Hamlet* was not offensive to Shakespeare's company. In fact, Ling, Simmes and Roberts were acquainted, Simmes's apprentice having transferred to Roberts in 1595.[7] Additionally, the printing rights for *Hamlet* are known to have passed from Roberts to Ling at some point prior to November of 1607.[8] It is possible this could have happened as early as 1603, the time of the printing of Q1 *Hamlet*.

Table 6.3 shows several points of evidence that were not available, or at least not in the foreground, in 1909. Alfred

Pollard assumed that there must have been a dispute between the parties involved and that the dispute had been 'patched up'. However, the evidence outlined above suggests there was unlikely to have been any contention between Roberts, Ling, Simmes and Shakespeare's company, over *Hamlet* or any other of Shakespeare's plays.

In the early 1880s, James Orchard Halliwell-Phillipps articulated the belief that Q1 *Hamlet* was a reported text, created by 'shorthand notes and other memoranda'.[9] Dealing first with the possibility of actor-reporters in Table 6.5, each horizontal bar represents a single page of Q2 text. Each bar has black, grey and light grey portions indicating the percentages of Q1 lines that are identical to lines in Q2, partially concordant, or unrelated. The shaded areas of each bar sum to 100 per cent. The full ninety-nine-line graphic is available online.[10] The Marcellus actor is onstage early, when the concordance is greatest, and the consensus for a century has been that actors were the source of Q1, with the Marcellus actor being a key contributor. In 1987, G. R. Hibbard noted that a bit-part hired player who was subsequently discharged 'would be exactly the sort of man . . . to concoct a version of *Hamlet*'.[11] However, as Paul Werstine subsequently noted, '[t]he failure to discover qualified [actor] reporters anywhere in the latter half of the play points to one of the glaring insufficiencies in the memorial-reconstruction hypothesis'.[12] Furthermore, in surveying the entire text, Terri Bourus notes that "the difference between variant and stable areas of the text cannot be plausibly graphed as a function of any conceivable intermediary of textual transmission."[13]

TABLE 6.5 *Q1 vs Q2 Concordance by Q2 Page.*

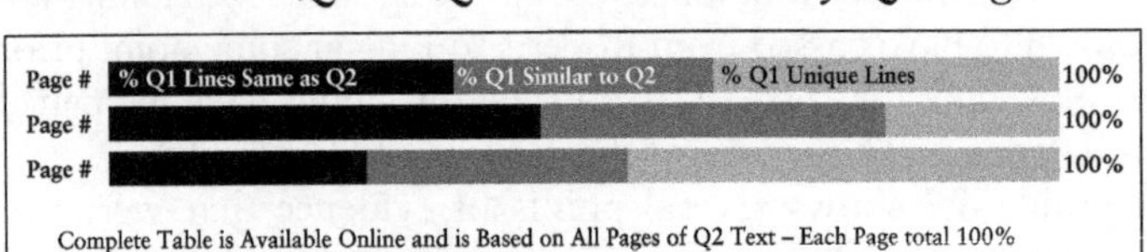

TABLE 6.6 ***Principal Actors in Chamberlain's Men / King's Men as Listed in F.***

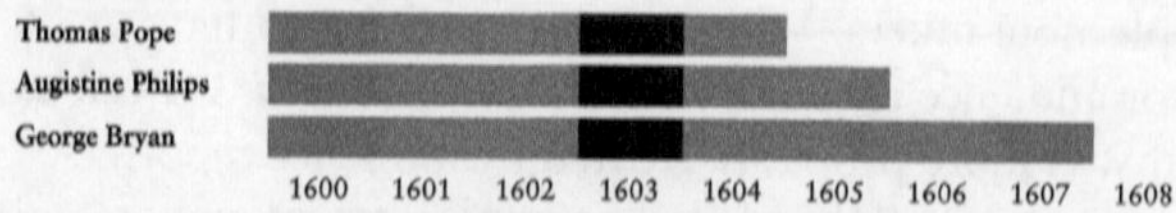

Complete Table is Available Online Showing 29 Individuals and spanning the Years 1594–1623

Additionally, it is highly probable that the Marcellus actor was not a bit-part player who was subsequently discharged, but rather that he was either a sharer or one of the loyal long-term hired men in Shakespeare's company. T. J. King's line counts by character show that the Marcellus role was the ninth most important adult role in the play.[14] Andrew Gurr's data on twenty-nine of Shakespeare's fellow players and their years with the company between 1594 and 1623 were charted in the manner of the three shown in Table 6.6.[15]

A fuller version of Table 6.6 is available online, and it illustrates that more than ten senior members of the company were working in 1603 and available to fill the nine most important roles in the play – including that of Marcellus.[16] Furthermore, the Marcellus actor hypothesis has been dealt another decisive blow by Paul Menzer's textual analysis,[17] which shows that the theorized actor-reporter, Marcellus, has failed to remember some of his own lines, and more notably, some of his cues.

Memorial reconstruction: The evidence against audience reporters

With the recognition emerging that the Marcellus actor was most probably a sharer or long-term hired actor, attention turns to the possibility of audience reporters. In 2013, Tiffany Stern outlined the variety of textual and possibly memorial relationships between corresponding portions of Q1 and Q2.

Her analysis makes the best case possible for the audience-note-taker hypothesis, as it takes into account the differing types and degrees of memory that must have been involved, hence implying multiple note-takers.[18] Stern does not claim to have made *the* case for audience reporters, but she claims that *if* Q1 is a 'noted' text, it was more probably created by audience reporters.

The line count of the Marcellus role is large enough statistically that the high concordance in the Q1 vs Q2 lines (93 per cent) must be accounted for in any narrative describing the relationship between the texts. In the audience note-taker narrative, the high Q1 vs Q2 concordance is accounted for by the assumption that the Marcellus actor must have been among those who 'were louder or clearer'.[19] Alternatively, the high early concordance might have resulted from Q1 being a draft of which the author revised the early portion. Some version of this possibility will emerge as the only unobstructed path through the evidence.

Focusing on the possibility of audience note-takers, another measurable characteristic of the text has recently been identified, which will impact the likelihood of this possibility. There are two roles with a significant number of lines both early and later in the play: the roles of Hamlet and Horatio. If the concordance of these two roles is relatively constant, early vs late, this will be consistent with the audience note-taker hypothesis. However, the concordance of Hamlet and Horatio drops off later in the play by an amount greater than can be accounted for by chance, as shown by Table 6.7.

As Table 6.7 indicates, the Q1 versus Q2 concordance is measured in the greater detail of words rather than lines. The early concordance for Hamlet is 87 per cent, and for Horatio 93 per cent. The percentage of drop-off in concordance for Hamlet is from 87 per cent to 56 per cent, and for Horatio, 93 per cent to 29 per cent.[20] Horatio's drop-off reinforces the Hamlet pattern, but the sample size of Horatio's lines, late in the play, is smaller. Other roles do not have large word counts early in the play. Fortunately, for statistical purposes, Hamlet has a high word count early and late, the drop-off in concordance is substantial, it occurs at a particular point in the

TABLE 6.7 *Q1 vs Q2 Concordance of Hamlet and Horatio, Early vs Late in the Play.*

Role	Total Q1 Words	Concordant with Q2	Unique to Q1	Early Concordance	Late Concordance	Comment
Marcellus						
Early	564	453	111	93%		Marcellus, Hamlet, and Horatio all have Q1 vs. Q2 concordance early in the play.
	NA	NA	NA		NA	Marcellus is on stage early in the play only.
Hamlet						
Early	1557	1353	204	87%		Hamlet's early vs. late concordance (87% vs. 56%)
Late	4645	2599	2046		56%	has a larger drop off than would occur by chance.
Horatio						Horatio's early vs. late concordance, by both measures, also drops off by more than would occur by chance.
Early	1043	967	76	93%		
Late	329	46	283		14%	Result including Horatio-Queen unique Q1 scene.
Adj. Late	159	46	113		29%	Result with unique Q1 Horatio scene removed.

Notes:

- Hamlet and Horatio are the two roles with statistically large line counts (and therefore word counts) early and late the play.
  The concordance of Hamlet and Horatio, following Act I, drops off by an amount greater than would occur by chance.
- This significant *infection point* must be accounted for in any theory of Q1 *Hamlet*, and it argues against audience reporters.
  The possibility of actor reporters, including the Marcellus actor, has already been ruled out as a possible source by other means.
  The remaining possibility is that Q1 is a pre-Q2 text, perhaps a draft the early portion of which has been revised.

text, and it is too great to have occurred by chance. Something caused it, and that *something* must be accounted for in any theory of Q1. The drop in the concordances occurs following the departure of the Marcellus actor, but the idea of the Marcellus actor as the source of Q1 has been eliminated. The remaining theory is of Q1 as a pre-Q2 text, which, in turns, reflects a partially revised draft.

Scholarship has been cautious in adopting the theory of Q1 as a pre-Q2 text, perhaps because of the long-held notion that Shakespeare, in his genius, created only a single text for each of his plays. Recognizing the improbability of both reported-text alternatives, the idea of Q1 as a pre-Q2 text is nevertheless emerging as the remaining option. It should also be noted that the idea of Q1 as a predecessor text is not new. When a copy of Q1 was uncovered in 1823 (and published in 1825), it was assumed that Shakespeare had 'afterwards altered and enlarged' the text.[21] In 2015, Zachary Lesser, in his comprehensive history of *Hamlet* after the discovery of Q1,

TABLE 6.8 *The 13 Passages of Three Lines or More Unique to Q2 vs F and F vs Q2.*

Passages Unique to Q2 vs. Folio	Passages Unique to Folio vs. Q2
Horatio discussion of Rome and Julius	
Hamlet soliloquy ... vicious mole of nature	
	Hamlet discussion of Denmark as a prison
	Description of child actors
Eyes without feeling, feeling without sight	
Hamlet: That monster custome	
Hamlet states his distrust of R & G	
Norwegian Captn and *How all occasions*	
Laertes offer to be *organ* of Hamlet's demise	
King's further manipulation of Laertes	
	is't not to be damned / Peace with Laertes
Hamlet's derision of Osric and Laertes	
Queen's request: Hamlet-Laertes reconcile	

concluded that 'our current editorial and textual theories about Q1 are constrained by blind spots of our own . . . that are preventing us from seeing alternatives'.[22] The findings outlined in Table 6.8 lead to the formal recognition of the collectively exhaustive lists of possible creators and possible sources of the text of Q1, introduced in Table 6.1.

Turning from possible creators of Q1 to the *collectively exhaustive* list of possible sources of the text, *Hamlet* offers an unusual statistical anomaly as a three-text play. There are thirteen passages (of three lines or more) that are unique to Q2 versus F or to F versus Q2. Ten of the passages are unique to Q2. These ten passages total 209 lines. The statistically important aspect of these 209 lines is that they have been identified by a standard that is independent of the existence of Q1. Therefore, it is appropriate to ask: how many of these 209 lines should be remembered *if* the text of Q1 was created from the memory of Q2? Since the text of Q1 contains 1,631[23] Q2 lines, or 41.8 per cent of text of Q2, approximately 41.8 per cent of the 209 Q2 lines (87 lines) should be remembered.

Approximately 87 is given because any *expected value* has a property called its *standard deviation*. In the present case, the standard deviation is 9.3. Plus or minus three standard deviations would produce a range of 59–115 lines. It is 99 per cent probable that between 59 and 115 of the 209-line sample would be remembered if Q1 was the product of Q2 memory. And, it is a *statistical certainty* that the number of lines remembered would fall in the range of six standard deviations, or 31–143 lines.[24] Yet, the number of these lines that appear in the text of Q1 is zero. Therefore, it is a statistical certainty that the lines did not exist in whatever text Q1 is related to. The lines were either not yet written, because the Q2 version of *Hamlet* was not yet written, or the lines were cut in a post-Q2 version of the play. This theorized, *intermediate* post-Q2 text, with the ten passages cut, is next to be considered.

The evidence against a cut version of Q2 as a possible Q1 source text

Between 1987 and 1992, Oxford editor George Hibbard wrestled with the same issue. Perhaps noticing, among other things, the absence of the 209 lines in the ten unique Q2 passages, Hibbard stated that the 'evidence is overwhelmingly in favor that [Q1] stems from the text behind F'.[25] Subsequently, perhaps focusing on the passages unique to F vs Q2, Hibbard wrote, 'Yet since writing those words, I have come to doubt their accuracy'.[26] Not considering the possibility of Q1 as a pre-Q2 text, Hibbard concluded that Q1's treatment of certain passages must be 'intermediate between Q2's and F's'.[27]

The idea of a post-Q2 cut text never gained widespread support, perhaps because some of the lines unique to F seem to have been written to replace passages that are unique to Q2. The first of the unique Q2 passages includes *honour* as Hamlet's stated motivation for killing King Claudius ('to find quarrell in a straw / When honour's at the stake, how stand I then' [sig. K3v]).[28] The second Q2 passage occurs when Hamlet and Laertes are about to meet for their fencing match.

Previously the two were so incensed they had to be physically separated, and the audience might expect this heated antagonism to resume. Perhaps recognizing this, the author created, in the Q2 text, a brief scene where an unnamed lord enters, inquires if Hamlet is ready, and advises him that his mother, the Queen, desires him to make peace with Laertes. Hamlet replies, 'Shee well instructs me' (sig. N3v).

In a single two-part passage, the author replaces both Q2 passages. In F, Hamlet has a new motivation for revenge, his salvation ('And is't not to be damn'd / To let this Canker of our nature come / In further euill?' [sig. 2P6r]). In the same F passage, the author solves the problem of the anticipated violence between Hamlet and Laertes by simply having Hamlet say, 'I am very sorry good *Horatio*, / That to *Laertes* I forgot myselfe' (sig. 2P6r), thus saving Q2's theatrically inconvenient (but necessary) entrance by the unnamed lord. The nature of these two related pairs of passages argues compellingly against the idea of an intermediate Q2–F text that Q1 is derived from. Such a text would lack either the Q2 or F motivation for revenge and would leave the audience anticipating renewed violence between Hamlet and Laertes as the two meet for their fencing match. F or a post-F text remain as possible source texts.

The evidence against F or a post-F text as a possible source of Q1

The statistical evidence against F as the source for Q1 parallels the Q2 case, only with different numbers. The three passages unique to F vs Q2 total fifty lines, with twenty-one being the *expected value* of lines to be remembered in Q1, if Q1 is a reported text. Again the result is zero. The sample size is smaller, so it lacks the overwhelming statistical certainty of the Q2 case, but the probability is nonetheless greater than 99 per cent that Q1 does not derive from F.

The remaining possible source text is a post-F text, and the evidence against this is as compelling as that against a Q2–F intermediate text. If one assumes the existence of a post-F text, missing all thirteen of the Q2-unique and F-unique passages, one is arguing that the author removed Q2's 'honour' as Hamlet's motivation for revenge, replaced it with F's motivation of divine salvation, and then somehow decided that the play was further improved by having neither. Likewise with Q2's and F's alternative ways of dealing with the anticipation of Hamlet's altercation with Laertes leading up to the fencing match. It is difficult to argue that Shakespeare would have found the text further improved, in a post-F text, by discarding both.

This completes the process of eliminating alternatives to the theory of Q1 as a pre-Q2 text. As exhibited in Table 6.1, all of the possible non-Shakespearean creators of Q1 and all of the possible sources of the text are two lists that are each *collectively exhaustive*. Thus, when compelling evidence *against* all possible alternatives is accepted, the remaining possibility must be accepted as more likely. With recent work by many scholars, this relationship is becoming recognized for both lists. Thus far, the case for Q1 as a pre-Q2 text has consisted of evidence *against* the possible creators and evidence against the theoretical range of possible sources. The balance of this essay will be devoted to evidence directly favouring Q1 as a pre-Q2 text (see Table 6.9).

The text of Q1 has often been referred to as *garbled*. However, when concordance arrows are drawn between lines in Q1 and Q2, the so-called garbling is found to be limited to sixteen passages, and is of three kinds: eight passages have minimal re-ordering of lines, seven passages have a larger number of reordered lines, and only one passage, the *To be* soliloquy, is truly garbled, with lines reordered and words mixed and even used differently. In the passage given in Table 6.9, concordance arrows revealed that what initially appeared as garbling was actually deft re-ordering, creating alternate versions of a 'split pentameter':

TABLE 6.9 *Example of Reordered (not Garbled) Passage.*

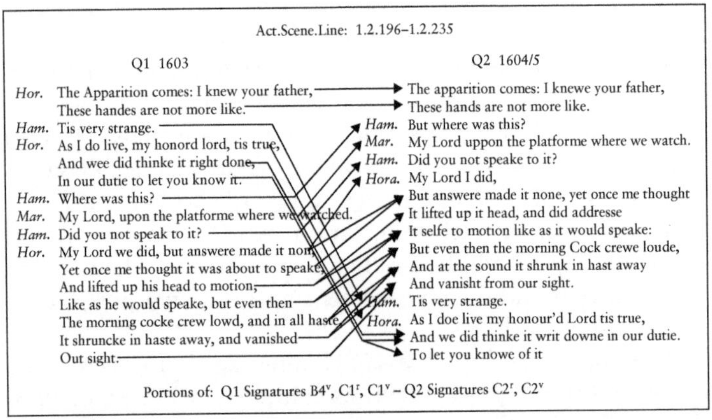

Q1 HORATIO These handes are not more like.
HAMLET Tis very strange.

(sig. C1r)

Q2 HORATIO These hands are not more like.
HAMLET But where was this?

(sig. C2v)

Further analysis of the same passage affects other split pentameters. As shown below, the Q1 'Where was this?' appears to be not yet refined to the Q2 four-syllable 'But where was this?' to produce in Q2 a split pentameter with an even number of syllables in both lines. Also, the 'Tis very strange' line receives more sophisticated handling in the Q2 version.

Q1 *Horatio* In our dutie to let you know it.
Hamlet Where was this?

(sig. C1r)

Q2 *Horatio* And vanisht from our sight.
Hamlet Tis very strange.

(sig. C2v)

With the perfect concordance of so many lines before and after the reordered portion, and the superior overall metering of the Q2 version of the reordered portion, the passage appears to be a Q1 → Q2 revision.

Turning to the *To be* soliloquy, the first line of Q1 is often pointed out as a botched recollection of Q2, 'To be or not to be, I there's the point' (sig. D4v). The Q1 version is often mocked for its crudeness. Yet, in *Othello* (3.3.234), the same phrase, 'I there's the point', is thought to be incisive. According to David Scott Kastan, 'the line marks a moment of unmistakably Shakespearean power . . . in *Hamlet* it marks a corruption of the text.'[29] As evidence, therefore, this factor does not add to the probability of either sequence of creation.

In an additional table available online,[30] concordance arrows illustrate the displacement of the handful of reordered lines and the relocation of several distinctive words. *Difference* between two texts does not indicate sequence of creation. And, a lack of sophistication in one text could indicate either that the simpler derived from the sophisticated or that the sophisticated is a revision of the simpler. However, in the portion of the *To be* soliloquy diagramed in Table 6.10, a characteristic is revealed that seems to be an indicator of sequence of creation, one which points in the direction of Q1 → Q2.

In the Q2 version of the soliloquy, there are nine lines (four early lines and five at the end) related to taking action and the consequences of not taking action. The Q1 version is missing all nine lines and the entire concept of taking action, making it seem most probable that the nine lines did not (yet) exist when the text of Q1 was created. The numbers involved are too small to produce a high level of *statistical confidence*, but the result supports what reason suggests. To argue for Q1 as a product of memory, one has to account for this mysteriously

TABLE 6.10 *The To Be Soliloquy in Q1 vs Q2/F.*

Q1 1603	Q2/F
Ham. To be or not to be, It there's the point, →	*Ham.* To be, or not to be, that is the quesetion:
? ______	Whether 'tis Nobler in the minde to suffer
? ______	The Slings and Arrows of outragious Fortune,
? ______	Or to take Armes Against a Sea of troubles,
? ______	And by opposing end them:
To die, to sleepe, is that all? I all:	to dye, to sleepe
Note 1: Core of *To be* soliloquy is substantially reordered, whatever the sequence of creation.	
Note 2: The concept of taking action and the consequence of not taking action are unique to Q2/F.	
? ______	And thus the Native hew of Resolution
? ______	Is sicklied o're, with the pale cast of Thought,
? ______	And enterprizes of great pith and moment,
? ______	With this regard their Currents turne away,
? ______	And lose the name of Action. Soft you now,

absent concept of taking action and the remarkably different soliloquy that results.

In 1996, Laurie Maguire called into question the entire idea of memorial reconstruction. She detailed her evaluation of each of the forty-one suspect texts and concluded that 'memorial reconstruction remains what it has always been: a possibility. It is an ingenious possibility and an attractive possibility, but let us not mistake it for a fact'.[31] Speaking specifically of *Hamlet,* and contrary to the firm opinions of editors such as Harold Jenkins and George Hibbard, Maguire would grant that *Hamlet* was only possibly created by memorial reconstruction, and then qualified that limited acknowledgement by stating that if it was, it was a very good one, implying a text very close to what was actually performed. Nothing in the line-by-line and word-by-word analysis of the *To be* soliloquy disputes the view of the Q1 version not deriving from the Q2/F version by any means. Margrethe Jolly supports objective full-text approaches when she comments on a common alternative approach: 'We can be amused by the descriptions of Q1 as a "mutilated corpse", and of its "To be" speech as a "farrago of nonsense", but perhaps we should be more suspicious of those rhetorical flourishes when practitioners see Q1 as the skeleton of Q2, as dynamic, and as having distinct energy.'[32]

The evidence for the *Brudermord* text (BB) as an early text

The BB text was taken from a 1709 German manuscript. There are not many clues to the date of the original, though two of Shakespeare's fellow players are known to have toured in Germany prior to 1600. In 1941, G. I. Duthie found twenty-one *correlates* in the BB text that coincide with Q1 (but not Q2) and thirty-six that coincide with Q2/F (but not Q1). He assumed that BB was not an earlier common original, and concluded that twenty-one Q1 vs thirty-six Q2/F was evidence that BB was derived primarily from Q2. He accounted for the twenty-one Q1 elements with a memorial theory involving contributions by touring players with a script of Q1.[33] However, the ratio of twenty-one to thirty-six is actually very close to the ratio of total lines in Q1 to Q2. Thus, the greater number of parallels in Q2 is no indication whatsoever that BB derived from Q2 with lesser contributions from Q1. To the contrary, the ratio of twenty-one to thirty-six suggests that BB might be an earlier text, elements of which carried through to Q1 and Q2 in the exact proportion of the number of lines in Q1 and Q2.

Duthie acknowledged that there were a few elements *unique* to BB, but did not search for them in similar detail to his search for Q1 and Q2 correlates. Recently, we rendered the BB text and Q1 as plot elements corresponding to 150 plot elements of Q2/F. The search for elements and details unique to the BB text revealed that there are in fact over fifty (see Table 6.11 for sample). No assumption that BB was derived from Q1 and Q2 accounts for how BB somehow gathered fifty unique plot elements and details. A sample of seven of these unique plot

TABLE 6.11 *Hamlet Variant Text Plot Element Analysis Chart for Brudermord, Q1, and Q2/F.*

Sample of BB Unique Plot Elements and Details

▲		King is offended by play, calls for torches, and departs
▲	△	Hamlet tells players that Horatio will reward them
▲		Hamlet instructs Corambus to reward players
	△	Hamlet tells Horatio he will find King alone and have his revenge
▲		King (alone) states that his conscience is awakened
▲		Hamlet elects not to kill King at the height of his devotions
	△	King states that his conscience is only somewhat lightened
	△	Corambus advises Queen that Hamlet is as made as ever
▲	△	Hamlet requests meeting with Queen in her chamber
▲	△	Queen requests Corambus hide behind arras
▲		Hamlet compares old king with his brother, the new King
▲	△	Corambus coughs behind arras, and Hamlet kills him

▲ Common to BB, Q1, and Q2/F

△ Unique to BB (Underline indicates portion Unique to BB)

elements and details is reproduced from the BB column in the large-scale table which is available online.[34] The analysis of BB vs Q1 vs Q2/F in the full parallel arrangement reveals several 'trajectories'[35] of revision passing from BB, through Q1, to Q2/F. These tend to further position BB as the earliest text, with Q1 at an intermediate point between BB and Q2/F, further marking Q1 as a pre-Q2 text.

Other evidence more easily reconciled with Q1 as a pre-Q2 text

Defending Q1 as a text based on a pre-existing Q2 requires an explanation for two name changes in the text. The first is *Corambis* (Q1), the name of the King's counsellor. The explanation from the memorial reconstruction theory is that the name change from *Polonius* (Q2) was necessary when *Hamlet* was played in Oxford, to avoid offence to the memory of Robert Pullen, the founder of Oxford; the character of Polonius is sometimes portrayed as pompous and foolish, and the similarity of his name to Pullen's could be argued to be offensive. According to the theory, Q1 was a reported text, taken from the version played at Oxford, and printed in London in 1603 without reverting to the *Polonius* of the assumed pre-existing London Q2 text.

This notion has two serious flaws. There is a second name change, *Reynaldo* (Q2) to *Montano* (Q1). Once the *Polonius* to *Corambis* name change had been postulated, the second was adopted based on the similarity between *Reynaldo* and the name of the founder of Corpus Christi College, John Reynolds. However, unlike Polonius, Reynaldo's name and role could not be offensive to anyone. He is onstage only briefly and with only thirteen lines. If his name (alone) could have offended, the problem could have been solved by simply addressing the character as 'my faithful servant'. As Q1 → Q2 becomes accepted as the sequence of creation, it might also be accepted that the Q1 names of Corambis and Montano might have been changed simply because audiences (and perhaps bit-part players) could have been confused by the similarity between the Q1 names of *Corambis* and *Claudius*, as well as *Montano* and *Marcellus*. If 1604 was the time of a major revision, and the drafting of the Q2 version, this might have been a convenient time to remedy the confusion.

Further undercutting the idea of *printing* a 'Corambis text' *if* a 'Polonius text' existed in 1603 is that Q1 was printed in London. Estimates of the population of London in 1600 range from 200,000 to 250,000, while estimates for Oxford range from 4,000 to 7,000.[36] The Oxford market represented a maximum of 3.4 per cent of the total. If one assumes a press run of 1,000 copies, the Oxford market (the 'Corambis market') would account for sales of only thirty-four copies. The idea of printing a 'Corambis text' in London if a 'Polonius text' already existed is difficult to rationalize.

A final argument against the idea of an Oxford-motivated name change is the emerging belief that the BB text is related to a pre-Q1 text, rather than being derived from pre-existing Q1 and Q2 texts. If BB derives from Q1 and Q2, and if the Polonius name was offensive only to Oxford audiences, why was it necessary to carry the Corambis name to Germany?

Another idea that has lost favour in recent years is that Q1 *Hamlet* might have been a 'touring script', designed to be played by a smaller number of players for less-sophisticated audiences. In 1992, T. J. King charted line counts by role for the texts of Shakespeare's plays, and his charts reveal that the same minimum number of players is required to perform both Q1 and Q2 *Hamlet*.[37] Furthermore, in 2006 Paul Werstine concluded that touring players performing at noble households were playing to many of the same people they played to in London, and that the 'standards of provincial performance can scarcely ever again be thought to differ from those of London . . .'.[38]

The early quartos have a range of textual relationships to their subsequent printings. To this point, and speaking of the short early quartos in general, Andrew Murphy noted that, 'We still do not know the provenance of these texts – or, indeed, whether they all share the same kind of history'.[39] The difficulty in identifying the provenance of any particular early text is compounded by possible authorial refinements, followed by alteration by players, scribes and compositors whose hands the texts passed through before appearing in print. In 2012, Paul Werstine concluded, '[w]hen a play survives only in print, it is impossible for an editor . . . to know if the manuscript behind the printed text had already been copied out either in the theatre or elsewhere before it became printer's copy'.[40] For every play, there will be a degree of speculation as to what lies behind the printed text.

Most of the stemmata created for the texts of *Hamlet* in the last century begin with the author's draft, by whatever term it was known (see Table 6.12). This text, representing the earliest state of the play, is often followed by various texts speculated to have existed, such as 'theatre manuscripts', 'theatrical abridgements', 'promptbooks', and 'memorial reconstructions'.

TABLE 6.12 *A Stemma for Hamlet Based Only on Texts Certain to Have Existed.*

A Stemma for *Hamlet* based only on texts certain to have existed – Implication for Several Early Quartos	
Author's Draft ⇩	The *author's draft* most certainly existed, whatever its degree of refinement. The term *foul papers* is less commonly used.
Allowed Book ⇩	A play could not be performed if a copy had not been reviewed and approed (the allowed book) by the Master of the Revels
???	Possible other texts: Stage Alteration, Prompt copy, Authorial Revision
1603 Q1 ⇩	Was Q1 *Hamlet* a pre-Q2 text, or was it created from memory of a pre-existing text of Q2, by actors or audience reporters?
1604/5 Q2 ⇩	Was the Q2 version Shakespeare's major development of his Q1 version of the text, or was Q2 his only text of *Hamlet*?
1623 Folio	Was the Folio text a refinement by the players seven years after Shakespeare's death, or did Shakespeare write it to refine Q2?

There are, however, two texts that are certain to have been a part of the provenance of every early printed play; although we do not have examples of either of them for any of Shakespeare's plays, Werstine calls attention to the author's *draft copy* and the *allowed book* in his discussion of security of the texts.[41]

These two texts might have been the first two extant texts in many instances. According to the theory of Q1 as a pre-Q2 text, Shakespeare would have reviewed his draft with the players. Then, the author or a scribe would have produced a copy for the censor's review; that copy becoming the *allowed book*. Once the players' roles had been written out, Shakespeare and the company would have enjoyed a level of security from loss, theft or fire. At that point, there was no need to save the draft copy.

Werstine suggests difficulty in 'imagining that the theatre would as a matter of custom take the trouble to preserve intact an author's copy of the play once it was replaced by the "[allowed] booke"'.[42] He cites a 1953 review by A. K. McIlwraith which deals with the earliest texts of John Fletcher's *Bonduca*. Although McIlwraith's conclusion about retaining authors' drafts was inconclusive, he raised the dichotomous issue of 'preserving the author's foul papers' (at least for some time, for the security of a backup copy) vs 'destroy[ing] them to prevent theft'.[43]

Now consider the process by which a new play was first published. Did the company let the allowed book out of their possession to be used as the printer's copy, or did they furnish the author's draft? If Q1 was Shakespeare's draft of the allowed book of that time, then the text would have been close to what its readers heard from the stage. This is but one narrative of Q1 *Hamlet* as a pre-Q2 text that offers an unobstructed path through the textual and non-textual evidence for the nature and source of the text. This narrative of Q1 *Hamlet* as a version of the author's draft, as the copy text for the early quarto, might emerge as a more plausible general model than the idea of the unauthorized printing of unauthorized memorial reconstructions.

Notes

1 Alfred W. Pollard, *Shakespeare's Folio and Quartos; A Study in the Bibliography of Shakespeare's Plays 1594–1685* (London: Methuen & Company, 1909), 65.

2 William Shakespeare, *Shakespeare's Merry Wives of Windsor, 1602,* ed. W. W. Greg (Oxford: Clarendon Press, 1910), xix.

3 Pollard, 74–5.

4 Laurie E. Maguire, *Shakespearean Suspect Texts* (Cambridge: Cambridge University Press, 1996).

5 Peter W. M. Blayney, 'The Publication of Play Books', in *A New History of Early English Drama*, ed. John D. Cox and David Scott Kastan (New York: Columbia University Press, 1997), 408–9.

6 David Scott Kastan, *Shakespeare and the Book* (Cambridge: Cambridge University Press, 2001), 29–30.

7 R. B. McKerrow, *A Dictionary of Printers and Booksellers in England, Scotland and Ireland, and of Foreign Printers of English Books 1557–1640* (London: Printed for the Bibliographical Society, 1910), 245.

8 Edward Arber, *A Transcript of the Registers of the Company of Stationers of London: 1554–1640 A.D.*, 5 vols. (London: 1875–94), 3: 161.

9 J. O. Halliwell-Phillipps, *Outlines of the Life of Shakespeare,* 5th edn. (London: Longmans, Green Co., 1885), 174.

10 The fuller version of Table 6.5 is available at https://www.bloomsburyonlineresources.com/hamlet-the-state-of-play.

11 William Shakespeare, *Hamlet*, The Oxford Shakespeare, ed. G. R. Hibbard (Oxford: Oxford University Press, [1987] 1998), 77.

12 Paul Werstine, 'A Century of "Bad" Shakespeare Quartos', *Shakespeare Quarterly* 50:3 (1999), 322.

13 Terri Bourus, *Young Shakespeare's Young Hamlet: Print, Piracy, and Performance* (New York: Palgrave MacMillian, 2014), 61.

14 T. J. King, *Casting Shakespeare's Plays: London Actors and their Roles 1590–1642* (Cambridge: Cambridge University Press, 1992), 206–9.

15 Andrew Gurr, *The Shakespeare Company 1594–1642* (Cambridge: Cambridge University Press, 2004), 217–46.

16 A fuller version of Table 6.6 is available online https://www.bloomsburyonlineresources.com/hamlet-the-state-of-play.

17 Paul Menzer, *The 'Hamlets': Cues, Qs, and Remembered Texts* (Newark: Delaware University Press, 2008).

18 Tiffany Stern, 'Sermons, Plays and Note-Takers: Hamlet Q1 as a "Noted" Text', *Shakespeare Survey* 66 (2013): 22–3.

19 Stern, 17.

20 The drop-off is 93 per cent to 14 per cent if Horatio's unique Q1 scene with the Queen is included.

21 William Shakespeare, *The First Edition of the Tragedy of Hamlet* (London: Payne and Foss, 1825), 1.

22 Zachery Lesser, *Hamlet After Q1, An Uncanny History of the Shakespearean Text* (Philadelphia: University of Pennsylvania Press, 2015), 220–1.

23 Charles Adams Kelly and Dayna Leigh Plehn, *The Evidence Matrix for the 1st Quarto of Shakespeare's Hamlet – 2nd Edition* (Ann Arbor: Triple Anvil Press, 2016), 17. 1,631 is the sum of 1,054 identical or nearly identical lines and 577 identifiably concordant lines.

24 Kelly and Plehn, Appendix E.

25 Hibbard, *Hamlet*, 88.

26 G. R. Hibbard, 'The Chronology of the Three Substantive Texts of Shakespeare's *Hamlet*', in *The Hamlet First Published*, ed. Thomas Clayton (Newark: University of Delaware Press, 1992), 79.

27 Hibbard, 'Chronology', 80.

28 Unless indicated otherwise, all quotations are from Q1, *The Tragicall Historie of Hamlet Prince of Denmarke* (London, 1603), Q2, *The Tragicall Historie of Hamlet, Prince of Denmarke* (London, 1604/5) and F, *Mr. William Shakespeare's Comedies, Histories, & Tragedies* (London, 1623).

29 Kastan, 27.

30 A fuller version of Table 6.10 is available online https://www.bloomsburyonlineresources.com/hamlet-the-state-of-play.

31 Maguire, 337–8.

32 Margrethe Jolly, *The First Two Quartos of Hamlet, A New View of the Origins and Relationship of the Texts* (Jefferson, North Carolina: McFarland & Co., 2014), 141.

33 G. I. Duthie, *The 'Bad' Quarto of Hamlet* (Cambridge: Cambridge University Press, 1941), 238–58.

34 A fuller version of Table 6.11 is available online https://www.bloomsburyonlineresources.com/hamlet-the-state-of-play.

35 The changes (BB vs Q1 vs Q2/F) in the circumstances surrounding the arrival of the players at Elsinore (2.2.380), distinct differences in Hamlet's lecture to the players (3.2.1), and the progression in the level of belligerence of Laertes when he confronts King Claudius (4.5.112).

36 Andrew Hinde, *England's Population: A History from the Domesday Survey to 1939* (London: Hodder Arnold, 2003), 169–70.

37 King, 206–9.

38 Paul Werstine, 'Margins to the Centre: REED and Shakespeare', *REED in Review* (Toronto: University of Toronto Press, 2006), 112.

39 Andrew Murphy, ed., *A Concise Companion to Shakespeare and the Text* (Oxford: Blackwell, 2007), 8.

40 Paul Werstine, *Early Modern Playhouse Manuscripts and the Editing of Shakespeare* (Cambridge: Cambridge University Press, 2012), 100.

41 Werstine, *Playhouse Manuscripts, 99*.

42 Ibid.

43 A. K. McIlwraith, 'Reviews', *The Review of English Studies*, 4(15) (1953): 283–4.

7

The *Hamlet* First Quarto Traces of Performance?

William Dodd

The impression that short or 'bad' first quartos like the 1603 *Hamlet* (Q1) preserve significant traces of performance is still widely shared by editors and textual scholars, however hard it is to come up with plausible accounts of how they got there. Among the more common kinds of evidence adduced are features sometimes referred to as actors' 'gag' or 'small change': seemingly banal interjections like *oh*, *nay*, *why*, *prithee*, *i'faith*, *look you*, *a pox*, and so on. These are often treated as little more than players' tics that debase the Shakespearean original. But what if such interpolations are more than simple padding or fudgings, what if they offer precious hints as to how Richard Burbage and his fellow players embodied their characters in performance? This is the question I will try to answer in the following pages. But first, how can we be sure it *was* the actors who left these traces in the text? Various scholars have warned of the risk of falling into circular logic here, of the kind: 'these must be post-performance texts because they carry traces left by actors, and we know they are traces left by actors, because these are post-performance texts'. Is there a way out of this vicious circle?

In 1996 Laurie Maguire took an important step in this direction when she examined actors' variants in the BBC *Shakespeare on Film* series. Since she was testing the validity of theories that a number of 'suspect' Shakespearean quartos were the product of memorial reconstruction by unauthorized actors, her main focus was on memory slips. By comparing what the BBC actors actually spoke with the published scripts, she was able to show that:

> twentieth-century actors, products of a print-based culture which values accuracy in textual reproduction, make errors of just the kind [that earlier scholars like W.W.] Greg *et al.* supposed actors would . . . [O]ther agents may make these errors too. But at least we can state unequivocally that actors do make these errors on a fairly large scale and not just that we imagine they might.[1]

From Maguire's standpoint it was reasonable to consider such departures from the original primarily as errors. However, I believe that many of them are best seen as variants on *pragmatic markers* typical of oral discourse, and hence as positive or creative modulations resulting from the actors' intuitive adaptation of written scripts to fluent stage interaction and to lively communication with the audience.

With this in mind, I classified and quantified the BBC film actors' pragmatic marker variants in five Shakespearean plays according to their specific interactional and textual functions. I chose *Romeo and Juliet*, *Richard III*, *Henry V*, *Hamlet* and *The Merry Wives of Windsor* because for each of these there exists a first quarto significantly different from a second quarto (Q2) and/or Folio edition (F). Four of them are short, so-called 'bad' quartos, which many (but not all) scholars believe reflect stage abridgements and adaptations of longer authorial texts.[2] Q1 *Richard III*, on the other hand, is both long and relatively 'good', but was argued by D. L. Patrick to be a post-performance text containing many of the kind of variants actors tend to produce.[3]

A preliminary count of the BBC *Hamlet* showed that the actors *added* sixty-six of these pragmatic items, and *omitted* twenty-five of those already present in their scripts, i.e. 72.5 per cent vs 27.5 per cent.[4] The BBC data for the five plays as a whole fully confirmed this ratio, showing a consistent prevalence of additions over omissions, a ratio of over 3 to 1. In other words, the BBC actors (all seasoned Shakespeare performers) show a far stronger tendency to increase the numbers of pragmatic markers than to omit them. They clearly feel intuitively that such tools play a significant role in *authenticating as oral* speeches which they initially encounter as written. It follows that if we can identify a similar pattern of additions vs omissions in the five first quartos it will be worthwhile exploring the hypothesis that these too may well be post-performance texts.

Maguire herself opted not to use this kind of parallel-text comparison in formulating her own data. Citing Alan Dessen's claim that the same evidence can be 'interpreted in diametrically opposed ways', she noted that:

> one can rarely have *a priori* confidence in the direction of influence between the two texts. It can be argued that Q1 *Hamlet*, for example, must have been revised to become Q2 just as it can be argued that Q2 must be the original of which Q1 is a derivative: evidence, in the form of variants, is readily to hand to support either interpretation.[5]

Regardless of what we consider to be the exact relationship between the two quartos,[6] I believe that *pragmatic* variants do point in one direction as regards traces of performance. Like the BBC actors' performed speeches as compared to their scripts, the first quartos of all five plays compared to their Q2/F counterparts show a significantly higher number of pragmatic markers in commensurable passages. It is thus legitimate to build on the hypothesis that these first quartos are in fact 'derivative' in at least one sense: namely, that they show clear signs of (further) oral adaptation of a prior written text, a 'mother' text whose more writerly aspect is preserved in the published editions.[7] As to whether the manuscript behind Q2 *Hamlet* itself was the mother text or a later revision of the mother text, the jury is still out.

With the direction of comparison established, it will also be possible to take into account pragmatic variants involving substitutions and displacements. We can look more confidently at these alternative first-quarto items as actors' replacements of the corresponding items in the later-published editions. But if we want to argue that actors are the most likely sources of pragmatic marker variants, we need to show first of all that there are plenty of them. As we will see from Table 7.1 below, the five earlier quartos contain a very substantial number of additional pragmatic markers. Conversely, far fewer pragmatic markers present in the maximal texts are absent from corresponding lines in the early quartos. Although some of the added Q1 markers may have been put there by other agents such as scribes, note-takers or compositors, only actors would have had a vested interest in producing *so many* positive variants of this particular kind. This is why I will be setting the Q1/Q2 *Hamlet* data against a backdrop of statistics derived from the BBC film versions (as well as from the 2018 Globe version cited in endnote 4), and from a collation of the five first quartos with their later counterparts as a whole.

In order to identify and classify pragmatic variants, I have slightly adapted an inventory of functions presented by Laurel J. Brinton in her 1996 book *Pragmatic Markers in English*, which is based on research into real oral discourse.[8] Pragmatic markers are not part of the grammatical structure of sentences as such but have a textual and interpersonal function. They are words whose original lexical meanings have come to be overshadowed by their functional, pragmatic role in discourse. I have grouped them under the following headings (the examples in brackets are all found in the five quartos, in various spellings):

A. *Openers/closers, attention-getters*: initiating or closing an exchange; claiming an addressee's attention (*come, go, how now, look you, prithee*);
B. *Floor access signals*: aiding speakers in acquiring or relinquishing their turns (the floor) in the exchange (*so go on*; *enough!*);
C. *Fillers*: holding the floor by using 'fillers' or delaying tactics (*and so forth*);
D. *Topic boundaries*: marking shifts in topic, etc. (*well, now*);
E. *Speech linkers*: marking 'sequential dependence': specifying how the forthcoming utterance relates to a previous one, etc. (*why*, *no/nay*, *ay*, *yea*);
F. *Deictics*: locating the speaker/hearer in the here-and-now of stage action (*here*, *this*, *now*);
G. *Subjective responses*: responding emotionally to preceding speech, back-channel signals of understanding and attention, etc. (O, *marry*, *God*, *i'faith*);
H. *Interpersonal cooperation*: indicating sharing, intimacy, deference or saving face (politeness), etc. (*I warrant you*, *and it please you*);
I. *Vocatives*: addressing the hearer with names, titles, pronouns (*father*, *my good lords*, *sirs*, *thou*).

Categories A, E, G and I account for 81.5 per cent of the variants in the BBC film versions and for 88.1 per cent of those in the 5Qs. I will thus focus mainly on these in the following discussion, mentioning the others only where they play a role in the Q1 passages I will be exploring. I have included a few lexical items that locally take on a pragmatic function. For example, *Class A* is extended to include some imperatives that serve either to close an exchange by leading or sending an addressee offstage (*come*, *go*, *begone*), or prolong an exchange by delaying an addressee's exit (*stay*, *hold*). In *Class G* I have included some repetitions of lexical terms when they have the effect of stressing a subjective response (*wormwood, wormwood*). Let's come now to the data.

Table 7.1 quantifies and classifies all categories of pragmatic variants according to the operation involved: i.e. whether they are added, substituted, displaced or omitted.[9] Expanded or repeated terms are counted here as additions, abbreviated terms as omissions.[10]

Unsurprisingly, the carefully-rehearsed BBC film versions show a far lower ratio of variants per line than the quartos, 1 per 20.4 vs 1 per 5.8, but the absolute number (693) is still fairly high.[11] As I have already pointed out, there is a very marked prevalence of additions over omissions across both corpora. The BBC actors made 431 additions vs 128 omissions (77.1 per cent vs 22.9 per cent). Of the five quartos' 1,871 variants, 779 are additions and 327 omissions (70.4 per cent vs 29.6 per cent). This pattern is confirmed by the specific figures for Q1 *Hamlet* (229 vs 81, or 73.9 per cent vs 26.1 per cent); and for the character Hamlet (124 vs 39, or 76.1 per cent vs 23.9 per cent). That the quarto data shows the same prevalence of additions over omissions as the BBC data (as does the Globe 2018 data given in endnote 4) is a strong first pointer towards the responsibility of early-modern players for the bulk of the quartos' pragmatic variants. In the 5Qs as whole, as well as in Q1 *Hamlet*, and Hamlet the character, we also find a large number, and high proportion, of *substitutions*, respectively 641 (34.3 per cent), 122 (26.6 per cent), and 55 (24.0 per cent), suggesting that Shakespeare's actors did a good deal of modulating and adapting of pragmatic markers to the felt needs of stage interaction. The BBC and Globe actors, trained in verbatim memorizing, apparently tend less to modify words they have already studied than to add pragmatic markers of their own that do not alter the semantics of their speeches.[12] Table 7.2 shows the distribution of variants across the eight pragmatic functions.

The BBC actors (like those of the Globe) vary (I) *Vocatives* proportionally far less than the 5Qs: 10.4 per cent vs 26.6 per cent. While in most other categories the proportion is very

TABLE 7.1 *Categories of Pragmatic Variants.*

	BBC Films	5 Quartos	Q1 Hamlet	Hamlet (character)
Total lines	14,114	10,897	2155	818
Total variants	693	1,871	459	229
Variants per line	1/20.4 (4.9%)	1/5.8 (17.2%)	1/4.7 (21.3%)	1/3.6 (28.0%)
Additions	431 (62.2%)	779 (41.6%)	229 (50.0%)	124 (54.1%)
Substitutions	105 (15.2%)	641 (34.3%)	122 (26.6%)	55 (24.0%)
Displacements	29 (4.2%)	124 (6.6%)	27 (5.9%)	11 (4.8%)
Omissions	128 (18.5%)	327 (17.5%)	81 (17.6%)	39 (17.0%)

similar, two are well above quarto averages, namely (E) *Speech linkers*: 34.9 per cent vs 19.8 per cent; and (C) *Fillers*: 11.4 per cent vs 0.3 per cent. The relatively low incidence of vocative variants is probably due again to typically accurate verbatim memorizing by modern actors, facilitated by the technical advantages of studio recording. On the other hand, their strong emphasis on *speech linkers* seems aimed at assisting a twentieth-century viewer's understanding of their uptake of previous speech acts, which may be less than transparent due to the rather archaic language.[13] The unusually high percentage of fillers is due to the fact that I was purposefully listening for, and transcribing them, whereas neither actors nor scribes would, in Shakespeare's time, have had any reason to record mumblings like *aahm* except in the rare cases they clearly connote a particular character (e.g. Corambis and some comic

TABLE 7.2 *Functions of Pragmatic Variants.*

	BBC Films	5 Quartos	Q1 Hamlet	Hamlet (character)
Tot. variants	*693*	*1,871*	*459*	*229*
A. Openers, closers, etc.	119 (17.2%)	408 (21.8%)	105 (22.9%)	56 (24.5%)
B. Floor access signals	1 (0.1%)	6 (0.3%)	5 (1.1%)	3 (1.3%)
C. Fillers	79 (11.4%)	5 (0.3%)	4 (0.9%)	3 (1.3%)
D. Topic Boundaries	14 (2.0%)	44 (2.4%)	11 (2.4%)	5 (2.2%)
E. Speech Linkers	242 (34.9%)	371 (19.8%)	93 (20.3%)	52 (22.7%)
F. Deictics	25 (3.6%)	84 (4.5%)	20 (4.4%)	11 (4.8%)
G. Subjective Responses	132 (19.0%)	308 (16.5%)	89 (19.4%)	52 (22.7%)
H. Interpers. Cooperation	9 (1.3%)	85 (4.5%)	12 (2.6%)	7 (3.1%)
I. Vocatives	72 (10.4%)	562 (30.0%)	122 (26.6%)	40 (17.5%)

personalities).[14] As regards the five quartos and *Hamlet*, four categories predominate: A, E, G and I. This suggests that the players were particularly focused on managing their interactions, showing their uptake of previous speeches, emphasizing their subjective responses, and nuancing politeness with superiors and inferiors. I will go into more detail when discussing Hamlet's role a little later.

Let's set numbers aside for a moment and take a preliminary look at some of these variants at work in a Q1 *Hamlet* passage that is very close to the Q2 version: the stichomythia in which Hamlet bombards Horatio and Marcellus with questions about his father's Ghost. (Underlined markers appear only in Q1. Where they are *substitutions* for a word or words in Q2/F, these are given in brackets. Other minor differences between Q1 and Q2/F are not signalled here.)

Ham. Indeed, indeed (also in F) sirs, but this troubles me:
Hold you the watch to night?
All. We do my Lord.
Ham. Armed say ye?
All. Armed my good Lord.
Ham. From top to toe?
All. My good Lord, from head to foote.
Ham. Why then saw you not his face?
Hor. Oh yes my Lord, he wore his bever vp.
Ham. How (Q2/F *What*) look't he, frowningly?
Hor. A countenance more in sorrow than in anger.
Ham. Pale, or red?
Hor. Nay, verie pal[e.]
Ham. And fixt his eies vpon you?
Hor. Most constantly.
Ham. I would I had beene there.
Hor. It would a much amazed you.
Ham. Yea very like, very like (also in F), staid it long?
Hor. While one with moderate pace (Q2/F *hast[e]*)
Might tell a hundred.
Mar. O longer, longer. (Q2: *Hor. Not when I saw't*)
Ham. His beard was grisled, no.
Hor. It was as I have seene it in his life,
A sable siluer.
Ham. I wil watch to night, perchance t'wil walke againe.
Hor. I warrant it will.[15]

Compared to Q2/F, Q1 has three added *speech linkers* (E) plus a substituted one: *Why*, *Yea*, *O*; *How* for Q2/F *What*. The first two slightly disturb the rhythm of the exchange, a possible symptom of interpolation.[16] As we have seen from the quantitative data, added and substituted markers of this kind are common throughout Q1. These are exactly the kind of variants the BBC and Globe actors inserted to stress and clarify their uptake of the preceding speech, so it seems most likely that the same types of variants in Q1 are the work of Shakespeare's players. We also find an expanded *vocative* (I), *My good Lord*, of which there are four examples elsewhere in Q1 (together with thirteen cases of interpolated *My lord* and one *My good lord* added whole). While emphatic repetitions are frequent in Q1, it is safer to disregard *indeed* and *very like* here since they both appear in F, and could simply have been overlooked by the Q2 compositor. In this passage, then, we seem to catch a glimpse of Richard Burbage portraying Hamlet as listening anxiously to his friends' account of the ghost and badgering them for rapid answers to his questions.[17] For their part, his interlocutors stress their affectionate loyalty to him (My *good* Lord), while the Marcellus actor is shown as *quick* to insist on his capacity for reliable observation: 'O longer, longer.'

As I have said, it is the cumulative weight of pragmatic variants in Q1 *Hamlet* as a whole that justifies our making such hypotheses about an individual actor's impact on the text of Q1. Their variants will need to be frequent enough to allow us to discount a certain proportion as possibly due to other agents.

As we can see from Table 7.1, Q1 *Hamlet* contains 459 pragmatic variants, 1 per 4.7 lines. No fewer than 229 of these, 49.9 per cent of the play's total, are produced by Hamlet himself. This is a very high proportion considering that Hamlet speaks 'only' 818 (38 per cent) of the play's lines. At one variant per 3.6 lines, he is thus well above the average of the play as a whole (1 per 4.7 lines), and of the rest of characters (1 per 5.8 lines). I will thus focus primarily on Hamlet's variants in what follows.[18]

Let us now take a closer look at Hamlet's own variants as listed in Table 7.2.

A. Openers/closers, attention-getters

This is the category in which the largest proportion of his variants appears. He has fifty-six in all, 1 per 14.6 lines, vs 1 per 27.3 of the remaining characters, and 1 per 26.7 in all five quartos. There are twenty-nine additions, thirteen substitutions and three displacements vs eleven omissions. Attention-claimers account for eleven of Hamlet's interpolations: *look you* (4), *do you hear?* (3), *behold* (2), *hark*, *mark* (1 each); of the five substituted attention-claimers, four are fairly neutral (*see* for *look*, *what* for *oh*,) while one shows increased authority: *take heed* for *pray you*; only four Q2 attention-claimers are omitted: *I say*, *hark you*, *heare you*, *what*). Of the remaining twenty-six additions + substitutions, sixteen are openers and ten closers, against seven omissions. Typically they enjoin Hamlet's interlocutors to take the floor or enter the physical space of dialogue (*speak*, *come*, *nay come*, *come on*, *I pray you*, *I prithee*, *etc.*), or to relinquish the floor, often by exiting: exchange-closing terms like *farewell*, *hoe*, *your loves.* To these must be added Q1 Hamlet's extra repetitions of *Go to a nunnery*, though these of course are rhetorical rather than actual.

What we see here, then, is a marked increase in the *management* of the dialogue by Burbage's Hamlet, as he repeatedly demands his listeners' attention, and instructs them to enter into speech with him or to exit from it. He seems to be showing rather more discourse authority than we might expect from an eighteen- to twenty-year-old boy prince, reminding us that Burbage himself in 1600 was actually thirty-three years old.

E. Speech linkers

Hamlet has fifty-two, 1 per 15.7 lines, vs 1 per 32.6 of the remaining characters, and the five quartos' 1 per 29.4 lines. He has thirty-two additions and thirteen substitutions against just six omissions. His most common interpolations are *why*, *O*

(6), *nay*, *no* (4), *I (=ay)* (4), together with one or two each of *yea*, *and*, *what*, *well*, and a few others. The substitutions of linkers (e.g. *but* for *and*, *how* for *what*, *then* for *and*, *yes* for *I*, etc.) tend towards greater precision. Taken together, the positive variants draw attention to the actor/character's *specific* uptake of the previous speech, clarifying the relationship of the forthcoming response to the words just spoken – signalling, for instance, that it will be adversative or logically consequent. Like the BBC actors, Burbage seems keen to transmit to the audience a sense that he is listening carefully to, and interpreting, his interlocutor's speech acts in real time, thereby facilitating the audience's grasp of the gist of the interaction. In 1664 Richard Flecknoe reported that Burbage would 'wholly transform himself into his Part . . . never falling in his Part when he had done speaking, but with his looks and gesture maintaining it still unto the heighth'.[19] These interpolated or adapted speech linkers seem to show Burbage doing just that: using his professional and empathetic skills to convey the impression of a mind interpreting what it hears in both the fictional exchange and the here-and-now of the theatrical action.

G. Subjective responses

This is the category with the second largest proportion of Hamlet's variants. He has fifty-two in all, 1 per 15.7 lines, vs 1 per 36.1 of the remaining characters, and the five quartos' 1 per 35.4 lines. They include thirty-two additions and fourteen substitutions (88.5 per cent) against just six omissions. The most common interpolation is *O* (6), together with a sprinkling of expressions like *marry* (4), *a poxe*, *O God*, *for God's sake*, *by my faith*, *why sure*, etc. *A poxe* also twice replaces milder exclamations. In this category, under additions, I have included eleven repetitions of lexical (as opposed to pragmatic) items, since they place a particular emotional emphasis on the meaning or referent of those items: for instance *wicked*, *my uncle*, *wonderful*, *wormwood*. Just as Burbage was keen to show his uptake of his interlocutor's speech acts, here he shows a strong tendency to stress the intensity of his subjective, emotional response to the ongoing exchange.

I. Vocatives

Hamlet's forty vocative variants, though a little below the average for Q1, are very close to that of the 5Qs: he has 1 per 20.5 lines, vs the five quartos' 1 per 19.4 lines. Again, positive variants predominate: additions 19, substitutions 7, omissions 8 (of which three are only partial, the vocative as such remaining intact). The most common additions are of *sir(s)* (6), *father* (5), *Horatio* (5). Since Hamlet is the social superior of all but the Ghost, the King and the Queen, if he wishes to be especially polite (or ironical) to others, *sir(s)*, *lady*, *my lords*, *gentlemen*, or the addressee's name, are practically his only options. What sticks out like a sore thumb here is his five-fold interpolation of *father* – addressed, not to the Ghost, but to his *uncle* the King, a point to which we will return later.

I believe that we have accumulated enough quantitative evidence by now to point confidently towards Shakespeare's players as the *primary* source of pragmatic marker variants. On this basis, we can now try to make some observations on how they performed their roles at specific moments in the play.

§

We can start with a glance at Hamlet's soliloquies. There are only five in Q1, and they are generally so much shorter than, and so different from Q2's, that I shall limit myself to a sampling of the main pragmatic variants there, rather than attempting a close reading. The opening of the most famous soliloquy contains some typical ones:

> To be, or not to be, I there's the point, (Q2/F *that is the question*,)

To Die, to sleepe, is that all? I all:
No, to sleepe, to dreame, I mary there it goes, (Q2/F *I there's the rub*)
For in that dreame of death, when wee awake,
And borne before an euerlasting Iudge,
From whence no passenger euer retur'nd,
The vndiscouered country, at whose sight
The happy smile, and the accursed damn'd.
(Q1, sig. D4v; see Q2, sig. G2r; F, sig. 2O5r)

This is clearly a *debased* version of a more coherent text. It has too many logical non sequiturs to represent an early draft directly. What *passenger* ever failed to return from an everlasting judge? And what kind of judge can suddenly turn into an undiscovered country that arouses a smile in the happy, and (leaves?) the accursed damned? If, as Richard Dutton argues,[20] Q2 is a Shakespearean revision-expansion for court performance, it is certainly not a revision of Q1 as we have it, but of a copy that already contained the main logical steps in Hamlet's soliloquy as preserved in Q2 and F. Q1's version is undeniably derivative in this respect, and from a manuscript where this speech is not radically different from that behind Q2. This is the case with several other Q1 passages containing logical glitches that can be solved by recourse to Q2. However we explain its transmission, the Q1 speech shows clear traces not only of faulty reporting, but also of performance, peppered as it is with the kind of pragmatic variants typically introduced by actors.[21] Here and later in the soliloquy we find interpolated/substituted speech linkers and subjective-response markers: *I*; *I all*; *No*; *I mary there it goes*; *I that...* This happens over all five soliloquies, where we see an increase in both types: *subjective responses*: eight added and two substituted; *speech linkers*: four added. They offer glimpses of Burbage stressing not only the Prince's emotional turmoil, but also the logic of his reasoning, as if he were deliberately bouncing it back off the audience in the process.[22]

Let's look now at how Q1 Hamlet interacts in conflictual dialogue with other characters, beginning with his treatment of Ofelia in the so-called nunnery scene.[23]

Ofel. My Lord, I haue sought opportunitie, which now
I haue, to redeliuer . . . such tokens which I haue receiued of you.
Ham. Are you faire?
Ofel. My Lord.
Ham. (Q2/F *Ha, ha*) Are you honest?
Ofel. What meanes my Lord? (Q2/F *your Lordship*)
Ham. That if you be faire and honest,
Your beauty should admit no discourse to your honesty.
Ofel. My Lord, can beauty (Q2/F *my Lord*) haue better priuiledge than with honesty?
Ham. Yea mary (Q2/F *I truly*) may it; for Beauty may transforme
Honesty, from what she was into a bawd: . . .
I neuer gave you nothing.
Ofel. My (Q2/F *honor'd*) Lord, you know right well you did, . . .
But now too true I finde,
Rich giftes wax poore, when giuers grow vnkinde.
Ham. I neuer loued you.
Ofel. (Q2/F *Indeed my Lord*) You made me beleeue you did.
Ham. O thou shouldst not a (Q2/F *You should not have*) beleeued me!
Go to a Nunnery goe (Q2/F *Get thee [to] a Nunry/ Nunnerie*), why shouldst thou
Be a breeder of sinners? . . .
To a Nunnery goe, we are arrant knaues all,
Beleeue none of vs, to a Nunnery goe (Q2/F *goe thy waies to a Nunry*).
Ofel. O heauens secure him!
Ham. Wher's thy father?
Ofel. At home my lord.

Ham. For Gods sake let the doores be shut on him,
He may play the foole no where but in his
Owne house: to a Nunnery goe.
Ofel. Help him good God.
Ham. If thou dost marry, Ile giue thee
This plague to thy dowry:
Be thou as chaste as yce, as pure as snowe,
Thou shalt not scape calumny, to a Nunnery goe.
Ofel. Alas, what change is this?
Ham. But if thou wilt needes marry, marry a foole,
For wise men know well enough,
What monsters you make of them, to a Nunnery goe.
Ofel. Pray God (Q2/F *[O] Heavenly powers)* restore him.
Ham. Nay, I haue heard of your paintings too,
God hath giuen you one face,
And you make your selues another,
You fig, and you amble, and you nickname Gods creatures,
Making your wantonnesse, your ignorance,
A pox, t'is scuruy (Q2/F *goe to*), Ile no more of it,
It hath made me madde: (Q2/F *I say*) Ile no more marriages,
All that are married but one, shall liue,
The rest shall keepe as they are, to a Nunnery, goe
To a Nunnery goe.
(Q1, sigs E1r–E2r; Q2, sigs G2v-G3r; F sigs 2O5r-v)

Although this dialogue is in a rather different order and shorter in Q1, it is close enough to Q2 to identify a number of significant pragmatic variants in Hamlet's speeches, together with a few minor ones in Ofelia's. The two extra repetitions of 'to a Nunnery go' and its reduction to a mechanical catchphrase compared with Q2's more varied forms make Hamlet appear more aggressive, while his Q1 curse *A pox, t'is scurvy* portrays him as downright ungallant. Although Q2's 'Ha, ha' (laughter? bulllying interjection?) is absent here, Q1 Hamlet has a number of extra or intensified speech linkers and subjective responses

(*Yea, mary, O, For Gods sake, Nay)* that stress his misogynous uptake of Ofelia's defensive responses.

To conclude, here is how Q1 presents Hamlet's clash with his uncle regarding the body of Corambis:

(*Enter Hamlet and the Lordes.*)[24]
Gil. My lord, we can by no meanes
Know of him where the body is.
King. Now sonne Hamlet, where is this dead body?
(Q2/F: *where's Polonius?*)
Ham. At supper, not where he is eating, but
Where he is eaten, a certaine company of politicke wormes
are even now at him.
Father, your fatte King, and your leane Beggar
Are but variable seruices, two dishes to one messe:
Looke you, a man may fish with that (Q2 *the*) worme
That hath eaten of a King,
And a Beggar eate that fish,
Which that worme hath caught.
King. What of this?
Ham. Nothing father, but to tell you, how a King
May go a progresse through the guttes of a Beggar.
King. But sonne *Hamlet*, where is this body? (Q2/F:
Where is Polonius?)
Ham. In heau'n, if you chance to misse him there,
Father, you had best looke in the other partes below
For him, and if you cannot finde him there,
You may chance to nose him as you go vp the lobby.
King. Make haste and finde him out. (Q2/F: *Goe seeke
him there.*)
Ham. Nay doe you hear? do not make too much haste,
I'le warrant you hee'le stay till you come.
King. Well sonne *Hamlet*, we in care of you: but specially
in tender preseruation of your health, . . .
It is our minde you forthwith goe for *England*, . . .
Ham. O with all my heart: farewel (Q2/F: *deere*) mother.
King. Your (Q2/F: *Thy*) loving father, *Hamlet*.

Ham. My mother I say: you married my mother,
My mother is your wife, man and wife is one flesh,
And so (my mother) farewel: for England hoe. (Q2/F: *Come for* England.)
(Q1, sigs G3v–G4; Q2, sigs K2r-v; F, sigs 2P2v-2P3r)

What first strikes the eye of course is Q1's special insistence on the *son/father* motif, which is absent from Q2/F until the last four lines. The six vocative additions/expansions suggest that the two actors played this episode as a kind of ritual duel, harping allusively on the concept of the King's 'incestuous' marriage to Hamlet's mother. It is a riff the King's actor has already begun to develop in Q1's Scene 2, where, in addition to the two *cosin/sonne* occurrences present in Q2, he interpolates a further *Sonne* before Hamlet's name. Later, in the lead-up to the play-within-the-play, the King substitutes *son Hamlet* for Q2's *cosin Hamlet*, to which Q1 Hamlet responds in kind with an added *I father*, as well as inserting another *Father* later on, when explaining the plot of the *Mouse-trap*. The reiterated vocatives suggest two actors stepping up the aggressiveness of their interaction: as we all know, even in less dramatic circumstances, to call a family member by name/relationship can often bear innuendoes of warning or menace. Emphatic interpolations like Hamlet's *Looke you*, *I'le warrant you*, *I say*, suggest that Burbage played Hamlet as bullying his stepfather here, whereas the King's use of sequential dependence markers, *But sonne Hamlet* and *Well sonne Hamlet*, suggests his actor was playing him as on the defensive, as if struggling to bring the exchange back on topic and under control.

A word on the added *deictics* (see item F). Here, as in many instances in the five quartos, they show actors contextualizing their speeches in the here-and-now of the stage action. They install the written script gesturally in the present and the physical location of performance: *where is this dead body?*; *politicke worms are even now at him*; *that worm*. . . Lastly we see the reinforcing of a couple of *closers* (see item A), which terminate a character's presence at an exchange by getting them offstage. Q1: *Make haste and finde him out* vs Q2/F: *Goe seeke him there*; Q1: *for England hoe* vs Q2: *Come for England*. Both actors are heightening the urgency and tension of the situation.

§

There is much more, I believe, to be gleaned from a study of Q1 *Hamlet's* pragmatic marker variants, but I hope to have shown: (a) that it is most likely that the actors were responsible for the bulk of them, and (b) that we can therefore catch precious glimpses of their performance habits, namely the way they animated their interactions and interpreted their roles. How these variants came to be recorded could be explained either by Tiffany Stern's scenario of Q1 as the product of note-takers in the audience or by that of Peter Blayney, who suggests (among other possibilities) that such texts may have been reconstructed by actors partly or wholly from memory for a friend or patron.[25] Once we recognize that Shakespeare's fellow actors are the most likely source of these pragmatic variants, we may begin, with greater confidence, to comb the mongrel texts of the short quartos for further traces of actors' skills (and, why not, shortcomings) in other linguistic and stylistic dimensions.

Notes

1 Laurie E. Maguire, *Shakespearean Suspect Texts: The 'Bad' Quartos and Their Contexts* (Cambridge: Cambridge University Press, 1996), 146.

2 Lene B. Petersen in her stylometric study of the Shakespeare canon, *Shakespeare's Errant Texts: Textual Form and Linguistic Style in Shakespearean 'Bad' Quartos and Co-authored Plays* (Cambridge: Cambridge University Press, 2010), showed that there was a significant increase in phenomena associated with oral transmission in two of the shorter quartos included in my data (*Hamlet*, *Romeo and Juliet*). She identified as oral-memorial

style-markers features like the transposition of phrases, the repetition of innocuous verbal features, and action-orientated formulae like 'look where he comes/goes'.

3 David Lyall Patrick, *The Textual History of 'Richard III'* (London: Oxford University Press, 1936). In his list of actors' memorial substitutions Patrick includes 'variations in the terms of address and reference, use of different exclamations and interjections, simplifications and colloquialisms' (18). His view that Q1 *R3* is based on some sort of (authorized) memorial reconstruction has, however, been seriously challenged.

4 I made a similar count of the filmed performance of the Globe's 2018 production of *Hamlet* directed by Federay Holmes and Elle While. Given the absence of published scripts, I compared it directly with Q2 and F, since it clearly draws on both. The data is thus probably less accurate but still indicative. The 169 pragmatic variants I located show an even higher proportion of additions vs omissions (86 per cent vs 14 per cent).

5 Maguire, 228.

6 For a detailed discussion of the relationship between the early editions of *Hamlet*, see Kelly and Plehn's essay in this collection. For recent, alternative accounts of the origins and relations among the three early versions of *Hamlet* preserved in Q1, Q2 and F, see, for example, Paul Menzer, *The Hamlets: Cues, Qs and Remembered Texts* (Newark: University of Delaware Press, 2008).

7 Of course, Shakespeare already provided a robust pragmatic scaffolding for stage interaction in his drafts. But his plays were also subject to another principle of cohesion, namely poetic structure. The end of one speech could be bound to the beginning of the next by rhythmic and phonic continuity – for instance, in the case of an iambic pentameter split between two or more characters. The two principles could sometimes pull in different directions.

8 Laurel J. Brinton, *Pragmatic Markers in English: Grammaticalization and Discourse Functions* (Berlin, New York: Mouton de Gruyter, 1996), 37–8.

9 Maguire, *Shakespearean Suspect Texts*, classified the BBC actors' 'memorial errors' according to the same four operations. In my

commentary, for want of space, I have ignored displacements (i.e. the anticipation or retarding of a pragmatic marker along a line or phrase; Maguire calls these transpositions).

10 In Q1 *Hamlet* expansions plus repetitions account for 13.5 per cent of the *Additions*; abbreviations and the elimination of Q2 repetitions account for 17.3 per cent of *Omissions*.

11 Likewise, the 2018 Globe *Hamlet*, a linguistically faithful performance, still reveals a significant number of pragmatic variants (169), roughly 1 per 15 lines. This is predictably higher than the 114 variants, 1 per 25 lines, of the BBC's studio-filmed *Hamlet*.

12 Table 7.3 listing all pragmatic variants between Q1 and Q2 *Hamlet* can be accessed online at https://www.bloomsburyonlineresources.com/hamlet-the-state-of-play.

13 This is confirmed by the Globe *Hamlet*'s high proportion of speech linkers: 47/169 (27.8 per cent).

14 Similarly, the Globe *Hamlet* has thirty-six fillers, most of them produced by Polonius or by the Claudius actor in his 'comic' mode.

15 *The Tragicall Historie of Hamlet Prince of Denmarke* (London, 1603), sigs C1r–C1v. For Q2 and F readings see *The Tragicall Historie of Hamlet, Prince of Denmarke* (London, 1604/5), sigs C2v-C3r, and *Mr. William Shakespeares Comedies, Histories, & Tragedies* (London, 1623), sig. 2N6r. All the other passages discussed use the same original editions.

16 Extrametricality has often been considered a sign of interpolation. I have counted twenty-eight extrametrical additions out of Q1's 459 (6.1 per cent) and one counter-example where Q2 is extrametrical and Q1 not. The rest of the variants appear in metrically incommensurable or ambiguous contexts. Terri Bourus, in *Young Shakespeare's Young Hamlet: Print, Piracy, and Performance* (New York: Palgrave Macmillan, 2014), 46–55, when dismantling Kathleen Irace's list of actors' extrametrical interpolations in Q1, provided her own counter-list of possible interpolations in Q2. She claimed that one could thus argue equally well that Q2 itself was a/the performance text. However, the radical *disproportion* in the distribution of interpolated pragmatic markers in the two texts as shown in my

data militates against this position. Moreover, a comparison of F *Hamlet* with Q2 results in less than half the pragmatic marker variants: 203 vs the 459 in Q1 vs Q2. Folio vs Q2 has a ratio of additions vs omissions of roughly 65 per cent to 35 per cent, which tends to confirm Harold Jenkins's view that the former carries traces of performance left by actors. See 'Playhouse Interpolations in the Folio Text of *Hamlet*', *Studies in Bibliography* 13 (1960): 31–47.

17 Maguire, *Shakespearean Suspect Texts*, quotes Harold Jenkins to the effect that: 'No one, as far as I know, has ever maintained that the debased Q1 text [of *Hamlet*] represents how Burbage and other leading actors of Shakespeare's Company spoke and remembered their lines . . .' (224). While Q1 contains various speeches likely to have been mauled by other intervening agents than the actors, there is no reason why Burbage and his fellows should not have left their imprint on pragmatic markers *in particular*.

18 Lack of space prevents me from discussing other characters here, but Corambis (51 variants) comes close to Hamlet with 1 per 4 lines. What his actor seems to be stressing is the fawning politician with a self-conscious, pompous manner of conversing. The other main characters, in descending order of frequency, are: *Laertes* 20 in 88 lines, 1 per 4.4 lines; *Queen* 16 in 89 lines, 1 per 5.6 lines; *King* 33 in 203 lines, 1 per 6.2 lines; *Ofelia* 17 in 135 lines, 1 per 7.9 lines; *Horatio* 25 in 199 lines, 1 per 8 lines; *Ghost* 7 in 74 lines, 1 per 10.6 lines.

19 Richard Flecknoe, 'A Short Discourse of the English Stage', in *Love's Kingdom*, vol. 2 of *Critical Esssays of the Seventeenth Century*, 1650–85, ed. J. E. Spingarn (London: Oxford University Press, 1964), 91–6.

20 Richard Dutton, *Shakespeare, Court Dramatist* (Oxford: Oxford University Press, 2016).

21 I use 'reporting' in W. W. Greg's sense of the term: 'any process of transmission which involves the memory no matter at what stage or in what manner' (W. W. Greg, *Two Elizabethan Stage Abridgements: The Battle of Alcazar & Orlando Furioso: An Essay in Critical Bibliography* [Oxford: Clarendon Press, 1923], 256).

22 Actor Christopher McCullough recalled: '"To be or not to be, I there's the *point*" actually only made sense if I said it *to the*

audience. In fact I was using the soliloquy as a way of putting an argument to the audience as to what was going on in the narrative'. Quoted in *Hamlet*, The Arden Shakespeare, ed. Ann Thompson and Neil Taylor, 2 vols (London: Thomson, 2006), vol. 1, 24.

23 To save space, lines have been cut where no variants can be pinpointed.

24 Where the wording or content (as opposed to the line order) of Q1 differs significantly from Q2 and/or F, it is shown in smaller type.

25 Tiffany Stern, 'Sermons, Plays and Note-takers: *Hamlet* Q1 as a "Noted" Text', in *Shakespeare Survey* 66 (2013): 1–23; Peter W. M. Blayney, 'The Publication of Playbooks', in *A New History of Early English Drama*, edited by John D. Cox and David Scott Kastan (New York: Columbia University Press, 1997), 383–422.

8

'You May Wear Your Rue With a Difference'

Gertrude, Ghazala and the Sati in *Haider*

Pompa Banerjee

Gertrude's part is famously underwritten in Shakespeare's longest play. For some readers, Gertrude is more powerful as the site for projected fantasies than as a fully realized independent character.[1] Indeed, there is a long history of clipping Gertrude's part on stage. From the mid-eighteenth to the early years of the twentieth century, acting editions and promptbooks systematically cut out Gertrude's lines, including the final twenty-eight lines from the Folio text, as well as the second Quarto's additional nine lines.[2] The most radical excisions occurred around the closet scene, weakening Gertrude's association with Hamlet, and leaving her an 'unresponsive, mindless figure, momentarily distraught by Hamlet's closet scene harangue, but ultimately unaffected by it'.[3]

Ghazala, a re-imagined Gertrude in the Indian film adaptation *Haider* (2014), rewrites Gertrude's role, stressing the tragic possibilities of a more fully delineated, more active Gertrude who drives the action of the play.[4] Directed by Vishal Bhardwaj, and co-written by Bhardwaj and Basharat Peer, the multi-language *Haider* is set in Kashmir in the 1990s. Claimed by both India and Pakistan, Kashmir is bloodied from decades of violence between two nations armed with nuclear weapons. In the film, Kashmir produces a powerfully reconfigured Gertrude in the character of Ghazala, whose fiery end as a suicide-bomber weaponizes Shakespeare's Gertrude.

Ghazala, who describes herself as a 'half-widow', seizes a devastating and self-annihilating agency; she wears a suicide-vest and blows herself up. I will argue that Ghazala is a version of the Hindu sati (a dual reference to the faithful Hindu good wife and the Hindu custom of burning widows at the pyre of their dead husbands). Ghazala's translation of the sati into a suicide-bomber is the key synecdoche for transporting the story of Hamlet to 1990s Kashmir, filling the vacuum in Gertrude's role with the cultural concerns of the film's own locus. Furthermore, by replacing the other memorable female suicide-bomber in *Hamlet* adaptations – Ophelia, who dies off-screen in Sulayman Al-Bassam's *Al-Hamlet Summit* (2004) – with Ghazala, *Haider* conflates the image of the feared Muslim female suicide-bomber with the non-threatening Hindu self-destructive wife who cannot live without her husband. Sati, used as a partial moral justification for the civilizing function of British rule in India, was precisely the sort of indigenous cultural violence that Western civilization and education, transmitted, for example, through the works of Shakespeare, would supposedly cure in India. Yet, *Haider* literalizes the Player Queen's admonition against widows marrying again, endorsing and amplifying early modern Europe's deep antagonism towards widow remarriage. In doing so, the film draws Shakespeare's early modern play into the nineteenth-century debates on sati. Interrogating the special place of Shakespeare's plays as entertainment and education in colonial India, *Haider* suggests that a rearticulated *Hamlet* does not merely speak to the loss and violence in Kashmir. Shakespeare's play is itself made to be a witness and participant, through visual iconography, in sati, India's own ritualized cultural violence against women.

India's *Hamlet*

Scholarship on Shakespeare's plays in India establishes their pervasive connection to the colonial and civilizing imperative of the British in India. Imported for the entertainment of East India Company officials, colonists and expatriates, Shakespeare's plays appeared in the English language repertoire theatres in Calcutta, the seat of the East India Company, and subsequently the capital of the colonial government (until 1911, when the colonial capital relocated to Delhi). From the late 1700s, Shakespeare's plays were regularly performed in venues such as *The Calcutta Theatre* or *The New Playhouse*, and later, the *Chowringhee*, and the *Sans Souci*.[5] Critical scrutiny of India's Shakespeare recognizes the special position of *Hamlet* in anglophone circles in late-eighteenth-century India. In the repertories of *The Calcutta Theatre/The New Playhouse*, a 1775 production of *Hamlet* marked its early influence and position of privilege among theatregoers of the time.[6] The *Calcutta Gazette* of 7 December 1786, recorded that the play was 'very high in public estimation', and there were requests for additional performances.[7] From the 1850s Shakespeare's plays were staged in Bombay's Parsi theatre, which in turn led to the development of what came to be recognized as Bollywood cinema.[8]

Although Shakespeare was already a fixture in popular entertainment venues, especially in the English-language repertory theatres in Calcutta and Bombay, his works also served as important pedagogical tools that sustained the imperial mission of civilizing and educating colonized British subjects. This mission advanced Englishness and English values through education in English language and literature, and championed the sort of schooling that eventually strengthened Western cultural hegemony.[9] After the Charter Act of 1813 advancing education for Indians under British rule, programmes specifically targeted towards native subjects in British India promoted 'the introduction among them of useful knowledge, and of religious and moral improvement'; subsequent debates and policies such as Macaulay's 'Minute of Indian Education' (1835), followed by Governor-General William Bentinck's 1835 English Education Act, formally institutionalized English as the medium of instruction in Indian education.[10] Imperial ideology was inscribed in the curriculum, and literary texts were chosen to enshrine the superiority of English over native literature and culture. Recall, for example, Macaulay's valuing 'a single shelf of a good European library' over all indigenous literatures of India and Arabia, the aim being to create a class of Indians 'in blood and colour, but English in taste, in opinions, in morals, and in intellect'.[11]

In the debates following Macaulay's 'Minute' and the 1835 Education Act, the importance of establishing this superiority became increasingly necessary: in 1838, J. Farish's 'Minute' from the Bombay Presidency proclaimed that 'The Natives must either be kept down by a sense of our power, or they must willingly submit from a conviction that we are more wise, more just, more humane, and more anxious to improve their condition than any other rulers they could possibly have'.[12] It is important to remember that the British mobilized the discourse of sati to justify colonial enterprise as another form of cultural education that established the moral superiority of English culture and values. These debates on sati also allowed their own advancement from 'a mercantile and commercial to a territorial and administrative British presence', in part, by citing the ethical obligation of 'White men saving brown women from brown men'.[13] *Hamlet* in India is inescapably bound to this British ideological restructuring of Indian education through which Shakespeare's works transferred English authority and English culture to define what it meant to be human and civilized.

Reading Shakespeare in colonial India also meant the 'marginalisation of the knowledge and belief systems of those who were conquered'.[14] Yet although Shakespeare and English literature were privileged over Indian languages and literatures, it was through the interpretations of Shakespeare in marginalized Indian languages that Shakespeare remained relevant in India. From the nineteenth century, an increasing number of translations and stage productions in Parsi theatre, and in various Indian languages, brought indigenous Shakespeares and many faces of *Hamlet* to Indian viewers.[15] With the technology of film, adaptations of Shakespeare also contributed to the growth and popularity of Bollywood.[16] Additionally, translations of Shakespeare's works participated in 'the complex production of the colonial subject'.[17] Yet, as is now increasingly evident, Shakespeare also became meaningful in India's own self-perception and sense of modernity.[18]

Unsettling *Hamlet* in *Haider*

If the use of Shakespeare in performance quickened the shift from colonialist ideology to alternate modernities in India, film adaptations continued to entrench the plays within contemporary geopolitical realities of their own regions and timeframes. Scholarship of Indian cinema and Shakespeare, both Bollywood and regional, has only recently been situated within the larger critical framework of Shakespeare criticism and film history, although the first Indian *Hamlet* film, Modi's *Khoon ka Khoon* (1935) appeared thirteen years before Olivier's iconic *Hamlet* (1948) and just thirty-six years after the world's first Shakespeare film, Herbert Beerbohm Tree's *King John* (1899).[19] Since Modi's *Khoon ka Khoon*, Indian filmmakers have taken up Shakespeare's play in various regional Indian languages and political situations, for instance in *Hamlet* (dir. Kishore Sahu, 1954; Urdu/Hindi languages), *Karmayogi* (dir. V. K. Prakash, 2012; Malayalam language) and *Hemanta* (dir. Anjan Dutt, 2016; Bengali language). These film adaptations of *Hamlet* augment the tradition of Indian performances of *Hamlet* on stage and screen even as they contribute to the growing influence of Shakespeare adaptations in world cinema.[20]

Haider occupies a key position in the sphere of Indian *Hamlet* adaptations. The film revises *Hamlet* in particularly disruptive ways. Such mutations of the original work, writes Jyotsna Singh, 'disturb Western viewers' epistemological certainties about the moral issues emanating from Shakespeare's play'.[21] The film tests the capacity of adaptations to unsettle the source text, and make it speak to the needs of its own cultural moment. Ghazala as a reconfigured Gertrude is a startling dislocation of Shakespeare's play, but there are other important departures. Most visibly, when Kashmir replaces Denmark, the play spills over from the contained Danish court to the blood-sodden mountains and valleys of Kashmir claimed by both India and Pakistan. The film's siting in Kashmir also connects it to other global and transnational adaptations which draw the viewers' attention to displaced peoples, migrants, refugees, and diasporic peoples whose loss of home is signalled but not recovered in debates of citizenship and conflicted borders.[22] Also disruptive is the film's use of the English language. As I have noted elsewhere, *Haider* radically shifts Shakespeare's early modern English into various linguistic registers, Urdu, Hindi, Kashmiri, Arabic and, briefly, Yiddish. A destabilized English alone is unable to express the scope of violence and loss in Kashmir.[23] Among other displacements, Hamlet's remarkable self-negotiation, specifically his 'To be, or not to be' soliloquy, is blared through a megaphone in the Kashmiri marketplace. *Haider* also shuffles and sometimes merges *Hamlet's* characters. Horatio and Ophelia are conflated into the character of Arshia, Haider's fiancée and a journalist; Rosencrantz and Guildenstern appear as the comically twinned Salmans (both share the same name and affect). Video-shop owners and purveyors of Hindi films, they are fans of the Bollywood star Salman Khan. Scenes from Hindi movies loop endlessly on a small screen in the video store, as incessant replays of a film-within-a film, the recurrent Bollywood excerpts distancing the viewer from Shakespeare's play even as they draw attention to their revisions of Hamlet's own play within a play.

Gertrude and Ghazala

As Ghazala, Gertrude assumes a new geopolitical significance far from Elsinore. Anglophone and non-anglophone *Hamlet* film adaptations variously project Gertrude as seductive, sexually active (Olivier, 1948; Kozintsev, 1964; Zeffirelli, 1990), ambitious, corporate (Almereyda, 2000; Al-Bassam, 2004) and murderous (Feng Ziaogang, 2006). Gertrude's death is accidental or perhaps suicidal (Almereyda, 2000; Doran, 2009).[24] In Bhardwaj's *Haider*, Ghazala dies as a suicide-bomber, unsettling *Hamlet* in important ways. The act of siting, or making local, Sonia Massai notes, challenges and modifies, and thereby facilitates the recovery of the creative possibilities of the Shakespearean text.[25] I suggest that Ghazala's visual representation and fiery self-immolation both extend and darken the latent potential of Shakespeare's Gertrude by pressing *Hamlet* into the painful cultural legacies of the film's location.

Haider's location in war-torn Kashmir defines the transformative shift from Gertrude of Elsinore to Ghazala as suicide-bomber. The narrative unfolds on the Indian side of the Line of Control between India and Pakistan. The army governs the militarized zone through AFSPA, the Armed Forces Special Powers Act, which suspends civil liberties in the Indian-controlled part of Kashmir under a special emergency anti-terrorism measure. In order to find terrorists and insurgents, the army employs surveillance, body searches, and rollcalls of residents. Some people are 'disappeared' or go missing without official explanation. Hand-written signs in English implore the UN and the world to help find spouses, parents, children: 'My father, where is he?'; 'Where are our loved ones?' Wives of disappeared men identify as 'half-widows'. Many young men join the insurgency or cross over to Pakistan to train as insurgents. Ghazala is instrumental in sending Haider/Hamlet off to university, far from his home in Indian-controlled Kashmir. When his father, Dr Meer, disappears after performing surgery on a suspected insurgent, Haider returns to find him. He discovers his mother with his uncle Khurram, the Claudius character of the film, soon to be married to him. As Haider finds his father in an unmarked grave, he also realizes that his uncle, a powerful figure in the army's counter-insurgency, informed on his father before his arrest and subsequent murder. The resulting violence, compounded by a visit by his father's vengeful ghost, and his fiancée Arshia's unravelling after the death of her brother and father, appears cyclical and fruitless until Ghazala intervenes. Whereas Shakespeare's Gertrude moves her son to kill Claudius with her dying words, 'The drink, the drink – I am poisoned' (5.2.295), Ghazala moves beyond words by resolving the situation with her own self-immolation. In the most basic sense then, Ghazala brings to fruition the plot-points that foreshadow her end.

Ghazala undercuts the film's largely masculine focus on violent extremism and a heightened father/son relationship. The cinematic gaze lingers on the Kashmiri landscape defaced by war and bloodshed, but the camera's eye repeatedly pivots to scenes of domestic interiority and familial relations. These shifts create a double narrative that buries a seemingly domestic account of home, mothers, wives and widows within the larger, global, story of bloodshed, loss, and the fragmentation of Kashmir. This narrative doubling forms a transitional arc that shifts Ghazala from an inadequate wife in the opening scenes to the sati at the end of the film, when Ghazala burns herself alive as the Hindu good wife who cannot live without her husband. The process shifts Ghazala Meer's Muslim identity into a Hindu one, stressing the crucial difference between the two communities. Muslims did not practice sati, whereas the wife/widow who burned herself alive was constructed as a virtuous Hindu woman.

FIGURE 8.1 *Wife and Mother.* Haider, *directed by Vishal Bhardwaj, UTV Pictures and Vishal Bhardwaj Pictures, 2014.*

The opening scene of the film stresses this connection between the violent strife in Kashmir and the twinned story of home, wife and mother. Before we see her home or meet Ghazala, home is already threatened, fragile and vulnerable to outside pressures. The fiery end of home and wife/mother (the sati) is anticipated in the first scene when Haider's father, Dr Meer, enters a patient's home. Later we are told the patient is a wanted militant in the area. One of the few discernible words the patient utters in pain is 'Mother!' Later, we will see how the complex ideation of the sati rests on the unlikely fusion of the wife and mother.

Dr Meer arranges to bring the patient home. Only when the outside – the hunted militant who needs medical attention – when *that* outside is already inside the walls of her home does Ghazala appear. What is a home, she asks her students as she looks out from the classroom and watches the ambulance making its way to her home, thereby setting off the chain of events that will reduce her home to rubble. Ghazala defines home as a space where a mother and father raise a child with love. When we first see her at home with her husband, the outsider, the hunted insurgent Latif is already inside. Her husband Dr Meer asks her to 'lower the flames' as she boils water to sterilize equipment for the medical procedure about

FIGURE 8.2 *Ashes to Ashes.* Haider, *directed by Vishal Bhardwaj, , UTV Pictures and Vishal Bhardwaj Pictures, 2014. All rights reserved.*

to take place in her home. As it turns out, the flames presage more than Ghazala's anger. Acting on a tip from their informant Khurram, Dr Meer's brother, the army blows up Ghazala's home in order to kill the suspected terrorist inside.

In response to her own question, 'What is a home?', Ghazala had identified home as the site of peaceful domestic interiority which housed parental love. Within the ashes of her ruined home, and among the objects randomly spared by the fire – a framed photograph, perhaps of her wedding day, a cricket bat, a battered sofa – are memories of her husband singing about love awakening a springtime garden, a lyric by the poet Faiz Abdul Faiz. At one level, the song speaks to the 'poetic and historical remnants of ruin, loss, and remembrance' by centring on the marital bed with its memories of home as a space where a mother and father raise a child with love, a definition that Ghazala offered her students.[26] Lyrical fragments evoking springtime and flowers also resurface in Khurram's house where Ghazala takes refuge. Khurram's house is not a home, and not a space for mothers. Memories of mothers are expunged. There is a fleeting shot of a photograph, presumably of the two brothers, Haider's father Dr Meer and his uncle Khurram, with their father. There is no mother in the photograph. As Haider enters the room in his uncle's house, he hears his mother sing about awakening a garden to life, in apparent betrayal of his father. The lyric's diegetic intervention allows the twinned narratives of the film – the larger war outside the home, and Ghazala's transformation into the singular figure of the sati – to collapse.

Despite her Muslim identity, the film visually constructs Ghazala as a version of the Hindu bad wife who remarries, then amends her to the sati, the eternal good wife, or self-sacrificing, virtuous Hindu widow. Although scriptural basis for the burning of widows was dubious at best, colonial reinterpretations of ancient Hindu texts produced the figure of the sati in binaries of 'good' and 'bad'. While a good wife may remain in ascetic widowhood or embrace the heroic martyrdom that many Western observers saw reflected in widow-burning, a bad wife may be a remarrying widow who desires a man other than her husband. Either way, these constructions foreclosed 'the possibility of a complex female agency'.[27] In *Haider*, Ghazala's desire to remarry brands her as a bad wife even as it invites Hindu disapproval of widow remarriage. Manu's laws (*c.* 100 CE), the authoritative source for the foundation of Hindu law, enjoined unquestioned devotion to a husband, a deity that was to be worshipped beyond death: 'Though of bad conduct or debauched, or even devoid of (good) qualities, a husband must always be worshipped like a god by a good wife'.[28] And if the god happened to die, the social conduct for widows required self-renunciation, fasting and celibacy. Upon her husband's death the good wife became an ascetic widow, a fading placeholder for her dead husband.

As a *remarried* widow, however, Ghazala becomes invisible. According to the logic that constructs Hindu widows into the sati, Ghazala's garden (in the lyric) cannot be permitted to be awakened as her song had entreated. Ghazala acknowledges that without her first husband, Haider's father, she will remain incomplete, 'half-widow and half-bride'. Ghazala does not expect to be whole, but it is unclear if she exists for her dead husband. In *Haider*, Ghazala appears to see the ghost, although her subsequent actions suggest she does not. The ghost ignores her, moves her hand, still marked by the mehndi from her wedding to his brother Khurram. The ghost tells Haider to aim the bullets between the eyes that entrapped his mother, indicating that it is Ghazala's betrayal that causes her widowhood. The wife who does not love enough brings his house, both the home and the family line, to ruin. In *Hamlet*, the ghost is equally certain that Gertrude was ensnared with witchcraft and 'traitorous gifts' (1.5.42). Shakespeare's Gertrude sees only 'vacancy' and 'incorporal air' (3.4.113–14) when her husband's ghost visits her son. She believes it is a 'bodiless creation' (3.4.135) of Hamlet's imagination. However, the ghost is keenly aware of his widow's body, her sexual 'falling off' (1.5.47), and her tumbling with 'an adulterate beast' while sating her 'ulcerous place' (1.5.41, 3.4.145). In *Haider*, Ghazala's desire to reawaken a garden rendered lifeless by the death of her husband connects her to early modern perceptions of the corrupt sexuality of widows through *Hamlet*'s metaphor of the 'unweeded garden / That grows to seed, things rank and gross in nature / Possess it merely' (1.2.135–7). Janet Adelman notes that the fear of the 'indiscriminately sexual maternal body' is localized in Hamlet's subsequent reference to the 'rank corruption' (3.4.146) of her erotic body.[29] In early modern Europe, reawakening the garden, or widow remarriage, although legal, was a complex and contentious issue that reflected the 'pluralistic contemporary attitudes toward widows',[30] pitting the claims of kinship and inheritance against the social management of women as constant and chaste.[31] Barbara Todd observes that many young widows, especially ones with small children, may have been encouraged to wed again, and a large number did remarry. The independent widow was an anomaly, for 'the ungoverned woman was a threat to social order'.[32] Yet, as Todd further observes, although the remarrying widow was a subject of comedy, 'remarriage of widows was becoming increasingly less common in the seventeenth century when stage widows flourished'.[33]

In *Hamlet*, the Player Queen foresees lasting strife if, once widowed, she were to marry again (3.2.216–17). Her dismissal of remarriage as obeying only the 'base respects of thrift, but none of love' (3.2.177) suggests that, in early modern Europe, the financial advantages of a second marriage may have been offset by a sense of betrayal to the first husband, what the Player Queen calls 'treason in my breast' (3.2.172). Although many European widows did remarry, and some commentators responded positively to their doing so, antipathy towards remarriage was expressed by both Catholic and Protestant writing on the conduct of widows. Spanish humanist Juan Luis Vives described a widow who remarried as lustful and a bad mother, one 'enflamed with vicious lust', one who 'forgetteth her own womb'.[34] For Protestant Thomas Overbury, the virtuous widow was holy and asexual, a 'relic, that, without any superstition in the world, though she will not be kissed, yet may be reverenced'.[35] Shakespeare's audiences would recognize both stereotypes of widows – the lascivious woman and bad mother as defined by Vives, and Overbury's widow devoted to a religious life, a woman who may not be kissed. Early modern widows were dually framed as both lecherous and simultaneously self-sacrificing, abstinent and filled with godly zeal, a dichotomy not dissimilar to the social constructions of Hindu widows in India.[36]

In Shakespeare's play, the widow who remarries is also a type of a bad wife and mother who does not love enough. Gertrude is Hamlet's 'cold mother' (1.2.77), a pitiless tiger who raises the 'Hyrcanian beast' (2.2.384–5), the savage animal that kills fathers. Shakespeare appears to associate *Hyrcania* with relentless inhumanity. Of the four variants of *Hyrcania* in the plays, two represent Hyrcanian beasts as physical entities with a corporal presence. Macbeth, for instance, would rather encounter the 'armed rhinoceros or th' Hyrcan tiger' than face Banquo's ghost' (3.4.102). Again, in *The Merchant of Venice*, Portia's taming influence subdues 'the Hyrcanian desert' so that her suitors may come from four corners of the world to worship at her shrine (2.4.45–7). However, when applied to female characters, the presumed inner qualities of Hyrcanian beasts are more potent than their physical attributes. In *3 Henry VI*, the Duke of York characterizes Queen Margaret as 'more inhuman more inexorable / O ten times more than tigers of Hyrcania' (1.4.159–60). In *Hamlet*, Gertrude's apparent lack of maternal love breeds Hyrcanian cruelty, a malignant, unfamilial unkindness that has no pity for her own kind, neither her murdered husband nor her grieving son. For Gertrude, Hyrcanian denotes faithlessness, the seal of a bad wife that brands her, like Claudius, as 'little more than kin, and less than kind' (1.2.65). Ironically, outside Shakespeare, in Marlowe and Nashe's *Dido, Queen of Carthage* for instance, the word often indicates inconstancy in a male character. Dido, another 'widow' who kills herself on the funeral pyre for the 'husband' who abandons her, characterizes the unfeeling Aeneas as bred by the 'Tygers of Hircania' (5.1.159).[37] In *Hamlet*, Gertrude's grief is not on public display. Unlike Player 1's grieving Hecuba, the 'mobled queen' who runs in barefooted frenzy, a 'clout' instead of a diadem on her head (2.2.440, 443–5), Gertrude remains silent. However, she comes to view her own desires as 'black and grieved spots' (3.4.88), more suited to bad wives than virtuous widows. This view is more in line with the Player Queen's avowal of constancy, 'A second time I kill my husband dead / When second husband kisses me in bed' (3.2.178–9).

In *Haider*, Ghazala moves inexorably towards the self-destruction that alters the bad wife into a virtuous one, or sati. Although her suicide-vest couples Ghazala with the menacing figure of the female suicide-bomber (coded as Muslim in the popular imagination), both early modern debates of bad wives as well as Hindu discourses of sati may be harnessed to read Ghazala as the manifestation of a deity possessing an abnormal and fearful female potency, one that makes her both untouchable and preternaturally powerful.[38] Many European observers of Hindu widow-burning found a redemptive pattern that amended the perceived bad wife into a good one. Although there is no prescribed ritual for widow-burning, and there are many cultural and regional differences in the social constructions of the burnings, for many spectators, the sati appeared to follow a recognizable arc of deliverance.[39] Thus transfigured, the sati placed 'herself in the context of a vivid temporal fiction' and experienced a personal transformation that exhibited her devotion in her death. The pyre purifies.[40] According to this cultural fiction, the shift, from bad wife to good, occurred at the moment of death, thereby assuring the sati's absolute (future) perfection. Presumably, the memory of her self-sacrifice cleansed her bodily trespasses. More than anything else, the self-sacrificing, self-immolating widow was a social and historical construct with 'mythological resonances'.[41] Through her self-immolation, it was thought, the widow's disruptive sexuality was extinguished. Her sinning body was refined into spirit, seared into the public imagination as a type of divine perfection. Reduced to ashes, the bad wife/widow could now be revived in cultural memory as the perfect and sacred exemplar of the devoted wife.

In *Haider*, Ghazala dies as both widow and bride. Before her self-immolation, the camera directs the viewer's gaze to the visible reminder of her bridal status, the red dye (*henna/mehndi*) on her hand presaging the blood to come. The *OED*'s earliest entry for *henna*, of Arabic etymology, is a usage recorded in 1600 in John Pory's *A Geographical History of Africa*. This buried referential web links henna with Leo Africanus' history of Africa via Pory's 1600 English translation, a source for *Othello*.[42] One may say that Ghazala's henna inserts into her location (Kashmir) early modern English perceptions of Africa and the constructions of racial and cultural difference elsewhere in the world. In India, the red dye is also commonly referred to as *mehndi*. Derived from the Sanskrit *mendhikā*, its first recorded entry in the *OED* dates from 1813, by which time it had become synonymous with *henna*.[43] The semantic transference of the red dye on Ghazala's hand from *henna* to *mehndi*, Arabic giving way to Hindi via Sanskrit, infers the linguistic pathway that maps Ghazala's shift from feared Muslim female suicide-bomber to the unthreatening Hindu sati.

In Fig. 8.3, the severed hand, still gripping the instrument of her death, encodes Ghazala simultaneously as bride and widow, echoing Ghazala's formulation of herself as 'half-widow, half-bride'. Ghazala's dismembered hand, blood replacing red dye, moves her towards the sanctified historicity of the social construction of sati as a voluntary sacrifice. If some in Shakespeare's audiences were aware of the practice of sati through the copious travelogues of India available in various European languages (and Englished regularly) from the 1500s, they would have encountered early modern eyewitness accounts inscribed in the vocabulary of heroic martyrdom.

The sati's complex epistemology also absorbs the idea of self-sacrificing motherhood. The process of dying transforms the woman into *sati-mata*, a mother and otherworldly being with special powers. Whether a widow was a mother or not, common chants of *sati-mata* elevated the widow into a sacred and protective mother of the community.[44] Through this remarkable apotheosis (see Fig. 8.4), the widow became sacred, a divine and terrible figure, a goddess/mother capable of

FIGURE 8.3 *By her own hand.* Haider, *directed by Vishal Bhardwaj, UTV Motion Pictures and Vishal Bhardwaj Pictures, 2014.*

FIGURE 8.4 *Apotheosis.* Haider, *directed by Vishal Bhardwaj, UTV Motion Pictures and Vishal Bhardwaj Pictures, 2014. All rights reserved.*

dispensing both benediction and curses. The archetypal sati, after all, is often seen as a version of the goddess Durga 'in her manifestation as a good wife'.[45] Such a figure is the subject of veneration, her devotion etched in stone, remembered in shrines and reproduced in the varied iconographies of the sati.[46] As a type of the sati Ghazala takes on some of these powers.[47] This process of elevation alters an erstwhile bad wife (one who did not love enough or wished to remarry) into a powerful, iconic and exalted figure. Ghazala foreshadows the link between a remarried wife and widow. Before her end as a suicide-bomber, she asks her son, 'Don't you want to see me as a widow again?'

Yet, Ghazala's decision to wear the suicide-vest complicates the narrative of the bad wife and sati I have outlined. Ghazala wears her 'rue with a difference' (4.5.175–6) by seizing her agency. She is not a victim. She is neither coerced nor manipulated nor yet compelled to the fire. Ghazala allows Shakespeare's Gertrude a powerful afterlife as a more fully realized character who asserts her multiple subject positions at a moment and place of her choosing. At the moment of her self-annihilation, Ghazala enacts both what it means to be and not to be a woman, a wife, a widow, a mother, a destroyer and creator. Like the cultural deity of the sati who was thought to bless the virtuous and punish the sinners in her community, Ghazala destroys her enemies. Haider survives, birthed into an improbable second life from the womb of the graveyard where his mother burns herself alive in violent self-sacrifice.

In *Haider*, Ghazala returns us more forcefully to *Hamlet's* tale of Hecuba and flaming Troy, a story transmitted through 'Aeneas's talk to Dido', a 'widow' who burns herself alive (2.2.384–5). In doing so, the film loops Shakespeare's play back to the 'contextual archeologies' of location that 'affectively and imaginatively reconstitute the fragments of Kashmir'.[48] Such an archaeology also illuminates the cross-cultural transfer from the colonial debates on sati taking place at the time of the early performances of Shakespeare, *Hamlet* prominently among those, in nineteenth-century Calcutta.[49] In my reading, this archaeology also fastens *Haider* to *Hamlet* through Ghazala's self-immolation, coupling Shakespeare's play to the modern versions of the cult of sati.[50]

In the final analysis, Gertrude refashioned as Ghazala may be read as an example of the way world cinema in general, and *Haider* in particular, take up *Hamlet* 'in order to allegorize the energies, instabilities, traumas and expectations that have defined the twentieth and twenty-first centuries'; in Mark Thornton Burnett's formulation, these rearticulated Shakespeares are 'traversed by resistant ideologies'.[51] Resistant ideologies in adaptations can be empowering, as Alexa Alice Joubin and Elizabeth Rivlin write, by licensing marginalized voices. However, they also note that Shakespeare's global reach invites pressing questions about the larger ethics of appropriation because non-Western productions can be viewed as 'fetishized commodities in the global marketplace'.[52] Concerning sati, one needs to be especially mindful of the ethics of appropriation. In the early modern context, the erotic spectacularity in eyewitness accounts of the practice often resulted in grotesque fetishizations and commodifications of the widow who burned herself alive. It was not uncommon for Europeans to collect relics and keepsakes for viewing at home.[53]

Through a fundamental remediation of Gertrude into Ghazala, *Haider* rearticulates and transports Shakespeare's play into the violent and fractured modernity of Kashmir. By insisting on turning viewers' gaze on the local, in this case, a fragmented Kashmir, the film also dislocates the original, Shakespeare's *Hamlet*, by reminding viewers of the play's own textual fragmentation. Reconstituted from Q1, Q2 and F, the splintered and revised *Hamlet* resists any sense of an original source text, thereby suggesting that Shakespeare's play is itself hybrid, shifting, altered and deeply responsive to adaptations.[54] However, one important question remains, can a fragmented Kashmir be reconstituted through this filmic process? Or is such a healing only and always in the viewers' imagination?

Notes

1 Janet Adelman, *Suffocating Mothers: Fantasies of Maternal Origin in Shakespeare's Plays, Hamlet to The Tempest* (New York: Routledge, 1992), 30.

2 Ellen J. O'Brien, 'Revision by excision: Rewriting Gertrude', *Shakespeare Survey* 45 (1992): 27–35 (27, 31–2).

3 Ibid., 34.

4 I have used the term 'Indian cinema' rather than 'Bollywood' or 'Hindi' cinema to preserve the film's multilingual emphasis and its Kashmiri setting. Terms such as Bollywood 'lead to the erasure and scholarly neglect' of the rich diversity of regional language cinemas in India. Poonam Trivedi and Paromita Chakravarti, 'Introduction', in *Shakespeare and Indian Cinemas: 'Local Habitations'*, ed. Poonam Trivedi and Paromita Chakravarti (New York: Routledge, 2019), 3. On differences in terminology between Bollywood, national, regional and local cinema in India, see also Craig Dionne and Parmita Kapadia, 'Introduction', in *Bollywood Shakespeares*, ed. Craig Dionne

and Parmita Kapadia (New York: Palgrave Macmillan, 2014), 1–18; Jyotsna Singh, *Shakespeare and Postcolonial Theory* (London: Arden Shakespeare, 2019), 178–9.

5 For a discussion of Shakespeare in colonial Indian theatres and the development of regional Indian drama and performances, see Jyotsna Singh, *Colonial Narratives Cultural Dialogues: 'Discoveries' of India in the Language of Colonialism* (London: Routledge, 1996), 120–52. See also Poonam Trivedi, 'Introduction', in *India's Shakespeare: Translation, Interpretation, and Performance*, ed. Poonam Trivedi and Dennis Bartholomeusz (Newark: University of Delaware Press, 2005), 13–43; Sukanta Chaudhuri, 'Shakespeare's India', in *India's Shakespeare*, ed. Trivedi and Bartholomeusz, 158–67.

6 Mark Thornton Burnett, *'Hamlet' and World Cinema* (Cambridge: Cambridge University Press, 2019), 153.

7 Quoted in Sarottama Majumdar, 'That Sublime "Old Gentleman"; Shakespeare's Plays in Calcutta, 1775–1930', in *India's Shakespeare*, ed. Trivedi and Bartholomeusz, 260–8.

8 On Shakespeare, Parsi theatre and early Bollywood, see Vikram Singh Thakur, 'Parsi Shakespeare: The Precursor to "Bollywood Shakespeare"', in *Bollywood Shakespeares,* ed. Dionne and Kapadia, 29–43.

9 Gauri Vishwanathan, *Masks of Conquest: Literary Study and British Rule in India* (New York: Columbia University Press, 1989), 2.

10 Ibid., 23, 44.

11 Thomas B. Macaulay, 'Minute on Indian Education', in *Selected Writings,* ed. John Clive and Thomas Pinney (1835; Chicago: University of Chicago Press, 1972), 241.

12 J. Farish quoted in Vishwanathan, *Masks of Conquest*, 2.

13 Gayatri Spivak, 'Can the Subaltern Speak?' in *Marxism and the Interpretation of Culture*, ed. Cary Nelson and Louis Grossberg (Urbana: University of Illinois Press, 1988), 271–313 (297).

14 Ania Loomba, *Colonialism/Postcolonialism* (London: Routledge, 1998), 66, 85.

15 See Supriya Chaudhuri, 'Shakespeare in India: Colonial and Postcolonial Memory', in *Celebrating Shakespeare:*

Commemoration and Cultural Memory, ed. Clara Calvo and Coppélia Kahn (Cambridge: Cambridge University Press, 2015), 101–20; Trivedi, 'Introduction', in *India's Shakespeare,* 6–8; Trivedi and Chakravarti, eds., *Shakespeare and Indian Cinemas*, 10.

16 Burnett, *Hamlet and World Cinema*, 154–5; Brinda Charry and Gitanjali Shahani, 'The Global as Local / Othello as Omkara', in *Bollywood Shakespeares*, ed. Dionne and Kapadia, 107–23.

17 Tejaswini Niranjana, 'Translation, Colonialism and the Rise of English', in *Rethinking English: Essays in Literature, Language, History* (Delhi: Oxford University Press, 1994), esp. 124, 126.

18 Partha Chatterjee, 'The Constitution of Indian Nationalist Discourse (1987)', in *Empire and Nation: Selected Essays* (New York: Columbia University Press, 2010); Jasodhara Bagchi, 'Shakespeare in Loin Cloths: English Literature and the Early Nationalist Consciousness in Bengal', in *Rethinking English: Essays in Literature, Language, History*, ed. Svati Joshi (Delhi: Oxford University Press, 1994), 146; Loomba, *Colonialism/ Postcolonialism*, 89–92.

19 Trivedi and Chakravarti, 'Introduction', 1. On Shakespeare, Bollywood and Hindi cinema, see also Rajiva Verma, 'Shakespeare in Hindi Cinema', in *India's Shakespeare*, ed. Trivedi and Bartholomeusz, 269–90; Paromita Chakravarti, 'Interrogating 'Bollywood Shakespeare': Reading Rituparno Ghosh's *The Last Lear*', in *Bollywood Shakespeares*, ed. Dionne and Kapadia, 127–45.

20 Burnett, *Hamlet and World Cinema*, 153–87.

21 Singh, *Shakespeare and Postcolonial Theory*, 182.

22 See Rosa M. Garcia-Periago, 'The Ambiguities of Bollywood Conventions and the Reading of Transnationalism in Vishal Bhardwaj's *Maqbool*', in *Bollywood Shakespeares*, ed. Dionne and Kapadia, 63–86.

23 Pompa Banerjee, '"Accents yet unknown": *Haider* and *Hamlet* in Kashmir', *Shakespeare Survey* 71 (2018): 405–9.

24 On Hamlet performances, see *Hamlet*, The Arden Shakespeare, ed. Ann Thompson and Neil Taylor (London: Thomson, 2006), vol. 1, 97–125, 161–8; Burnett, '*Hamlet*' *and World Cinema*. For representations of Gertrude as a remarrying widow in films and in

different versions of the text, see Dorothea Kehler, *Shakespeare's Widows* (New York: Palgrave Macmillan, 2009), 139–69.

25 Sonia Massai, 'Defining Local Shakespeares', in *World-wide Shakespeares: Local Appropriations in Film and Performance*, ed. Sonia Massai (London: Routledge, 2005), 3–11.

26 Singh, *Shakespeare and Postcolonial Theory*, 181.

27 Lata Mani, *Contentious Traditions: The Debate on Sati in Colonial India* (New Delhi: Oxford University Press, 1998), 31, 32–41.

28 *The Ordinance of Manu*, trans. A. C. Burnell, ed. E. W. Hopkins (New Delhi: Munshiram Manoharlal, 1995), 130.

29 Adelman, *Suffocating Mothers*, 14, 17.

30 For commentators who encouraged widow remarriage, see Elizabeth Oakes, '*The Duchess of Malfi* as a Tragedy of Identity', *Studies in Philology* 96(1) (1999): 51–67 (53).

31 Lisa Jardine, *Still Harping on Daughters: Women and Drama in the Age of Shakespeare* (Brighton: Harvester, 1983), 84–93; Karen Newman, *Fashioning Femininity and English Renaissance Drama* (Chicago: University of Chicago Press, 1991).

32 Barbara Todd, 'The Remarrying Widow: A Stereotype Reconsidered', in *Women in English Society 1500–1800*, ed. Mary Prior (London: Methuen, 1985), 54–83 (55–6).

33 Ibid., 61, 68.

34 Juan Luis Vives, 'The Instruction of a Christian Woman' (1529), in *Renaissance Woman: A Sourcebook*, ed. Kate Aughterson (London: Routledge, 1995), 74. In contrast, see the analysis of Jennifer Panek, where remarriage was both common and socially, economically and morally approved, and the lusty widow stereotype 'worked as an enabler rather than a preventer of remarriage', in *Widows and Suitors in Early Modern English Comedy* (Cambridge: Cambridge University Press, 2004), 10–11.

35 Thomas Overbury, 'The Good Wife' (1614), in *The Cultural Identity of Seventeenth-Century Woman: A Reader*, ed. N. H. Keeble (London: Routledge, 1994), 253–4.

36 For the social construction of early modern widowhood on stage, see also Kehler, *Shakespeare's Widows*. For similarities between the sati and early modern European widows, see Pompa

Banerjee, *Burning Women: Widows, Witches, and Early Modern European Travellers in India* (New York, Palgrave Macmillan, 2003), 127–35.

37 Cited in *Hamlet*, ed. Thompson and Taylor, vol. 1, 297, n. 388.

38 Deborah Willis, *Malevolent Nurture: Witch-Hunting and Maternal Power in Early Modern England* (Ithaca: Cornell University Press, 1995), 14, 65–81.

39 Dorothy M. Figuera, 'Die Flambierte Frau: Sati in European Culture', in *Sati: The Blessing and the Curse,* ed. John S. Hawley (Oxford: Oxford University Press, 1994), 55–78 (67).

40 Lindsey Harlan, 'Perfection and Devotion: Sati Tradition in Rajasthan', in *Sati: The Blessing and the Curse,* 81.

41 See Veena Talwar Oldenburg, 'The Continuing Invention of the Sati Tradition', in *Sati: The Blessing and the Curse*, 159–73 (169).

42 See Emily C. Bartels, 'Making More of the Moor: Aaron, Othello, and Renaissance Refashionings of Race', *Shakespeare Quarterly* 41(4) (Winter 1990): 433–54, esp. 435.

43 *OED* online, accessed 24 November 2019.

44 Harlan, 'Perfection and Devotion', 79–99.

45 Gayatri Spivak, A *Critique of Postcolonial Reason* (Cambridge: Harvad University Press, 1999), 305.

46 See Paul B. Courtright, 'The Iconographies of the Sati', in *Sati: The Blessing and the Curse,* 27–53

47 Scholars connect her to other powerful maternal figures as well. Poonam Trivedi sees Ghazala as a type of the heroic female warrior and avenger: 'Woman as Avenger: "Indianising" the Shakespearean Tragic in the Films of Vishal Bhardwaj', in *Shakespeare and Indian Cinemas*, ed. Trivedi and Chakravarti, 23–44.

48 Singh, *Shakespeare and Postcolonial Theory*, 179.

49 See Spivak, 'Can the Subaltern Speak?', 271–313; Mani, *Contentious Traditions.*

50 On contemporary discourses of sati in India, including the case of Roop Kanwar (1987), see Veena T. Oldenburg, 'The Roop Kanwar Case: Feminist Responses', in *Sati: The Blessing and the Curse,* 101–30.

51 Burnett, *'Hamlet' and World Cinema,* 2, 158

52 Alexa Alice Joubin and Elizabeth Rivlin, 'Introduction', in *Shakespeare and the Ethics of Appropriation*, eds. Alexa Alice Joubin and Elizabeth Rivlin (New York: Palgrave Macmillan, 2014), 1–20 (1).

53 For early modern souvenir hunters, see Banerjee, *Burning Women*, 200–10. For the commercial exploitation of the 1987 Roop Kanwar case, see Oldenburg, 'The Roop Kanwar Case', esp. 107.

54 For the play's textual challenges, and the relationship between Q1, Q2, and F, see Thompson and Taylor's notes in *Hamlet*, vol. 1, esp. 76–96.

9

'Most Eloquent Music' (and Multiple Texts)

The 2017 Glyndebourne Opera of *Hamlet*

Neil Taylor and Ann Thompson

'Many composers have tried to make an opera out of *Hamlet*, but none has been able to make one stick. Until now? Brett Dean's *Hamlet* – his second opera, and Glyndebourne's first new commission in nearly a decade – feels like it has a better shot at longevity than most,' wrote Erica Jeal in *The Guardian* on 12 June 2017. This was typical of the very positive reviews garnered by the opera which opened on 11 June, had a live cinema broadcast on 6 July, and was televised on BBC4 on 22 October that year. The production also toured from 21 October to 1 December to Canterbury, Norwich, Milton Keynes and Plymouth. It is now available as a DVD.[1]

We attended the Final Dress Rehearsal on 8 June; Ann had previously been involved on 11 May in a one-off event called

'*Hamlet* and the Test of Time' at the Sam Wanamaker Playhouse, presented jointly by Glyndebourne and Shakespeare's Globe. It began with an introduction to the opera by the composer and two of the principal singers, Allan Clayton (Hamlet) and Barbara Hannigan (Ophelia), who performed excerpts to a piano accompaniment. This was followed by a panel discussion on the enduring appeal of *Hamlet* and on the variety of ways in which it has been presented, adapted and interpreted. The panel was hosted by the television and radio presenter Melvyn Bragg and featured Neil Armfield, the director of the opera, Ian McEwan, author of a recent novel, *Nutshell*, a retelling of the Hamlet story,[2] Simon Russell Beale, a memorable Hamlet at London's National Theatre in 2000, and Tom Bird, Executive Producer at Shakespeare's Globe and producer of the Globe's *Hamlet* world tour which visited 197 countries between 2014 and 2016. Ann was included on the panel because of having co-edited, with Neil, all three texts of *Hamlet* for the Arden Shakespeare third series.

We should at the outset emphasize that we are not specialists in music or opera but editors in a series which, after much argument, eventually allowed us to edit and publish those three texts – the 1603 'bad' Quarto, the 1604/5 'good' Quarto and the 1623 Folio (hereinafter referred to as Q1, Q2 and F). Our particular interest is in Matthew Jocelyn's libretto for the opera which offered an unusually eclectic text and constituted a striking development of (or departure from) the editorial tradition to which our edition(s) responded and contributed. We are also intrigued by the extensive but largely forgotten tradition of operatic versions of *Hamlet*. The standard reference work, *A Shakespeare Music Catalogue*, edited by Bryan N. S. Gooch, David Thatcher and Odean Long,[3] contains 1,406 entries for *Hamlet*, mainly for symphonies, musicals, settings of songs, incidental music for stage productions and film scores, but including 139 for 'operas and related music'. The most familiar *Hamlet*-related music today is probably by Dmitri Shostakovich: his Fifth Symphony (1937, known as 'the Hamlet Symphony' in the former Soviet Union) and his score for Grigori Kozintsev's 1964 film. Recent books on 'Shakespeare and music' typically contain very few or no references to *Hamlet*.[4] We shall have a little more to say below about one of the previous *Hamlet* operas which has arguably 'stuck' (at least a little), the one by Ambroise Thomas and librettists Jules Barbier and Michel Carré, which premièred in Paris in 1868.[5] But our main focus is on the Dean/Jocelyn version and its approach to the multiple texts of the play.

The plot

Matthew Jocelyn explains in the leaflet issued with the DVD of the Glyndebourne production that

> the first thing that I said to Brett in our very first conversation was that, to my belief, there is no such thing as *Hamlet* . . . any production we've ever seen and any edition we've ever read is actually a conflation of some form or another. That, for me, was a great liberation because it meant that what we have is a whole bunch of raw material and nobody can tell us, 'No, that's not *Hamlet*'.
>
> (7)

Nevertheless, despite knowing there are three *Hamlet* texts, Jocelyn and Dean began their collaboration by writing down the principal ideas they felt to be essential for 'telling the *Hamlet* story' (ibid., 8). In other words, they couldn't rid themselves of the assumption that there is a single '*Hamlet* story', and they came up with a simplified version of the plot lines operating in Shakespeare's texts – a version they described as an 'intense psychological thriller' (Neil Armfield, the director, speaking in the BBC4 broadcast) in twelve scenes:

1. The Funeral [an invented scene]. Hamlet is at the graveside, lamenting his father's death and tempted to

commit suicide. He sings 'What ceremony else?' introducing a parallel with Laertes in The Second Funeral.

2 The Wedding [drawing on 1.2, 1.3]. Laertes warns Ophelia against believing Hamlet's professions of love. Hamlet learns that Horatio and Marcellus have seen his father's Ghost.

3 The Visitation [1.5]. The Ghost tells Hamlet that Claudius poisoned him. Hamlet promises to take revenge.

4 The Conspiracy Theory [2.1, 2.3, 3.1]. Rosencrantz and Guildenstern arrive. Polonius reckons his daughter has sent Hamlet mad by rejecting his love letters. Spying on Hamlet when he is with Ophelia, Claudius and Polonius witness him brutally telling her to enter a nunnery, but then join her, singing snatches of 'But yet I do believe' and 'There's something in his soul' while she sings 'Never doubt I love.'

5 The Players [2.2]. Hamlet asks some itinerant actors to perform his version of *The Murder of Gonzago* before Claudius. He and Horatio agree that, by means of the play, 'we'll catch the conscience of the King'.

6 The Play's the Thing [3.2]. Claudius stops the performance and Hamlet calls out 'Murderer!'

7 The Confession [3.3]. Hamlet discovers Claudius at prayer, thinks of killing him but decides to do it when he is less likely to go to Heaven.

8 Murder and Incest [3.4]. Hamlet enters his mother's ante-chamber, unaware that Polonius is hiding there. Mother and son quarrel, Polonius calls out and Hamlet, believing it is Claudius, kills him. Hamlet accuses Gertrude of betraying his father and the Ghost appears to Hamlet, chiding him for failing to kill Claudius. Hamlet tells Gertrude not to sleep with Claudius and leaves his mother lamenting that he has 'cleft her heart in twain'.

9 Madness and Mad Plans [4.5, 4.7]. Having learnt that Hamlet killed Polonius, and seeing that his sister is demented, Laertes conspires with Claudius to engineer Hamlet's death. Gertrude enters with the news that Ophelia is drowned.

10 The Second Funeral [5.1]. Hamlet and Horatio come across a man digging Ophelia's grave. When the funeral party arrives Hamlet launches into a fight with Laertes, proclaiming his love for Ophelia.

11 The Wager [5.2]. Hamlet is told that Claudius has laid a bet that he cannot beat Laertes in a fencing match. Hamlet accepts the challenge but Horatio is full of foreboding.

12 Death [5.2]. As Hamlet and Laertes begin fencing, Claudius poisons a cup of wine and offers it to Hamlet. But Gertrude takes it, drinks and dies. Having been wounded, Hamlet picks up Laertes's rapier, which has a poisoned tip, wounds Laertes (who confesses his and Claudius' treachery), kills Rosencrantz and Guildenstern, then stabs Claudius and forces him to drink from the poisoned cup. He asks the dying Laertes for forgiveness, then makes Horatio promise to tell his story to the world. Horatio sings 'flights of angels sing thee to thy rest' while Hamlet sings 'The rest is silence', the two 'rests' overlapping. Hamlet dies.

Hamlet is one of Shakespeare's longest and most complex plays, and attempts to make an opera out of it are pretty well bound to involve simplification, and therefore reinvention, not only of the dialogue but of the plot itself. As this synopsis makes clear, Jocelyn's libretto presents a reduced version of the action embodied in Q1, Q2 and F. It skips the play's opening scene on the castle battlements and uses only one scene (Ophelia's mad scene) of the seven scenes which make up Act 4. The chief reason for these omissions is the decision to (a) drop Fortinbras from the cast list and (b) strip out the plot element involving the King's failed attempt to send Hamlet to his death in England.

Both these excisions have long histories in theatrical tradition. Fortinbras was normally cut from productions of the play in England from 1732 until 1897. In France, the same cut was made in Alexandre Dumas's influential 1847 production, which also omitted Claudius's attempt on Hamlet's life, while heightening attention on Hamlet and Ophelia's love affair and trying to bring symmetry, moral clarity and neo-classical unity to the play's action, time and place. This involved bringing the Ghost back at the end to see that justice is done and seen to be done: Claudius, Laertes and Gertrude must die, but Hamlet will live on as King of Denmark.[6]

In 1868, the composer Ambroise Thomas had a great success with his French version. As well as further reducing the cast list by dropping Rosencrantz and Guildenstern, his librettists decided that Hamlet does not kill Polonius or Laërte, while Gertrude is not poisoned but is told by the Ghost that she should get to a nunnery instead. And there are many more modifications. For example, having delivered the 'To be or not to be' soliloquy while alone in his mother's bedroom, Hamlet hears her approaching with Polonius, slips behind an arras and discovers that they are both fully aware that Claudius murdered his father. As a consequence Hamlet refuses to carry out his mother's wish that he marry Polonius' daughter. Act 4 is effectively devoted to the staging of Ophélie's reaction to this decision, and it is Hamlet's rejection alone which unhinges her. Her death by drowning is no longer an offstage event and the whole act becomes in many ways the musical and theatrical showpiece of the opera. Act 5 continues the emphasis on Hamlet's love for Ophélie. The Ghost appears, proclaiming Claudius' guilt, instructing Gertrude to get to a nunnery, and telling Hamlet that he is now the rightful King of Denmark. Amid the celebrations, Hamlet sings 'Mon âme est dans la tombe, hélas!'

Both Dumas's play and Thomas's opera alter not just the plot but the moral, political and psychological compass of

Shakespeare's play. The absence of Fortinbras removes the ambiguities raised by Fortinbras's appearance as both *deus ex machina* and foreign invader at the play's end. And, by not including the plot in which Claudius attempts to banish Hamlet from Denmark and have him killed in England, both versions reduce or at least alter some of the complexity in our attitude to Hamlet. We no longer have to weigh the significance of the fact that he is perfectly capable of ingenious, pragmatic, decisive and callous action – outwitting his enemy, escaping his treacherous friends, and, before seizing the opportunity to jump ship and find his way home, deliberately sending Rosencrantz and Guildenstern to premeditated deaths ('They are not near my conscience', 5.2.57).

Dean's opera tops and tails the opening and closing of the play, and it adopts the French strategy of simplification, dropping Fortinbras and the English adventure. But, as the synopsis above makes clear, there are comparatively few major changes to the broad outlines of 'the Hamlet story' and scenes 2 to 12 follow the order of Shakespeare's twenty, though the scene between Hamlet and Ophelia and 'To be or not to be' follow the Q1 (earlier) placing rather than Q2/F. Dean's major innovation is to allow Rosencrantz and Guildenstern to live until Hamlet discovers what he takes to be their treachery in the final scene, and then for Hamlet to kill them. He also omits Hamlet's decision at 1.5.170 to put on an antic disposition, and in its absence we are forced (at least in the Glyndebourne production) to regard Hamlet's eccentric manner and gestures as either innate or the symptoms of a conflicted psyche brought on by recent traumas. Ophelia's mad scene (at least in Armfield's direction) is the theatrical highpoint of the opera and Hamlet's relationship with her is even more complex than in Shakespeare, for amidst the cruelty of the nunnery scene (scene 4) there is a point at which each sings 'Never, never, never, never, never / Doubt I love'. Another feature of the opera's narrative is the increased presence of Horatio and the strengthening of Hamlet's relationship with him (they jointly plot to incriminate Claudius and the opera ends with a duet – Hamlet's final words sung simultaneously with Horatio's valediction). Dean and Jocelyn do not, however, take up the opportunity offered by Q1 to expand on the role of the Queen, for example in the scene unique to Q1 (scene 14) in which she meets secretly with Horatio, hears about Hamlet's return to Denmark and determines to deceive her husband.

Dean also adds a new, important member to the cast list by accepting the convention of the operatic chorus, using it sometimes to give voice to Shakespeare's anonymous and usually silent characters, but more often allowing his singers to repeat and emphasize certain phrases supplied by the named characters – lines which point up a 'reading' of the action. In scene 3, for example, the chorus is offstage but echoing Hamlet's fear at the appearance of the Ghost ('Angels and ministers of grace, defend us!'). In scene 9, the semi-chorus repeats Ophelia's insistent repetitions of the word 'never'. 'Never' comes from two quite different sources and contexts in the play – Hamlet's letter in which he had proclaimed 'Never doubt I love' (2.2.117) and the lament she sings about Polonius, 'And will a' not come again?' (4.5.182). The effect is to reinforce the convergence of the two events which have driven her mad, her lover's rejection and her father's death. A few lines later, when she leaves the stage, the semi-chorus repeats the phrase 'Mad as the sea' (4.1.7), which Jocelyn gives, not only to Gertrude, but to Rosencrantz and Guildenstern as well. The phrase in Shakespeare's play is Gertrude's comment to Claudius, not on Ophelia but on Hamlet – a comment now rendered ironic in multiple ways, because: (a) Ophelia's madness is of a different kind and order to Hamlet's; (b) in the play Gertrude's account of Hamlet's behaviour to Claudius was full of possible ambiguities (for example, Hamlet has told her that he isn't really mad, but she apparently protects him by telling her husband that he is) and these may here bleed into her more straightforward response to Ophelia's behaviour; and (c) Rosencrantz and Guildenstern's response must be still more straightforward.

The words

Winston Dean argued in 1964 that 'a scrupulous respect for Shakespeare's text and a refusal to tamper with it except for a few cuts . . . sounds admirable, but it makes the task of the composer very much harder.'[7] Humphrey Searle's 1968 serial *Hamlet* kept close to Shakespeare's text but was not highly rated, and Andrew Clements, who reviewed Dean's Glyndebourne version, wrote that the more successful recent operas of Shakespeare's plays 'have opted for texts that put some distance between their librettos and Shakespeare's words'.[8] Jocelyn's libretto deals only in Shakespeare's words, but, as these examples from the chorus's contributions reveal, he creates 'distance' by not always placing the words where Shakespeare placed them.

Hamlet editors before our 2006 multiple-text Arden edition assumed their task was to bring to light a single lost play, clues to which could be found in Q1, Q2 and F; they therefore constructed a theory to explain how those texts emerged and then produced an eclectic fourth text conforming with that theory. Our decision to refuse to prioritize one text over another, but treat each as an independent entity and eschew eclecticism, has been described as both the culmination and the exhaustion of the dominant postmodern approach to editing.[9] Jocelyn's libretto is a return to a form of eclecticism, drawing as it does on all three early texts. But, at the same time, it is a further development of a postmodern approach by treating Q1, Q2 and F as one great textual treasure trove, selecting particular words, lines or speeches from across all three texts. We will focus on three scenes which nicely illustrate Jocelyn's method in action – scenes 1, 4 and 5.

Scene 1: The Funeral

We find ourselves at the tail end of the late King of Denmark's burial and the scene closes with an introduction to the next scene (The Wedding), in which the new King hosts a celebration of his marriage to the late King's widow. But while the scene has a narrative function, it has another, very different function, for it establishes immediately the nature of the libretto's relationship to Shakespeare's words.

What both Hamlet and a chorus of mourners sing in this opening scene is made up entirely of phrases extracted from speeches by Hamlet within Shakespeare's play, with the one exception we have mentioned above, Laertes' 'What ceremony else?' This means that the audience is required to focus simultaneously on three things – (1) the unfolding events on the stage before them, (2) events yet to unfold in the 'Hamlet story', and (3) events in another text altogether. Anyone reasonably familiar with Shakespeare's text will realize that these phrases come from scenes right across the play and are delivered out of sequence – the order being 5.1, 2.2, 3.1, 1.4, 3.4, 5.1, 1.2, 3.4, 1.2, 1.5, 5.2, 1.4. When they appear again in the opera almost all appear in the appropriate place within the unfolding action. Sometimes, however, they appear more than once, and not always as utterances by Hamlet.

Nineteenth-century operettas and twentieth-century musicals often included as an overture a medley of the tunes to come later in the work. This first scene is a verbal overture of that kind, selecting, condensing and refining material from the scenes ahead. Neil Armfield described the play of *Hamlet* as 'Shakespeare's great poem, which . . . Matthew [Jocelyn] has turned into his own great poem' (DVD leaflet, 10). If the opera is a poem, then this scene is a modernist poem within a poem – fragmented, cryptic and self-referential.

The DVD of Armfield's Glyndebourne production begins with a close-up of Hamlet's head in his hands, his face despairing and wild. The camera begins to pull back and we find that, while he is otherwise engulfed in the blackness of a darkened stage, his face is lit from below. The source is not footlights, as one might suspect, but his father's grave, into which he is staring and groping. Whereas Shakespeare's play begins with external events, with soldiers up on the battlements and national preparations for an international impending war, Dean's opera is focused on one man and the emotional war within his head.

Hamlet begins to sing – '. . . or not to be. / . . . or not to be. / . . . or not to be'. A few lines later he returns to the phrase, sandwiched between a repeated '. . . or not'. The effect is complex. When we hear him sing '. . . or not to be', we inevitably think of the whole phrase 'To be, or not to be', words which Shakespeare's Hamlet is speaking at 3.1.55 as he walks onto the stage, so that we know we are tuning in to a train of thought already running in his mind. Here in the opera, we can't help imagining that we have just tuned in, but one or two seconds late, to that soliloquy in the play, where the train of thought is primarily a debate Hamlet has been having with himself about the merits and demerits of committing suicide. Indeed, this might seem to be confirmed by the fact that, half-way through his aria, Hamlet is singing 'O that the Everlasting had not fix'd / His canon 'gainst self-slaughter'. But these lines have been extracted from a different soliloquy in the play, delivered the moment Hamlet is first alone on stage (1.2.129–59). However, that first soliloquy in the play is much more about his mother's marriage than it is about suicide. So the allusions to the two spoken soliloquies invoked in the sung soliloquy lead us in different directions. And while these 'quotations' from the play indicate that the Hamlet of the opera is struggling to cope with ideas about incest and self-slaughter, his persistent invocation of the concept 'not to be', along with the physical staging of the man with his head in a grave, indicate that, more than anything else, he is overwhelmed by his confrontation with death, the condition of no longer being, of being not. The aria ends 'The rest is . . . / The rest is . . . / The readiness is all'. Thus the scene looks forward stoically to the opera's last scene ('Death'), whose final line completes the phrase he is here adumbrating, 'the rest is silence'.

Scene 4: The Conspiracy Theory

It is three scenes later and Hamlet is once again playing over that same half phrase, '. . . or not to be'. Only after he has repeated it twice more do we finally hear 'To be . . .' and get the satisfaction of a kind of closure. But it is a perverse closure, for the resulting phrase is 'or not to be. / To be' (like an extremely compressed version of the opening and closing of *Finnegans Wake*, in which the end is the beginning). However, just when we might expect the words 'To be' to herald the familiar Hamlet soliloquy we've been waiting for, we get instead

To be . . . ay, there's the point.

We've suddenly stumbled into the text of Q1 rather than Q2 or F. Andrew Clements was wrong to write in his *Opera* review that Dean and Jocelyn were 'basing their text on the less familiar first quarto' (1076) – only 449 words out of the libretto's 7,797 come from Q1 – but he was surely right to invoke the concept of reduced familiarity, for, as Jonathan Cross put it in a review of the Glyndebourne touring production, Dean sets out to 'defamiliarise the all-too-familiar'.[10] Using much of Q1's version of the most familiar of familiar soliloquies certainly has that effect. Jocelyn felt that there was enough material across the three-text treasury to arrange and 'rhythmically rethink' *Hamlet* (DVD leaflet, 7), and one of Q1's features is its departures from Q2's rhythms as well as its words. But Jocelyn doesn't stick to Q1's words or rhythms either, and the opera's lines tend to be shorter than those in the play because, even though every line is a Shakespeare line, the whole of that line is not always used.[11]

Once Polonius has instructed Ophelia to 'walk you here – / Read on this book' (3.1.42–3), the libretto describes Hamlet as entering '*in his own world, as is Ophelia . . . despite the overlap of thoughts*'. The idea of 'overlap' has been there from the beginning of the opera. The DVD's recording of the Glyndebourne production slowly reveals the fact that, while scene 1 focuses on Hamlet's tormented vigil at his father's graveside outdoors, the full chorus can be dimly seen simultaneously in the background, seated indoors at his stepfather's wedding feast. Thus two 'worlds', one exterior and one interior, are presented simultaneously. Similarly, the libretto identifies three groups of characters present at the feast in scene 2, labelling them 'A' (Claudius, Gertrude, Polonius and the chorus), 'B' (Laertes and Ophelia) and 'C' (Hamlet, Horatio and Marcellus). Their lines come from two different scenes (A is drawn largely from 1.2.1–128, B from 1.2.42–57 and 1.3.2–111, and C from 1.2.135–243), but the action moves back and forth between all three groups (ABABCACABA) and there is some interaction between some members of different groups. And in scene 3, where Hamlet meets and listens to the Ghost, the libretto departs from Shakespeare by not leaving the two of them alone on stage for the whole of their tête-à-tête: after 43 lines, '*Horatio arrives – though not in the same time-space frame as Hamlet and the Ghost*' and what then follows is described as a duet/trio, in which '*Hamlet is at once hearing the story from his father and reporting what he has heard from his father to Horatio*'. The 'overlap' in scene 4 is evidenced by Ophelia punctuating Hamlet's soliloquy by, on three occasions, supplying the line 'But for this, the joyful hope of this' (Q1: 7.123), which is rightly Hamlet's but which he omits.

Hamlet has to cope with trying to hold together, and make sense of, utterly contradictory emotional and intellectual material. His lover rejects him. He loves his mother but she loves his hated stepfather. His revered father tells him to kill Claudius (his King/uncle/stepfather), while not hurting Gertrude (his Queen/aunt/mother). This conflicted psychological state finds musical expression in Dean's repeated 'Hamlet chord' – 'a four-note, sometimes five-note chord that is intended to convey uncertainty, indecision, ambiguity and possibility.'[12] And, throughout the opera, we are often in a conflicted state too, occupying two worlds at once. At the same time that we're hearing Shakespeare's text we hear that it's not his text as we know it. We're hearing Q1, Q2 and F in a perverse conflation which is trying to depart from, rather than get back to, the original text.

Scene 5: The Players

The players enter the stage reciting lines from a play. Perhaps they have been rehearsing it, or perhaps they just can't have enough of it. As it happens, the play is Shakespeare's *Hamlet*. Player 1 begins with the Ghost's line at 1.5.23, 'If thou didst ever thy dear father love', shifting then to Hamlet's line at 3.2.378, ''Tis now the very witching time of night.' Player 2 counters with Ophelia's line from 3.1.149, 'O, what a noble mind is here o'erthrown', at which Player 3 picks up the last word and repeats it (but as 'overthrown', which spoils the iambic pentameter. Is he attempting to turn Player 2's verse into prose? Is he acting as director, voice coach or textual editor? Or is he simply cloth-eared?). The next line is Player 4's, 'Blasted with ecstasy' (from Ophelia at 3.1.159), which prompts Polonius to question the phrase 'with ecstasy' and then the longer phrase 'Blasted with ecstasy', much as Shakespeare's Polonius objects to Hamlet's vile phraseology at 2.2.110. So, these characters are running through lines from a play eerily related to the opera in which they have their being.

Hamlet now asks the players for a speech from their 'very best play'. Unsurprisingly the play turns out to be the one they have already been reciting, Shakespeare's *Hamlet*. Player 1 embarks on Hamlet's 'To be or not to be' soliloquy, of course. He supplies the first six words, but Player 2 completes the line. However, his contribution comes out as 'Ay, that is the question', which ruins the metre. Hamlet himself steps in, trying to improve the line, but his version turns out to be Q1's 'ay, there's the point' (7.115), to which Player 3 responds 'Nay there's the rub', seemingly suggesting that the problem wasn't with 'question' but with 'Ay'. The line he is quoting from the play is itself a misquotation of 'ay, there's the rub' which comes later in the soliloquy at 3.1.64. Polonius ignores the issue of misquotation. He likes 'There's the rub' (in the same way that he likes 'the mobled queen' at 2.2.440 in Shakespeare's play), commenting 'That's good. Faith, very good.' By so-doing he conflates Shakespeare's three texts of *Hamlet*, for 'That's good' is from Q2 (2.2.442) and F (2.2.500), while 'Faith, very good' is from Q1 (7.365).

The players suddenly shift their ground to a different soliloquy, Hamlet's first. Player 2 quotes the opening line, 'O that this too too sullied flesh would melt' (1.2.129), but Player 3 counters with a correction: '. . . this too too solid flesh . . .'. A trio of Players 2, 3 and 4 now competes between these two readings

. . . this sullied flesh/solid flesh/sullied/solid/sullied/solid

but Player 1 puts an end to this debate with the observation that 'All is not well', Hamlet's later line from his soliloquy at 1.2.253. Player 3 finally abandons Hamlet's words and quotes Ophelia's exclamation at 3.1.159–60, 'O woe is me / T'have seen what I have seen.' Horatio now throws in Marcellus's observation from 1.4.90, 'Something is rotten in the state of Denmark', whereupon Player 1 leads in Hamlet, Horatio and all the other players to repeating Marcellus's line, but in Latin.

Now Player 1 deploys the final words of the Ghost's departing line in scene 3 (The Visitation): 'adieu, adieu, remember me' (1.5.91). Hamlet responds with his own line, 'Remember thee?' (1.5.95), but he and we might as well reply 'Of course we do!', since, in the Glyndebourne production at least, the same singer, John Tomlinson, played both Player 1 and the Ghost. His appearance, gestures, stance, voice and the notes he sings, all make Tomlinson unmistakably the same man and the same character.

At this point, Player 1 turns to yet another of Hamlet's soliloquies for the question 'What is a man?' (4.4.32). The answer, however, is supplied from earlier in the play (2.2.270–4), where Hamlet describes man as noble in reason, infinite in faculties, like an angel, the beauty of the world. the paragon of animals, and, finally, the quintessence of dust. Each of these phrases is shared out among the players, finally including Hamlet and Horatio too. Horatio's exclamation of Hamlet's line 'that it should come to this!' (F 1.2.135; Q2 has 'come thus' at 1.2.137), is taken up, first by Player 3, then by Player 2, and finally by everyone on stage except Polonius.

Hamlet calls a halt to this elaborate display of wit and erudition by people who can only speak quotations from plays. He uses a line from Polonius, 'Prithee no more' (2.2.458). The players leave the stage, and Polonius goes too, but as he goes he is clearly re-running in his head, and puzzling over, what are to him two key phrases from earlier in the scene, for he is muttering '. . . or not to be?' and 'That it should come to what?' And so, perhaps are we. It's not quite the end, though. Hamlet keeps Player 1 back, asks him to put on a play, and then says 'Go, make you ready' (3.2.43). The player replies with Hamlet's line at 5.2.200, 'The readiness is all'.

For us, as editors of *Hamlet*, the most delicious line in the opera has to be its editorial in-joke:

> . . . this sullied flesh/solid flesh/sullied/solid/sullied/solid

These players have really researched their play and are quarrelling over its most famous editorial crux – did Shakespeare intend 'sullied' or 'solid'? Editors before us were always faced with that choice. Because we were editing all three early texts we were faced with a different one. F prints 'solid', but both Q1 and Q2 print 'sallied'. Previous editors have almost always dismissed 'sallied' as a misprint for 'sullied', since they have been unable to find any use of the adjective 'sallied' elsewhere. We printed 'sallied' in our Q1 and Q2 texts and 'solid' in our F text (and we were heavily criticized for doing so!). Another example of an editorial in-joke occurs in Scene 10: The Second Funeral, when the Gravedigger speaks Hamlet's line from much earlier in Q1, 'what a dunghill idiot slave am I' (7.404) and Hamlet 'corrects' him with the Q2/F version 'what a rogue and peasant slave' (2.2.485), whereupon the Gravedigger, '*as to excuse himself*', continues with Hamlet's expression later in the same speech, 'A dull and muddy-mettled rascal' (2.2.502). And in Scene 11: The Wager, there is a hilarious comedy quartet in which Hamlet, Horatio, Rosencrantz and Guildenstern puzzle over the terms of the wager on the fencing match proposed by the King, repeating phrases like 'twelve for nine', 'six against six', 'three for twelve', very much as editors have struggled to make sense of these details (5.2.130–50). In his review of the Glyndebourne touring production, Jonathan Cross argued that 'the opera is as much commentary on as presentation of Shakespeare' and called it 'a piece about theatre'.[13] At some points, however, we could also call it 'a piece about textual editing.'

Conclusion: Hamlet in pieces

Brett Dean, Matthew Jocelyn and the Glyndebourne team were not, of course, the first people to offer a version of Hamlet that made a collage or kaleidoscope of the text(s). On one level, the vast majority of staged or filmed productions have been 'adaptations' of the play, simply because of the (usually) inevitable process of selecting from the longest possible version ('the entirety' or 'the eternity' as the Victorians called it), cutting some passages and emphasizing others. But the practice became more overt and ambitious in the second half of the twentieth century. Charles Marowitz dis-assembled the play in *Hamlet Collage* and *Ham-omlet* (both 1972), while Peter Brook's *Qui est la?* (1996) presented fragments modified by voices of past directors. Heiner Muller's *Hamletmachine*, first published in 1977 and premièred on stage in Paris in 1979, became, by the time he had built it up to a seven-hour performance at the Deutsches Theater in Berlin in 1990, not only a collage of *Hamlet* but 'a fragmentary collage of cultural history' as Anthony B. Dawson puts it:

> There were projections of famous paintings, neo-classical arcades, nineteenth-century railway stations; references to

> the Stalinist legacy of East Germany laced the production; the eclectic costuming evoked both modern and classical drama; and the staging, such as the slow-motion duel of Hamlet and Laertes or the reappearance of Ophelia as Electra at the end, suggested ritual forms of theatre.[14]

More recently, in 2007 the Wooster Group in New York took as their inspiration the 1964 film of the stage production directed by John Gielgud and starring Richard Burton. This version was partly a re-enactment of the film, digitally re-edited on onstage screens, but also a more complicated layering with other films (Grigori Kozintsev's 1964 version, Kenneth Branagh's from 1996 and Michael Almereyda's from 2000), putting the focus on Hamlet's past and its constant remediation. In London in 2012 another 'remix' of the play called *The Rest is Silence* was directed by Tristan Sharps for dreamthinkspeak which presented all the scenes behind glass panels and allowed the promenading audience to create their own collage by choosing when to spy on the characters both onstage and offstage.

Perhaps our own presentation of all three texts of *Hamlet* has contributed to the ongoing disintegration and reintegration of Shakespeare's most famous work. We were delighted to find such an eloquent, as well as ingenious, example of the phenomenon in Brett Dean's wonderful opera.

Notes

We would like to thank Matthew Jocelyn, for permission to quote from the libretto and for kindly offering some suggestions and corrections. (Of course any remaining errors are our own.) We also thank Serena Davies in the Glyndebourne Press Office for help with arrangements and contacts for both the Sam Wanamaker event and the Final Dress Rehearsal.

1 *Hamlet*, an Opus Arte DVD (OA1254D), published by Royal Opera House Enterprises, 2018.

2 Ian McEwan, *Nutshell* (London: Jonathan Cape, 2016).

3 Bryan N. S. Gooch, David Thatcher and Odean Long, eds, *A Shakespeare Music Catalogue*, 5 vols (Oxford: Oxford University Press, 1991).

4 See, for example, Daniel Albright, *Musicking Shakespeare: a Conflict of Theatres* (Rochester, NY: University of Rochester Press, 2007), which has a brief discussion of the Ambroise Thomas opera; Bill Barclay and David Lindley, eds, *Shakespeare, Music and Performance* (Cambridge: Cambridge University Press, 2017), which has an essay on Ophelia's songs; Arthur Graham, *Shakespeare in Opera, Ballet, Orchestral Music and Song* (Lampeter: Edwin Mellon Press, 1997), which does not mention *Hamlet* at all; and Julie Sanders, *Shakespeare and Music: Afterlives and Borrowings* (Cambridge: Polity Press, 2007), which has a chapter on opera, concentrating on Verdi and Britten, but its few references to *Hamlet* focus on film music.

5 Thomas's opera was most recently revived in the UK at Covent Garden in 2003. Another *Hamlet* opera, by composer Franco Faccio and librettist Arrigo Boito, very famous for a few years after its première in Genoa in 1865, was revived at the Bregenz Festival in 2016 and broadcast on BBC Radio 3 on 8 June 2017. One reviewer of the Glyndebourne version, Rupert Christiansen, writing in *The Telegraph* on 6 July 2017, claimed to have been far more emotionally involved by Faccio's 'romantically overheated' *Amleto* than by 'this clean, lean and unambiguous version of a tragedy that should plumb the darkness of life'.

6 Matthew Jocelyn tells us that in a version of the Glyndebourne opera staged at Oper Koln in November 2019 the Ghost reappeared in scene 4, apparently to prompt Hamlet to tell Ophelia 'Get thee to a nunnery', much as he appears in scene 8 to remind his son of his obligation to kill the king.

7 'Shakespeare in the Opera House', in *Essays on Opera* (Oxford: Clarendon Press, 1990), 237–51; 250. This chapter was based on a lecture given at the International Shakespeare Conference at Stratford-upon-Avon on 2 September 1964.

8 *Opera* 68.8 (August 2017): 1075–7; 1075.

9 Zachary Lesser, *'Hamlet' after Q1: An Uncanny History of the Shakespearean Text* (Philadelphia, PA: University of Pennsylvania Press, 2015), 207.

10 *Opera* 68.12 (December 2017): 1640–1; 1640.

11 According to Michael Shmith, both composer and librettist loved 'the way Shakespeare is forever changing the form, inverting his own iambic pentameter, repositioning the accents so that sometimes the verse becomes prose' ('"To Thine Own Self Be True": Brett Dean and Matthew Jocelyn tell Michael Shmith how they cut *Hamlet* down to size', *Opera* 68.6 [June 2017]: 706–9; 707). In the introduction to the BBC4 broadcast, Dean spoke of 'a wonderful liberty that one has with opera', but his use of that liberty was controlled by musical considerations and he made sure that 'the singer's breath [is] not beholden to iambic pentameters'.

12 Shmith, 708.

13 As cited in note 10, 1640.

14 Anthony B. Dawson, *Shakespeare in Performance: 'Hamlet'* (Manchester: Manchester University Press, 1995), 232.

INDEX